The Canon of Benjamin Franklin 1722–1776

NEW ATTRIBUTIONS AND
RECONSIDERATIONS

J. A. Leo Lemay

NEWARK: UNIVERSITY OF DELAWARE PRESS
LONDON AND TORONTO: ASSOCIATED UNIVERSITY
PRESSES

© 1986 by Associated University Presses, Inc.

Associated University Presses
440 Forsgate Drive
Cranbury, NJ 08512

Associated University Presses
25 Sicilian Avenue
London WC1A 2QH, England

Associated University Presses
2133 Royal Windsor Drive
Unit 1
Mississauga, Ontario
Canada L5J 1K5

The paper used in this publication meets the minimum requirements of the American National Standard for Permanence of Paper for Printed Library Materials Z39.48-1984.

Library of Congress Cataloging-in-Publication Data

Lemay, J. A. Leo (Joseph A. Leo), 1935–
  The canon of Benjamin Franklin, 1722–1776.

  Bibliography: p.
  Includes index.
  1. Franklin, Benjamin, 1706–1790—Bibliography.
I. Title.
Z8313.L45   1986   016.9733'092'4 [B]   85-40530
ISBN 0-87413-290-8 (alk. paper)

Printed in the United States of America

The Canon
of Benjamin Franklin
1722–1776

For
Lee Clarke Lemay

ACKNOWLEDGMENTS

This book was the subject of a meeting at the Modern Language Association in Washington, D.C., on 29 December 1984. I am greatly indebted to the chairman of that session, Professor Joel Myerson of the University of South Carolina, and to the three commentators, Professor Alfred Owen Aldridge of the University of Illinois, Professor Ronald A. Bosco of the State University of New York, Albany, and Professor Marcus Cunliffe of the George Washington University. In addition, both Professor Aldridge and Professor Paul M. Zall of the State University of California, Los Angeles, sent me their comments on and corrections of the manuscript.

At the Library of America, Mr. Christopher Looby made several suggestions. Professor Alan Tully of the University of British Columbia kindly answered my query concerning the satire in no. 68, below. Professor David S. Shields kindly sent me a suggestion concerning the poem against party malice (no. 53). My research assistant, James M. Hutchisson, has read and reread the entire manuscript for me, made numerous suggestions, fetched and returned books, compiled the initial index, and did innumerable other chores faithfully and efficiently.

I wish that I could blame someone else for all the remaining errors of omission and commission, but I fear that they are mine alone.

CONTENTS

Acknowledgments
List of Items Considered   10
Introduction   15
    Background   15
    Categories of Items Included   17
    Bases for Attribution   19
    Method   24
Text   27
Conclusion   127
Appendix   138
Bibliography   141
    1. Items Attributed to Franklin   141
    2. Items Rejected from the Canon   143
    3. Scholarly References   144
Index   152

LIST OF ITEMS CONSIDERED

1. Philomusus to Dr. John Herrick on his incomparable Elegy, 25 June 1722
2. Hugo Grim on Silence Dogood, 3 December 1722
3. "A, B, C, &c." suggests "Rules" for the *New England Courant*, 28 January 1722/3
4. Juba to "your Honour" [Samuel Sewall], 4 February 1722/3
5. Proceedings against the *Courant*, 26 February 1722/3
6. High Tide in Boston, 4 March 1722/3
7. On Tattlers and Talebearers, 18 March 1722/3
8. Timothy Wagstaff on the Influence of Education and Custom, 15 April 1723
9. Abigail Twitterfield replies to the Sin of Barrenness, 8 July 1723
10. Bridget Bifrons on Lecture Day Visiting, 19 August 1723
11. Suppressed Addition to Busy-Body No. 8, 27 March 1729
12. Burlesque Ballad Criticism, 16 December 1729
13. The Trial and Reprieve of Prouse and Mitchel, 23 December 1729 and 20 January 1729/30
14. News Note Jeu d'Esprit on "a gallant Duel," 10 February 1729/30
15. The Letter of the Drum, 23 April 1730
16. Philoclerus on that odd Letter of the Drum, 7 May 1730
17. News Note Jeu d'Esprit on an unlucky She-Wrestler, 23 July 1730
18. Poem on the Rats and the Cheese, 24 September 1730
19. Rules and Maxims for promoting matrimonial Happiness, 8 October 1730
20. On Conversation, 15 October 1730
21. News Report on the Aurora Borealis, 29 October 1730
22. Why the earliest New Englanders came to America, 5 November 1730
23. On Swearing, 12 November 1730
24. The Lying of Shopkeepers, 19 November 1730

List of Items Considered

25. Betty Diligent and Mercator on the Lying of Shopkeepers, 3 December 1730
26. An ironic Comment on Astrology, 8 December 1730
27. Compassion and Regard for the Sick, 25 March 1731
28. The Conduct of Common Life, 1 April 1731
29. English Officials for America, 27 May 1731
30. The Effects of the Molasses Bill, 17 June 1731
31. Death Rates in Boston, 26 August 1731
32. Apollo and Daphne, A Dialogue, 4 November 1731
33. Hints on Fairs, 27 November 1731
34. News Note Jeu d'Esprit on a Lion, 25 January 1731/2
35. News Note Jeu d'Esprit on a Burnt-Offering, 15 February 1731/2
36. Marcus burlesques Portius, 30 March 1732
37. Simplicity, 13 April 1732
38. *"This is the Practice at home":* a second Satire on Portius, 20 April 1732
39. Prosit satirizes Prosit, 4 May 1732
40. A glorious Passage in Persius, 25 May 1732
41. A Quaker Lady on a Lover's Threat, 25 May 1732
42. A Discourse on Argumentations from California or the Moon, 1 June 1732
43. On Declamation, 1 June 1732
44. Philanthropos on helping young Men, 26 June 1732
45. Belinda on a too-bashful Suitor, 26 June 1732
46. Praise for William Penn, 14 August 1732
47. Censure or Backbiting, 7 September 1732
48. "Y.Z." on the Benevolence as well as Selfishness of Man, 30 November 1732
49. Chatterbox on the Family of Boxes, 11 January 1732/3
50. On Drunkenness, 1 February 1732/3
51. A Meditation on a Quart Mugg, 19 July 1733
52. "Blackamore" on Molatto Gentlemen, 30 August 1733
53. Poem by Pennsylvanus against Party-Malice, 28 September 1733
54. Pennsylvanus on brave Men at Fires, 20 December 1733
55. "Queries" urging establishing a Pennsylvania Militia, 6 March 1733/4
56. On Constancy, 4 April 1734
57. The Death of Infants, 20 June 1734
58. Parody of and Reply to a melancholy religious Meditation, 8 August 1734
59. Note on a Thunderstorm, 25 September 1734
60. Report on the Murder of a Daughter, 24 October 1734
61. Exaggerating Body Counts in Battle Reports, 19 December 1734

62. Veridicus on a pertinacious Obstinacy in Opinion, 27 March 1735
63. Statistics on Trade in Colonial Ports, 8 April 1736
64. Report of a Sea Monster, 29 April 1736
65. David's Lamentation, 22 September 1737
66. Philomath on the Talents requisite in an Almanac Writer, 20 October 1737
67. The Origin of the English Constitution, 30 March 1738
68. "A.B." writes "Dear Ned" on Pennsylvania Politics, 4 May, 6 July, 12 October 1738; 29 March and 5 April 1739
69. News Note on the Compassion of Captain Croak, 10 August 1738
70. News Note Jeu d'Esprit on Octuplets, 24 November 1738
71. The New Jersey House of Representatives' Address to Governor Lewis Morris, 28 April 1740
72. Obadiah Plainman defends the Meaner Sort, 5 May 1740
73. Obadiah Plainman to Tom Trueman, 29 May 1740
74. Paper Currency in the American Colonies, February 1741
75. Theophilus Misodaemon on the Wandering Spirit, February 1741
76. Letter from Theophilus, Relating to the Divine Prescience, March 1741
77. An infallible Receipt to make a new Kind of a Convert, by Esculapius, June 1741
78. Introduction and "Remark" on "What is True?" 24 February 1742/3
79. An Apology for the Young Man in Goal and in Shackles, 15 September 1743
80. The New Jersey House of Representatives' Address to Governor Lewis Morris, 18 April 1745
81. Cut of Louisburg, 6 June 1745
82. Appreciation of George Whitefield, 31 July 1746
83. George Whitefield's financial Accounts, 23 April 1747
84. On Barclay's *Apology*, 22 October 1747
85. The Necessity for Self-Defense, 29 December 1747
86. A Course of Experiments on the newly discovered electrical Fire, 10 May 1749
87. News Notes on three Natives of Greenland, 15 June and 7 September 1749
88. Rules Proper to be observed in Trade, 20 February 1749/50
89. Ebenezer Kinnersley's "Course of Experiments on the newly-discovered *Electrical* Fire," 11 April 1751
90. A New and Mild Method totally to Extirpate the Indians, 6 February 1764
91. The Vision of Mirza, 13 February 1769

List of Items Considered

92. The Colonist's Advocate Essay Series, 4 January to 2 March 1770
93. An Act for the more effectual keeping of his Majesty's American Colonies dependent on the Crown of Great Britain, 29 June 1774
94. Method of making Salt-Petre, 2 August 1775
95. The Devices on the Continental Bills, 20 September 1775
96. The Rattlesnake as a Symbol of America, by an American Guesser, 27 December 1775

Appendix
97. The degenerating Times, 8 April 1723
98. On New England Church Discipline, 9 September 1723

INTRODUCTION

Background

This book grew out of a long-standing interest in the problem of the canon of Benjamin Franklin, but the immediate occasion for the book was the request that I edit the Library of America's *Benjamin Franklin*. I agreed, partly because it would give me the opportunity to print a number of interesting pieces that I was sure were by Franklin but that were not included in the standard edition of his writings. Since the Library of America volume was to be a popular anthology, without space for scholarly attribution arguments, I realized I must no longer put off a study of Franklin's periodical writings.

In the eighteenth century, authors rarely signed contributions to newspapers or magazines with their own names. Instead, they used pseudonyms or attached no signature to the piece. Franklin followed the normal practice. His periodical writings are anonymous or pseudonymous. During his life no attempt was made to gather all his writings. Even for Franklin, the task would have been impossible. In 1767, when his sister asked for copies of all his published work, he replied, "I could as easily make a Collection for you of all the past Parings of my Nails" (*The Papers of Benjamin Franklin*, vol. 14, p. 345 [hereafter cited as *P* 14:345]; full references for all works cited below are in the Bibliography, part 3). Every major Franklin editor and many individual scholars have made judgments concerning which pieces in the eighteenth-century periodicals are by Franklin.

The great nineteenth-century editions of Franklin's writings by Jared Sparks (first published 1836–40) and by John Bigelow (1887–88) primarily reprint the periodical pieces contained in the editions of Benjamin Vaughan (1779), William Duane (1808–18), and William Temple Franklin (1817–18). Sparks sometimes doubted previous attributions (e.g., 2:278n), but he chose to err on the side of inclusiveness: "Though written with ability, and probably expressing the sentiments of Franklin, yet the characteristics of the style are not such as to make it evident, on that ground alone, that the performance came from his pen. It is proper to state, however, that Mr. Duane has included it in his edition, and thus given it the sanction of his judgment" (2:285n). Bigelow, however, omitted Sparks's reservations—and his own, if he had any. In his *Franklin Bibliography* (1888), Paul Leicester Ford indirectly took Sparks and Bigelow to task when he said that no collection which did not gather Franklin's contributions to periodicals could pretend to be complete. He conceded, however, that the task was nearly impossible (lv, 3, 9, 281–89). Albert Henry Smyth critically read *The Pennsylvania Gazette* for his edition of *The Writings of Benjamin Franklin* (1905–7), but he nevertheless mainly followed the judgments of previous editors (see Crane 1950, lv). Indeed, as important as Smyth's additions to the Franklin canon was his rejection of a number of essays printed by Duane, Temple Franklin, Sparks, and Bigelow. Smyth bluntly judged that some writings "have been ascribed to Franklin on insufficient evidence, and are at any rate dull and trivial" (2:v). But in making this evaluation, Smyth inadvertently dismissed one of Franklin's most interesting philosophical pieces (*P* 2:19–210; Aldridge 1949b, 157n).

The editors of *The Papers of Benjamin Franklin* faced the same insurmountable obstacle that has bedeviled earlier Franklinists. But for a major segment of Franklin's life (the English years between 1758 and 1775), the task was greatly simplified. The one extraordinarily painstaking examination of various periodicals for Franklin's writings was made by Verner W. Crane in the 1930s and 1940s. Crane focused on Franklin's years in England because earlier scholars had paid the least attention to that period. The result, Crane's *Benjamin Franklin's Letters to the Press 1758–1775* (1950), has been enormously useful to subsequent Franklinists. The editors of the *Papers* have reexamined the basic periodicals (particularly the *New England Courant* and the *Pennsylvania Gazette*), but the editors' early policy was deliberately conservative (influenced, I suspect, by the voluminous Franklin materials that they knew would not reach publication within their own lifetimes). Although the editors sometimes cite past authorities for the periodical pieces they print (e.g., Parton and Van Doren [*P* 1:51 n.6]; McMaster [*P* 1:182]), they do not mention all the works that such scholars attribute to Franklin. Instead, they systematically consider only those periodical writings that have appeared in previous editions of Franklin, and they evidently overlooked two items in William Duane's revised editions (24 and 25, below). Since the publication of the first two volumes of the *Papers*, one major Franklinist, Alfred Owen Aldridge, has attributed a number of additional periodical pieces to

Franklin, especially in his landmark essay of 1962, "Benjamin Franklin and the *Pennsylvania Gazette*," but subsequent scholars have generally ignored these new attributions, perhaps because they are not conveniently available in an edition of Franklin's writings.

Categories of Items Included

Nearly twenty years ago I suggested that all past attributions not dealt with in the *Papers* should be systematically listed and critically evaluated (Lemay 1967, 186–88). There are twenty-seven such items in the following discussion (1, 5, 8, 12, 15, 16, 18, 19, 23, 24, 25, 27, 28, 31, 36, 38, 39, 44, 49, 51, 65, 66, 68, 77, 88, 89, and 93). Of these, I argue that nineteen are by Franklin and I reject eight from the canon (5, 12, 23, 28, 44, 65, 68, and 77). Naturally there is no point in reconsidering past attributions dealt with in *The Papers of Benjamin Franklin* unless I believe the editors are in error. In one case, 51, the editors consider a past attribution but reject it. Therefore they do not print it. I believe, however, that it is by Franklin and so consider it within this category. Here too are items that have been reexamined by scholars since the publication of the relevant volume of the *Papers* but that were attributed to Franklin (usually without any detailed reasons being given) by earlier authorities.

Besides the attributions made before the publication of volume one of *The Papers of Benjamin Franklin* by such scholars as James Parton, John Bach McMaster, Elizabeth Christine Cook, Carl Van Doren, and Alfred Owen Aldridge, a number of attributions have been made since the publication of the relevant volume of the *Papers* (most notably by Aldridge). I urged in 1967 that these too should be gathered together and critically examined. A total of twenty-four items have been attributed to Franklin since the publication of the relevant volume of the *Papers* (11, 22, 26, 32, 34, 45, 53, 54, 55, 58, 67, 72, 73, 74, 75, 80, 84, 86, 87, 90, 91, 94, 95, and 96). I believe that sixteen of these attributions are correct and reject seven (45, 67, 75, 80, 84, 90, and 91). Arguments for a few attributions have been definitively made in scholarly journals. In such cases, I merely identify the piece, cite the scholarship, and say the attribution is definitive. But many attributions have been made in a brief manner, without giving any reasons. I hope to advance the state of our knowledge of the Franklin canon by giving whatever substantial reasons I can think of—either for or against the attribution—in the annotated checklist below.

In addition to the attributions ignored by the editors of the *Papers* and the attributions made since the appearance of the relevant volume of the *Papers*, the following list includes a small (two items only, 20 and 92) but important third category of materials—those items printed in the *Papers* that should be rejected from Franklin's canon. In reviewing volume one of *The Papers of Benjamin Franklin*, Alfred Owen Aldridge showed that a piece printed therein was not by Franklin, but subsequent scholars who have published books on Franklin have generally overlooked this information, perhaps because hundreds of reviews of various volumes of the *Papers* have appeared, and few reviews make any scholarly contribution.

I do not devote separate attention to those cases where the editors of the *Papers* print a piece but cast doubt upon the attribution, because such pieces are generally regarded by Franklinists as part of the canon. Notable examples include the "*golden Extract* from a favourite OLD BOOK (*P* 8:124), "The Captivity of William Henry" (*P* 15:145–57), and "The Sale of the Hessians" (*P* 23:480–84). I see reasons for attributing at least these three items to Franklin (e.g., Lemay 1967, 187).

A fourth category dealt with below is the items that the editors of the *Papers* suggested might be by Franklin. They examined the basic periodicals (the *New England Courant* and the *Pennsylvania Gazette*) and speculated that Franklin wrote five additional essays in the *Courant*. The editors did not print them but invited future scholars "to examine them anew and prove or disprove his authorship" (*P* 1:53). I attempt to respond to their challlenge below (see 6, 7, 9, and 10). I believe that two of these are by Franklin and reject two (7 and 10). Although the editors suggested that number 8 also might be by Franklin, James Parton previously attributed it to him, so I include it within the first category. Unfortunately, the editors published no comparable list of items from the *Pennsylvania Gazette* that they thought might be by Franklin. They did, however, suggest that number 49 might be Franklin's—only to reject it. But since McMaster had previously attributed it to Franklin, I include it with the previous attributions.

The fifth category dealt with below are new attributions to Franklin. Thirty-nine (2, 3, 4, 13, 14, 17, 21, 29, 30, 33, 35, 37, 40, 41, 42, 43, 46, 47, 48, 50, 52, 56, 57, 59, 60, 61, 62, 63, 64, 69, 70, 71, 76, 78, 79, 81, 82, 83, and 85) of the ninety-six items examined fall within this category. Although I have in the past read through all the colonial newspapers and periodicals, for the purposes of this study I reread only the *New England Courant* and the *Pennsylvania Gazette*—and only for the years that Franklin was directly involved with them. I also wanted to read through all the London periodicals for the year

1725 and the first half of 1726 (the months that Franklin spent in London when he was nineteen and twenty). I suspect that the ambitious young Franklin would have wanted to try his pen among the London wits, but I have not yet had the time and opportunity for this additional study.

Bases for Attribution

How does one tell that an anonymous or pseudonymous periodical piece is by Franklin? The best possible evidence is the existence of a draft in Franklin's hand (but despite this and other overwhelming evidence, the editors of the *Papers* nevertheless doubt that Franklin wrote "The Captivity of William Henry" [*P* 15:145–57]). One item below, identified by Alfred Owen Aldridge as Franklin's (74), falls in this category. The next best evidence is Franklin's own statement that he wrote the piece. (He seems never to have claimed writing anything that he did not write.) Franklin noted in the outline for his autobiography that he wrote for the New Jersey Assembly, and he gave a number of circumstantial details about the speech in a conversation with John Jay. I believe that these details, together with the internal evidence, enable us to identify that speech (71; cf. 81). He directly stated in the *Autobiography* that he drew up an outline of lectures on electricity for Ebenezer Kinnersley (87 and 90). And finally, I think that in a confusing passage in the *Autobiography*, he claims two additional essays that appeared in the *New England Courant* (3 and 4).

Perhaps the third best type of external evidence comes from the testimony of knowledgeable contemporaries (78, 93, and 94); but of course, they can be wrong or can even have some reason to misrepresent the facts (84). And a contemporary's attribution of a piece to someone else can be used to deny Franklin's authorship (92). Besides the direct statements, contemporaries sometimes hint that Franklin wrote a piece (36, 40, 42, and 72). Essays that are part of Franklin's known writings, such as the Silence Dogood series (1, and, in a way, 2) or the Busy-Body series (11) are almost positively by him on this basis alone. So too, I think, must be an essay that prepares for another one he is known to have written (47). Similarly, if one can be certain that Franklin wrote one essay in a series, then one must think it probable that he wrote the others (24 and 25; 36, 38, 39, 40, 42, and 43; 72 and 73). But we know that he collaborated with Joseph Breintnall in the Busy-Body essays, and it is always possible that he collaborated with Breintnall or someone else in other series. Of course the definitive ways of rejecting items from Franklin's canon are to show either that someone else wrote them or that they were first printed earlier and elsewhere (12, 20, 44, and 45).

Naturally, when the item is an editorial comment in the *Gazette*, it would seem that Franklin wrote it, especially if it also reveals his characteristic style and opinions (22, 26, 29, 30, 61, 63, and 83). Papers that defend his newspaper, the *Pennsylvania Gazette*, and attack the rival paper, the *American Weekly Mercury*, point to Franklin as the likely author (38, 39, and 42), as does a reply to an attack on Franklin (36). One must also suspect Franklin is the author when a piece demands especial cooperation from the editor in layout, printing or prefatory remarks (24, 25, 38, 39, 50, and 78).

News items from the *Pennsylvania Gazette* present a special difficulty. Even if Franklin wrote almost all the local news items from 1729 to 1740 and many thereafter until he left Pennsylvania in 1757, so what? Why preserve the reports of suicide, murders of bastard children, thefts, and counterfeits that are a constant staple of news in the colonial times, as in the present? Most of these items are indistinguishable from comparable reports in other papers. The editors of the *Papers* selected from the news reports those items that they judged to "reflect Franklin's interests, his activities, or his sense of humor" (*P* 1:xxxvii). But nearly a dozen additional news reports seem to be quite as revealing. As the editors said concerning official documents, "The ultimate test to be applied . . . is whether the contents are in any sense the product of his mind" (*P* 1:xxxv). The editors did not need to justify their selections of news items, but I believe I must justify rewinnowing the grain (see below 13, 14, 21, 31, 46, 59, 60, 63, 69, 82, and 87). A similar category—but, of course, more fun—are the news note hoaxes (17, 34, 35, 41, 64, and 70).

Biographical facts often strengthen an attribution. Thus Franklin's organizing the Associators (55 and 85); his later scientific theories and speculations (21, 59, 86, and 89); his friendships (82 and 83); his interest in a Northwest Passage (87); his special expertise (81, 94, 95, and 96); the sickly condition of his son (57)—and even his deliberate cultivation of simplicity (37)—all may aid in attributing a work to him. In view of his systematic attempts to apply logic and discipline to his own behavior, the appearance of the "Rules and Maxims for promoting Matrimonial Happiness" (19) only five weeks after his marriage to Deborah Read seems significant. So too may his custom of writing in favor of a project in his paper before attempting to have the Pennsylvania legislature enact a bill concerning it (33). If one believes that Franklin satirized Samuel Sewall in the Silence Dogood essays, then one suspects him of being the author of a later, similar but more direct satire on Sewall (4). If one notices that the *Pennsylvania Gazette* pays more attention to a particular crime than the other two Philadelphia newspapers, then one wonders if Franklin may not be the author of the fine grotesque poem about the crime (79). And if one finds that Franklin spoke to his grandson about the elite airs of a Philadelphia club, then one suspects that Franklin wrote the two satires upon the aristocratic tendencies of that club (72 and 73).

Biographical evidence can also be used to reject works from his canon. The fact that the "Dear Ned" series of letters attacks his friends and patrons, as well as the Pennsylvania assembly (to which he had just been appointed clerk), effectively eliminates him from consideration as the author (68). And for reasons that will be offered below, it seems to me that he would not directly attack George Whitefield (75 and 77). But despite the fact that he was out of the province when a poem against party malice appeared (53), I nevertheless suspect that he was probably the author.

Of course these judgments are easier to make in colonial Philadelphia than in eighteenth-century London, for comparatively few good writers lived in Philadelphia in 1730—and no other colonial American possessed Franklin's literary genius. But even if these essays had appeared in a London paper that Franklin was publishing, I suspect I would still, after reading all the other contemporary papers, believe that Franklin wrote these essays. Any extremely well-written local essay that appears in the *Gazette* in the 1730s or 1740s must be suspected to be by Franklin. But, as in London, external circumstances can be misleading, and one fine poem (79), which I am sure is by Franklin, actually appeared in his rival's newspaper. Finally, although external evidence is generally more reliable than internal evidence, no piece that I assign to Franklin is attributed to him solely on the basis of external evidence. Internal evidence supports each contribution—or else I would detail my reasons for rejecting the piece from the canon of Benjamin Franklin.

Internal evidence (the content and style of the piece) is extremely important in making attributions. It may be surprising for many students of Franklin to learn that for most periodical publications attributed to him in *The Papers of Benjamin Franklin*, no positive external evidence of his authorship exists, only the necessarily doubtful internal evidence, supplemented by circumstantial external evidence such as the time and place of publication.

Stylistic evidence is notoriously tricky. A reprinted piece in the *Pennsylvania Gazette* for 7 August 1736 said: "There is nothing more uncertain than the Guesses made at the Author of an anonymous Piece. The Sentiments and the Stile are the only two Things we have to found a conjecture on, and we are frequently deceiv'd in both." Franklin was a master of different styles, varied to meet the different needs of the subject and the occasion. In his essay on style he wrote, "After all, if the Author does not intend his Piece for general Reading, he must exactly suit his Stile and Manner to the particular Taste of those he proposes for his Readers" (*P* 1:330–31). Franklin could imitate past styles brilliantly, as his gulling even some ministers with his biblical counterfeits proves. (See "A Parable against Persecution" [*P* 6:114–24] and "A Parable on Brotherly Love" [*P* 6:124–28]). Nor is subject matter a positive indication of Franklin's authorship. Aldridge (1949b, 154–55), followed by Jorgenson and Mott (clix), pointed out that editors of periodicals especially reprint pieces that support their own views. Moreover, Franklin tended to reserve his best *jeux d'esprit* for private circulation, especially after 1740, by which time his *Pennsylvania Gazette* had become the *New York Times* of colonial America. When such pieces as Franklin's biblical imitations, "Old Mistressees Apologue" (*P* 3:27–31), "The Speech of Miss Polly Baker" (*P* 3:120–25), or "Verses on the Virginia Capitol Fire" (*P* 3:135–40) appeared in the periodicals, other newspapers printed them, not Franklin's *Pennsylvania Gazette* (cf. 79).

Of course, style, content, place, and date of publication may indicate authorship; and, at least in Franklin's earlier years, not many people in any colony possessed great verbal ability and literary inclinations. Franklin wrote in his *Autobiography* that when his older brother and the other established writers for the *New England Courant* tried to guess who had composed Franklin's "Silence Dogood" essays, "none were named but men of some Character among us for Learning and Ingenuity" (p. 18). The tests of style and content are in some cases nearly indisputable: few would doubt that Franklin wrote "The Drinker's Dictionary" (*P* 2:173–78), for it expands a passage in his Silence Dogood No. 12 (*P* 1:39). And Franklin himself used the test of style in identifying opponents in the contemporary papers (see nos. 36 and no. 73). Perhaps the editors of *The Papers of Benjamin Franklin* furnish the best example of the efficacy of internal evidence. In an anonymous extract of a letter in the *Pennsylvania Gazette* in 1770, the editors believe they can tell, three sentences before the end of a newspaper extract, exactly where Franklin's writing ends and another author's starts (*P* 17:215 n.3); and I agree with their judgment.

Of the kinds of internal evidence, probably the most significant is the repetition of the same words and phrases concerning the same subjects. Fifteen items below contain some of the exact words and phrases Franklin uses in similar contexts in his known writings (2, 22,

33, 37, 47, 49, 56, 57, 58, 62, 66, 76, 87, 93, and 95). Two pieces below repeat unusual quotations found elsewhere in Franklin's writings (8 and 56; cf. 40). To quote the same proverb does not seem to me as significant, although it also indicates that the same author may be responsible for both writings (4, 19, 54, and 56). To link together the same classical figure with the same historical figures (56) or to use the same classical quotation in the same context (95) seems quite telling.

Franklin's delight in wordplay, coinages, and his burlesque of periphrasis and jargon appear in several items below (6, 24, 30, 49, 51, 73, 74, 93, and 96). His characteristic humor, irony, and ironic personae occur repeatedly (1, 2, 3, 9, 15, 17, 24, 25, 34, 35, 36, 41, 47, 49, 50, 51, 52, 64, 66, 71, 79, 85, and 96). An ability to create sententiae (4, 24, 37, 47, and 57), an interest in proverbs (3, 4, 15, 24, and 34), the use of anecdotes (38, 41, and 54), ironic, extravagant praise (36, 66, and 78), the pushing of logic far beyond the expected (and simply the use of superior logic [3, 8, 16, 32, 36, 38, 42, 73, and 76]), an expert knowledge of rhetoric (39 and 73), a delight in witty antimetaboles (3), the use of paralipses (15) and of *reductio ad absurdum* (6 and 36)—all are characteristic of Franklin. And since he frequently writes an editorial disclaimer before his known compositions, one must suspect any piece preceded by a disclaimer to be Franklin's (32, 39, and 58). One finds too that certain of Franklin's favorite ways of organizing writing turn up (e.g., the "rules" structure, 3, 19, and 87; the ironic queries, 56; and the framework structure, 15).

Of course clear syntax, the use of a precise word, colloquial expressions, and (where appropriate) specialized vocabularies generally characterize his style (15, 19, 21, 29, 42, 43, 46, 62, 69, 71, 72, 79, 82, 83, 88, and 95).

Subject matter and attitudes may also indicate Franklin's authorship. An interest in philosophical issues (3, 13, 48, and 54), a freedom of speculation about metaphysics (37, 42, and 72), the satire of religion (3, 6, 8, 9, 16, 38, 40, 47, 50, 51, 57, 72, 85, 90, and 96), and satire of ministers (15, 16, 40, and 76) are all common in Franklin. A philosohy of deliberate optimism (3, 19, 54, and 58), a burlesque of astrology (26 and 66), an interest in statistics (31 and 63), an underlying contempt for the pride of man (16, 18, 39, 47, and 79), an occasional breaking-forth of scurrility (49, 52, and 79), a proto-nationalism (29, 30, 38, 39, 93, 95, and 96), an outspoken Whiggism (11, 46, and 73), a political shrewdness and ability to judge economic implications (30), and emphasis upon the compassionate nature of man (13, 48, 54, 60, 64, and 69), a concern with appearance versus reality (37 and 72), and a belief in relativism (8 and 61)—all also characterize his thought. Perhaps the most fundamental of all his attitudes, however, is his egalitarianism (most apparent in 8, 19, 37, 42, 48, 52, 54, 72, 73, and 95). On the other hand, a writer who seems to believe in Christ and who makes the mistake of preaching at the reader (7, 10, 44, and 65) could hardly be Franklin. One who uses and evidently believes in the common eighteenth-century discriminations between the "vulgar sort," the "common sort," and the "better sort" could not be Franklin (23 and 28).

But no one of Franklin's characteristics, most of which are not extremely uncommon, would be enough to make me identify a piece as his unless the style and the circumstantial external evidence also suggested that he was the author. In all cases, ony the totality of different kinds of evidence makes me attribute a piece to Franklin. Indeed, in two or three cases I suspect that subsequent Franklinists may judge that I have been too conservative, particularly with those items that I say are "probably" or "probably not" by Franklin (see 18, 53, 64, 84).

I hope that future scholars with special expertise in computer applications to stylistics will test these attributions (as well as others currently in the Franklin canon), but of course no existing computer programs can critically judge irony, humor, and satire, just as no existing program could test a burlesque of other styles. Nevertheless, it would be good to have the results of computer-generated stylistic analysis, and I hope someone will make such an analysis. A precondition, however, of a computer analysis is to have such a list as this one, which selects Franklin's likely writings from among the thousands of periodical pieces in the colonial American newspapers and magazines.

This examination does not include letters and documents by Franklin that have turned up since the publication of the relevant volume of the *Papers*. (The editorial office of the *Papers* at Yale's Sterling Library maintains such a list). I include only periodical publications. The dates 1722–76 are my chronological limits simply because I know of no new attributions before 1722 and because *The Papers of Benjamin Franklin* are only up to 1777 (the beginning of Franklin's French period) in the ongoing publication of that greatest edition of Franklin's writings.

Method

Items appear in chronological order. When two entries have the same date, the item that appears first in the newspaper source also appears first here (e.g., 40 and 41). In addition to the title, pseudonym (if any), and place and date of publication, the headnote lists the approximate length of the item and notes any previous attributions. Scholarship is cited in chronological order so that credit can be concisely given to previous Franklinists who have made the attribution. All scholarly references are fully expanded in the Bibliography, part 3. The body of each discussion begins with a brief summary of previous reasons (if any were given) for the attribution. When my references to certain characteristics of Franklin would simply repeat those made elsewhere in the study, I merely give the cross-reference. When previous authorities have attributed a writing to Franklin and I disagree with the attribution, I attempt to present not only their evidence but also (if, like McMaster, they give no reasons) whatever occurs to me in favor of the attribution. For such cases are not absolutely certain. But when the evidence for the attribution or the rejection is indisputable (e.g., 12, below), I give it in the briefest possible form. Each item ends with a terse conclusion, saying whether or not I believe the item is by Franklin. In those cases where the item is part of a continuing series, I call attention to the other item(s) in a final parenthetical note. Naturally each conclusion reflects the entire discussion.

THE CANON OF BENJAMIN FRANKLIN

1. **"To the Sage and Immortal Doctor [John] H[erric]k, on his incomparable ELEGY, upon the Death of Mrs. Mehitabel Kitel, &c. A *PANEGYRICK*."** By "Philomusus." In *The New England Courant*, 25 June 1722, p. 2. *Length:* 32 lines of iambic pentameter. *Previous attributions:* Davy 21n; Lemay 1969, no. 25.

The appearance of this mock panegyric poem in the same issue of the *Courant* that first printed Silence Dogood No. 7 (which satirized Herrick's elegy) constitutes external evidence that Franklin wrote it. Two other possibilities could account for the poem's appearing at this time. First, someone independently could have chosen to satirize Dr. Herrick's elegy at the same time Franklin did; but since the elegy evidently had been written nearly four years earlier (Mehitabel Kittle died on 15 September 1718 [*P* 1:24n]), and since the poem generally echoes the essay, we may discount this possibility. Second, James Franklin, Nathaniel Gardner, or another Couranteer could have written the poem after Franklin slipped the manuscript of Silence Dogood No. 7 under the door of the *Courant* office (*Autobiography*, 18) and before this *Courant* appeared. But James Franklin was in jail from 12 June to 7 July, and Franklin was editing the *Courant*. Therefore the editor's prefatory note, saying that "The following Lines" came "to Hand soon after I had receiv'd the above Letter from Mrs. *Dogood*," must also be by Franklin. Franklin had already written two successful broadside ballads ("The Lighthouse Tragedy" in 1718 and "The Taking of Teach or Blackbeard the Pirate" in 1719 [*P* 1:6–7], and he continued to write poetry throughout his life (e.g., *P* 8:126, 129–30, 443–44; 12:431–32; 22:274–77). He is the logical author. *Conclusion*—by Franklin.

2. **Hugo Grim on Silence Dogood.** In *New England Courant*, 3 December 1722, p. 2. *Length:* 373 words. *No previous attribution.*

This punning author writes Mrs. Dogood, under cover of a letter to the editor ("Mr. *Couranto*"), asking her to resume her essays. The mocking remarks on Silence Dogood typify the humor and especially the strong element of self-satire commonly found in Franklin (cf. *P* 1:219; 4:82–83, 467; 6:88; 23:299; see also Aldridge 1957, 178; and Brodwin 136 and 150) and in many of his ironic personae (e.g., the Casuist, *P* 1:234–37; Poor Richard, passim; Polly Baker, *P* 3:120–26; the "*great* Person" of the Cravenstreet Gazette, *P* 17:220–26; and the old man who, if tempted, would once again "very easily be led to ruin . . . and find that I had once more given too much for the *whistle*," Smyth 7:416; and nos. 15, 36, 47, 52, 66, and 85, below).

The author displays a thorough familiarity with the Silence Dogood essays, echoing phrases from various numbers. It is unlikely that James Franklin, Nathaniel Gardner, or any other Couranteer could have written the essay without rereading the series. And it seems quite unlikely that any other Couranteer would compliment the young Franklin by carring on the Silence Dogood fiction. Indeed, James Franklin evidently became somewhat jealous of his young brother once Franklin revealed his authorship of the Dogood essays: "I began to be considered a little more by my Brother's Acquaintance, and in a manner that did not quite please him, as he thought, probably with reason, that it tended to make me too vain" (*Autobiography*, 18). Benjamin Franklin is the only person who knew the series well enough to write the essay offhand, and he is certainly the person who cared most about the series and would want to recall it with a further fiction.

The author chides Silence Dogood by asking, "Is your Common-Place Wit all Exhausted, your stock of matter all spent?" In recalling the ending of the series in the *Autobiography*, Franklin uses similar diction: "I kept my Secret [of authorship] till my small Fund of Sense for such Performances was pretty well exhausted" (18). The editors of the *Papers* mention the publication of Hugo Grim's letter and comment that James Franklin took part in the fiction by advertising for a "true Account of Mrs. Silence Dogood" (*P* 1:45). But it seems to me more probable that the advertisement, which nicely complements the letter printed immediately above it, is by the same person who wrote the letter itself. *Conclusion*—by Franklin.

3. "Rules" to "render your Paper . . . pleasant and agreeable." By "A, B, C, &c." In *New England Courant*, 28 January 1722/3, pp. 1–2. *Length:* 1,288 words. *No previous attribution.*

This author cleverly defends the *New England Courant* and satirizes its opponents. The first sentence's parenthetical comparison between the *Courant* and the "Primitive Christians" is witty and highly original, admirably setting the mock-serious tone for the essay. The second paragraph says, "It is a common saying; *that it is a bad thing to have a Bad Name;* when a Man has once got a bad Name, people are apt to misrepresent, and misconstrue whatever he says or does, tho' it be Innocent, nay, good and laudable in it self, and tho' it proceed from a good Intention, which is absolutely necessary to denominate any Action Good." The use of the cliché and the commonsense application of it are both typical of Franklin (e.g., *Poor Richard*, passim; cf. Crane 1950, xxvi), but both are common in eighteenth-century prose. The final dependent clauses, however, are extraordinary. The pushing of the logic beyond the expected conclusion, the consciousness of and concern with underlying philosophical problems, and the nice discrimination are all unexpected—but typical of the young Franklin (cf. *P* 1:57–71, 264–70; 2:15–21; 3:84–89; and nos. 48, 54, and 76, below). No other Couranteer, not even Nathaniel Gardner, had these characteristics and interests.

In the third paragraph, the author (recalling the attack by Samuel Mather or Mather Byles of 15 January 1721/2) says that "many good people . . . say . . . *there can be no good thing come out of that Paper.*" He claims that discourses good in themselves "and strengthen'd by many Texts of Scripture, and quotations from the Works of the most *Eminent Divines,* who have *great Names* in all the Universities of Europe" are nevertheless condemned as "base and vile" when they appear in the *Courant.* Such discourses have been said to have a "wicked Tendency" and to be "written with a bad intention, with a design to mock and deride Religion, and the serious, consciencious professors of it." The reader must begin to suspect that something is radically wrong with the "serious, consciencious professors" of religion who discover satire in works that are good in themselves and buttressed with scripture and authoritative learning. Thus this author, like Franklin (cf. no. 16 and its references), manages to satirize religion and its "pious" professors at the very time that he is defending himself from the charge of satirizing them.

In the fourth paragraph, the author continues his seemingly reasonable persona by saying he is "of Opinion that this matter has been strain'd a little too far, by persons whose Zeal is not sufficiently poized with Knowledge and Prudence." The tone is so reasonable ("of Opinion . . . a little too far") that one hardly realizes the author is saying that the *Courant*'s opposers are imprudent, stupid zealots. "Yet," he continues, "it may be very proper to lay before you some Rules, which if duly observ'd will render your Paper not only inoffensive, but pleasant and agreeable." Franklin had already used a variant of the "Rules" structure in Silence Dogood No. 7 (*P*

1:25–27), and later used it twice in *Poor Richard* (*P* 2:339–40, 340–41), in "Rules for Making Oneself a Disagreeable Companion" (*P* 4:73–74) and in "Rules by Which a Great Empire May be Reduced to a Small One" (*P* 20:389–99), as well as in two items below (nos. 19 and 88).

The first rule is to "be very tender of the *Religion of the Country*," for "The Honour of Religion ought ever to ly near our Hearts; nor should any thing grieve us so much as to see That reflected on, and brought into contempt." The underlying implication is that religion can easily be "reflected on, and brought into contempt" (see no. 16 and its references). The author also implies that New England prides itself too greatly upon its religion ("our strength and Glory"). Franklin similarly burlesqued New England provinciality in the Silence Dogood essays (*P* 1:23–26 and passim).

Rule two is "TAKE great care that you do not cast injurious Reflections on the *Reverend and Faithful Ministers of the Gospel*." The author claims that "New-England may boast of almost an unparallel'd Happiness in its MINISTERS," for "take them in general, there is scarce a more *Candid, Learned, Pious*, and *Laborious* Set of Men under Heaven." Of course, all this sounds not only a little too boastful—but also dreadfully provincial. It burlesques the usual self-congratulatory praise of New England ministers by New England ministers (especially the third book of Cotton Mather's *Magnalia*, devoted entirely to New England ministers' hagiography). Franklin earlier had satirized Mather, not only in the pseudonym "Silence Dogood" (which glances at both Mather's *Silentiarius* and his *Bonifacius* or *Essays to Do Good*), but also in the humorous account of Silence Dogood's birth ("for as he, poor Man, stood upon the Deck rejoycing at my Birth, a merciless Wave entred the Ship, and in one Moment carry'd him beyond Reprieve" [*P* 1:10]), which burlesques Mather's account of "The Death of Mr. John Avery" (*Magnalia*, 3, pt. 2, chap. 2:367). Further, this rule mocks Cotton Mather's diatribe to James Franklin, which had appeared in the *Courant* on 4 December 1721. The author continues with a clever antimetabole: "But tho' they are the *Best of Men*, yet they are but Men at the best, and by consequence subject to like *Frailties* and *Passions* as other Men." Franklin similarly delights in antimetaboles (e.g., "to be grieving for nothing"—*P* 1:10; the "Horse Casuist"—*P* 1:237; and "no Credit to give"—*Autobiography*, 41).

The author then allows his underlying complaint about the excessive pride in ministers to become obvious: "And when we hear of the *Imprudencies* of any of them, we should cover them with the mantle of Love and Charity, and not profanely expose and Aggravate them."

The author is evidently complaining that ministers and other "pious People" do just the opposite when speaking of the *New England Courant*—while, in fact, deliberately overlooking the ministers' "Imprudencies." Such an indirect but vicious attack is typical of Franklin's rhetorical genius—and his turn of mind. The author concludes the second rule: "*Charity covers a multitude of Sins.* Besides, when you abuse the Clergy you do not consult your own Interest, for you may be sure they will improve their influence to the uttermost, to suppress your Paper." Here the author not only says that "a *multitude of sins*" of the ministers are overlooked but that they are selfish and without charity. They have even been labeled as powerful instruments of repression, "sure . . . to suppress your Paper" if criticized. The seemingly innocuous "Rules" are, in fact, vicious anticlerical propaganda, typical of Franklin (see no. 15 and its references).

Rule number three is "BE very careful of the reputation of the People of this Land in general," for, the writer implies, these provincials are extraordinarily self-satisfied and proud. Then he burlesques the usual message of the jeremiad (Nathaniel Gardner had earlier burlesqued the genre in the *Courant*, 20 November 1721): "Indeed, it must be confess'd that there is a visible Declension and Apostacy among us, from the good ways of our Fore-Fathers." This author then reassures the audience that despite the declension, "a great number of serious Christians" dwell in New England. "Here it may be you will say, there has been more said and printed in some Sermons on this Head, than ever you published." (Of course! The author jokes and at the same time he calls the jeremiads boringly repetitive.) "To this we Answer, that there are many things good and proper in the *Pulpit*, which would be vile and wicked in a *Courant*." The irony here is that the author thinks this situation absurd. He is indirectly pointing out that the paper should have a greater range of subjects than the pulpit. Almost all contemporaries would have agreed. Samuel Sewall, for example, thought it "inconvenient" for ministers to make science the subject of their discourse (Sewall 2:779). "And what if all men are not moulded according to your Humour? must you presently stigmatize them as Knaves and Hypocrites? Certainly on no Account whatsoever." But this was exactly what the Mathers had repeatedly done to the Couranteers. Thus the author not only complains against the double standard applied to the Couranteers but also lectures the ministers about how they should behave.

The fourth rule says, "BY no means cast any Reflections on the *Civil Government.*" If you do, says this writer, "we think you ought to smart for it." The author refers to James Franklin's former imprisonment and his present troubles: "And here we would caution you to avoid with care those Rocks, on which you have once and again almost suffered Shipwrack." Franklin used similar metaphorical language (but it is, of course, commonplace) in the *Autobiography:* "So tho' we had escap'd a sunken Rock which we scrap'd upon in the Passage, I thought this Escape of rather more Importance to me" (32). Then the author burlesques the old-fashioned interpretation of the biblical injunction to honor and obey one's parents as applying also to civil and religious authorities (the *Geneva* Bible gloss of Exodus 20:12 says, "By the parents also is meant all that have authority over us"). "Furthermore, when you abuse and villify Rulers, you do in some sense resist a *Divine Ordinance,* and *he that resisteth shall receive to himself Damnation.*" The author follows this overstatement with a satirical sentence revealing his egalitarian and Whiggish principles: "Princes, Magistrates, and Grandees, can by no means endure their Conduct should be scann'd by the meanest of their Subjects; and such may justly be offended when private Men, of as private parts, presume to intermeddle with their *Arcana,* and fault their Administration." Such sentiments were becoming outdated by the 1720s, especially in America, and this author is satirizing the old-fashioned beliefs of Sewall and the Massachusetts General Court in ordering James Franklin's arrest. He also, like the Rabelasian Franklin, puns about investigating their "private parts."

The fifth rule advises the editor "to avoid Quotations from prophane and scandalous Authors," especially Butler's *Hudibras,* for Butler lampooned "the *Brethren*" and "the *Saints.*" The author refers to the *locus classicus* of anti-Puritan satire, reminding his readers that Puritans generally (and all New Englanders) were regarded as laughingstocks by others. The author further says that it is "very unsuitable to bring in Texts of *Sacred Scripture* into your Paper." Thus the *Courant* can quote neither sacred nor profane authors, clearly an absurd position. The "Rules" essay splendidly satirizes the ministers, magistrates, religion, government, and provinciality of New England. This brilliant satire discloses an ability that Nathaniel Gardner and James Franklin did not quite have. And the sentiments and expression are entirely Franklinian.

There is also some external evidence. Previous scholars have assumed that James Franklin wrote this essay (e.g., Perry Miller 339–40; *P* 1:47–48; Tourtellot 427). But James Franklin was hiding from the sheriff when it (and the following essay, no. 4) appeared. I believe that Franklin claims these two works as his own compositions in a confusing passage in the *Autobiography.* He says that while his brother was confined, "I had the Management of the Paper, and I made bold to give our Rulers some Rubs in it." Commentators on this passage have assumed that Franklin refers to the four weeks in the summer of 1722 when James Franklin was in jail, rather than the two-and-a-half weeks in the winter of 1722–23 while he was in hiding. The *Autobiography* confuses the two times. Franklin began by talking about the earlier time, when James Franklin "was taken up, censur'd and imprison'd for a Month by the Speaker's Warrant" (19) but concludes by talking of the later time: "My Brother's Discharge was accompany'd with an Order of the House, (a very odd one) *that James Franklin should no longer print the Paper called the New England Courant*" (19). No wonder scholars have been misled. But a careful examination of the evidence may resolve the confusion.

Although James Franklin was imprisoned from 12 June to 7 July 1722, he was given "the Liberty of the Prison House and Yard" beginning on 18 June (*Journals of the House of Representatives* 4:35). He may have had some role in editing the *Courant* (although not the actual typesetting and printing) during the period from 18 June until his release from prison on 7 July. If so, Benjamin Franklin really had "the Management of the Paper" for only six days during the summer of 1722, 12 June to 18 June. More significantly, no "Rubs" against the authorities appeared during the weeks that James Franklin spent in jail (see also Tourtellot 402). Franklin's only essay published during the entire four weeks was his literary satire on the New England funeral elegy, Silence Dogood No. 7. It is certainly the best essay in the colonial American newspaper press to that date, but it contains only indirect and minor "Rubs" against the authorities.

The editors of the *Papers* thought that the "Rubs" Franklin referred to were Silence Dogood essays 8 and 9 (*P* 1:27). But they both appeared after James Franklin was released from jail—and they are relatively tame. No. 8 (which came out two days after James Franklin was released) deals with the issue. But it consists almost entirely of a reprint from Trenchard and Gordon's *Cato's Letters* on liberty of speech. Franklin could hardly have recalled this reprinted essay with pride. No. 9 (which came out two weeks later), on hypocrisy in religion and government, also consists in part of a quotation from *Cato's Letters*. If the editors of the *Papers* are correct and the latter Dogood essay points only at the widely detested but recently deceased Governor Joseph Dudley (1647–1720), then it is pretty weak stuff. But if Lemay (1972, 208) and Tourtellot (408) are correct and its underlying butt is the powerful Chief Justice Samuel Sewall (1652–1730), then it has considerable bite. But in either case, the essay does not match Franklin's statement in the *Autobiography,* for it appeared on 23 July, not "During my Brother's Confinement" (19). And if it does indeed satirize Sewall, then it is the boldest satire in the

Courant before the appearance of this and the following essay (no. 4), and it makes their attribution to Franklin more probable.

But previous scholars who have commented on the *Autobiography*'s confusing passage have overlooked the possibility that Benjamin Franklin could be referring to the time when he again managed the *New England Courant*, 24 January to 12 February 1722/3. James Franklin got into trouble with the Massachusetts authorities for the second time on 14 January 1722/3 by printing Nathaniel Gardner's essay on religious hypocrites and Gardner's attack on the absconding Governor Samuel Shute. On 16 January the General Court resolved that "*James Franklin* . . . be strictly forbidden by this Court to print, or publish the *New-England* Courant . . . except it be first Supervised by the Secretary of this Province" (*Journals of the House of Representatives* 4:208). James Franklin flouted the ruling by publishing the next *Courant* on 21 January without the Secretary's approval, causing Sewall to record in his diary, "The Courant comes out very impudently" (Sewall 1004; cf. Tourtellot 425–26). On Thursday, 24 January 1722/3, the Court ordered the arrest of James Franklin. Undersheriff John Darrell testified on Monday, 28 January, that he had made a "Diligent Search" for James Franklin but could not find him (Duniway 165). Tourtellot believes that James Franklin did not go into hiding until the sheriff of Suffolk County was ordered to arrest him on Monday, 28 January, the day that Darrell reported he could not be found. Therefore Tourtellot believes James Franklin was in full charge of the *Courant* for 28 January (Tourtellot 427–28). But I should think that if he did intend to evade arrest, he would have closeted himself before the sheriff began searching for him. I therefore suspect that Benjamin Franklin was in charge of the *Courant* of the 28th, but even if he was not, I think he wrote this essay.

Franklin noted in the *Autobiography* that "it was finally concluded on . . . to let it [the *Courant*] be printed for the future under the Name of *Benjamin Franklin*" (19). And so the *Courant* for 11 February 1722/3 appeared under Benjamin Franklin's name. The following day, 12 February, James Franklin came out of hiding, appeared in court, and posted a bond of £100 for his "Good Behaviour."

Franklin's statement in the *Autobiography* (that he "had the Management of the Paper" and "made bold to give our Rulers some Rubs in it" while his brother was confined) matches perfectly with this essay of 28 January and with the following one of 4 February 1722/3. Although James Franklin may have had some slight hand in the *Courant* even while in jail during the earlier period, Benjamin Franklin obviously edited the paper during the later period (24 January to 12 February). These two essays contain the most severe (and the latter contains the most open and direct) "Rubs" in the entire existing *Courant*. Unlike any earlier essays, these would have caused Franklin to be considered (as he recalled in the *Autobiography*) "in an unfavourable Light, as a young Genius that had a Turn for Libelling and Satyr" (19).

To be sure, despite hiding from the authorities during these weeks, James Franklin could have found the time to write essays and probably had some means to deliver them to Benjamin Franklin for publication in the *Courant*. But the cool irony and the vicious satire of this essay seem much more likely to have come from the young genius Franklin than his talented older brother. Indeed, I suspect that James Franklin is responsible for the lead, rather graceless, and even somewhat confusing essay on 4 February on King Alfred's hanging the judge who hung "Franckling." That essay seems to reveal an outraged and frightened state of mind on the part of its author—and such, I suspect, was James Franklin's condition.

Another bit of inconclusive contemporary evidence should be considered. Advertising in the *Boston News Letter* for 4 February 1722/3, Christopher Taylor said that "a Certain Skinner of this Town, who is said to be a Corporal [Nathaniel Gardner], was the author of the two first Letters in the Courant of the 14th of January last [the essay on religious hypocrites and the ironic jeremiad beginning "The ancient"]; assisted by Others: And (no doubt 'tis believed) those very men were the Authors of the Courant of the 10th of December last, as well as the two Courants [21 January, on Psalm 56; and this essay, 28 January] that came out since what the General Court did in that affair, and many more of the same nature formerly."

The difficulty with Taylor's evidence is that he only clearly credits Gardner with the two essays on 14 January. All the others he attributes to "those very men" (i.e., Gardner or the other Couranteers). Nathaniel Gardner was the most prolific Couranteer, but James Franklin and Benjamin Franklin also wrote regularly for the *Courant*. All Taylor tells us is that the 21 and 28 January issues of the *Courant* were also by regular writers for the *Courant*—and that includes, of course, Benjamin Franklin. To sum up, I believe that Franklin claims this and the following essay as his compositions in the *Autobiography* and that internal evidence supports Franklin's authorship. *Conclusion*—by Franklin. (Cf. no. 4.)

4. **Juba to "Your Honour" [Samuel Sewall].** In *New England Courant*, 4 February 1722/3, pp. 1–2. *Length:* 466 words. *No previous attribution.*

This is the most direct attack on any "ruler" (as opposed to minister) in the *Courant*. Everyone in New England would immediately have recognized that the person directly addressed—but not named—was Chief Justice Samuel Sewall, age seventy. The letter is prefaced by a brief paragraph by "JUBA" claiming that the following "rough Draught of a Letter" has "lately been found in the Street." But the paragraph must really have been written by the editor, for it refers to the lead essay (on King Alfred's hanging judges as murderers for their false judgments), saying that "this Case seems to be set in a true light" by the following letter. Since James Franklin had been hiding from the authorities for at least a week (see no. 3), Franklin was editing the *Courant*. The letter opens: "Sir, I am inform'd that your Honour was a leading Man in the late Extraordinary procedure against F[rankli]n the Printer: And inasmuch as it cannot be long before you must appear at *Christ*'s enlightned Tribunal, where every Man's work shall be tryed, I humbly beseech you, in the Fear of GOD, to consider and Examine, whether that Procedure be according to *the strict Rules of Justice and Equity?*" This double-edged satire not only points out that the elderly Sewall (who must have seemed aged indeed to Franklin, just turned seventeen) would soon have to justify his actions before the ultimate judge, but it also echoes and mocks Increase Mather's condemnation of James Franklin: "I cannot but pity poor Franklin, who tho' but a Young Man, it may be Speedily he must appear before the Judgment Seat of God" (*Boston Gazette*, 29 January 1721/2, p. 2). The author then claims: "It is manifest, that this Man had broke no *Law;* and you know, Sir, that where there is no Law, there can be no Transgression." The use of the apothegm is typical of Franklin, who cited the identical maxim in 1735 (*P* 2:119). It has also been said that this maxim contains the basic theme of "The Speech of Miss Polly Baker" (Lemay 1976, 119; and see Hall 51–52).

The author says that "it is highly *unjust* to punish a Man by a *Law*, to which the Fact committed is *Antecedent.*" And then he writes an absolutely clear, well-balanced, and colloquial sententiae: "The Law ever looks *forward*, but never *backward*." Franklin had just this ability—and desire—to make difficult subjects familiar, as when he explained the Copernican system by comparing Ptolemy to "a whimsical Cook, who, instead of Turning his Meat in Roasting, should fix That, and contrive to have his whole Fire, Kitchen and all, whirling continually round it" (*P* 3:249; cf. the observation on Franklin's democratic aesthetic, no. 19). The identification of Samuel Sewall as the person addressed becomes absolutely clear in the last paragraph, where this author refers to Sewall's role in the Salem witchcraft trials and to his confession of "Blame and Shame" at the Old South Church on 14 January 1696/7 (Sewall 1:366–67): "I would also humbly remind your Honour, that you were formerly led into an Error, which you afterwards Publickly and Solemnly (and I doubt not, Sincerely) Confess'd and repented of." Tourtellot says that this essay is "the work of an unknown but sure hand, very possibly that of Mr. Gardner," but he gives no reasons for the attribution (Tourtellot 429). In addition to the internal evidence, it is significant that Franklin had earlier made Sewall the underlying subject of Silence Dogood no. 9 *Conclusion*—by Franklin. (Cf. no. 3.)

5. **Proceedings against the *Courant*.** In *American Weekly Mercury*, 26 February 1722/3, pp. 3–4. *Length:* 244 words. *Previous attribution:* Suggested by Eliot 146.

In 1799, John Eliot, continuing his "Narrative of the Newspapers printed in New England," called attention to the *American Weekly Mercury* editorial of 26 February 1722/3 against James Franklin's being "forbidden to print or publish the New England Courant." Eliot speculated that the editorial "might have come from the pen of Dr. Franklin." In his *History of Printing in America* (1812), Isaiah Thomas agreed that the remarks "were unquestionably furnished by the Courant club in Boston" (240). But in saying this, Thomas implicitly cast doubt upon Eliot's ascription of the piece to Franklin. I think Thomas was right. James Franklin or Nathaniel Gardner, rather than Benjamin Franklin, was probably the author. James Franklin probably had already established some communication with Bradford. And, according to Captain Christopher Taylor in the *Boston News Letter* of 4 February 1722/3, Gardner wrote both essays that caused the General Court of Massachusetts to prosecute James Franklin. *Conclusion*—not by Franklin.

6. **High Tide in Boston** In *New England Courant*, 4 March 1722/3, p. 2. *Length:* 435 words. *Previous attributions:* Suggested by *P* 1:53; Granger agreed 38n.

The news notice itself is extraordinarily well-written, filled with graphic details. It also burlesques the *Boston News Letter*'s article on the high tide. The author writes a *reductio ad absurdum* of the logic behind the *News Letter* account, piling one incredible explanation upon another in a manner that anticipates Franklin's satire of British news writers' nonsense about America (*P* 12:132–35). Meanwhile, revealing the rhetorical genius of Franklin, the author buries the obvious explanation in a parenthetical remark: "(the Wind blowing hard at North-East)." Franklin also uses parenthesis for rhetorical purposes in "The Speech of Miss Polly Baker" (Lemay 1976, 109). The author, probably reflecting Dr. John Keill's *Examination*, mocks religious arguments by Thomas Burnet, Erasmus Warren, and William Whiston and makes a clever coinage ("Hypothesimania"). Both the religious satire (cf. nos. 15, 16, and 76) and the wordplay (see nos. 30 and 96 and the latter's references) are typical of Franklin. *Conclusion*—by Franklin.

7. **On Tattlers and Talebearers.** In *New England Courant*, 18 March 1722/3, p. 1. *Length:* 578 words. *Previous attributions:* Suggested by *P* 1:53; Granger agreed 38n.

The categories of "tattlers and Tale-bearers" confusingly change to "Lyar" and "Tale-bearer," so that the reader cannot be sure if a "lyar" is meant to be synonymous with a "Tattler" or if a "lyar" is a subcategory of a "Tale-bearer." The author discriminates between those of "inferior Station" and those "of a higher Rank." Although this dichotomy was common in the eighteenth century, Franklin scorned it (see no. 72 and its references). The author also reveals an insensitivity and antifeminism atypical of Franklin when he refers to "silly Women in a Kitchen" (cf. no. 19 and its references). Further, the author parades his learning in unclear etymological remarks. Both the display and the obscurity are atypical of Franklin. Finally, the piece consists mainly of religious quotations from "the excellent Bishop [Joseph] *Hall*," an unlikely author for Franklin to praise or to quote at length. *Conclusion*—not by Franklin.

8. **Timothy Wagstaff on the Influence of Education and Custom.** In *New England Courant*, 15 April 1723, pp. 1–2. *Length:* 1,290 words. *Previous attributions:* Suggested by Parton 1:94; and by *P* 1:53; Granger agreed 38n.

The relativism (which John Locke made widely acceptable) implied by the first sentence on "the Influence of Education and Custom" is typical of Franklin. He remarked in a letter to his parents on "the unavoidable Influence of Education, Custom, Books, and Company upon our Ways of thinking" (*P* 2:203). And in his speech at the close of the Constitutional Convention, he wrote, "when you assemble a number of men . . . you inevitably assemble with those men all their prejudices, their passions, their errors of opinion, their local interests, and their selfish views" (Smyth 9:608). In the second sentence the author's irritation with the social hierarchy (he sarcastically refers to "some Gentlemen of the best Reputation in our Country") is also characteristic (see the references in no. 72 below). In the body of the essay, the author cleverly refutes the "Anti-Couranteer" criticism by showing how the Reverend Thomas Symmes (1677/8–1725), the widely respected author of *Utile Dulci, Or, A Joco-Serious Dialogue*,

Concerning Regular Singing (1723), could be criticized on the same grounds. The excellence of the logic and the humorous tone are both typical of Franklin. And the concluding lengthy quotation from the deistic *Essays* of the notorious freethinker Sir Thomas Pope Blount (1649–97) suggests Franklin's readings and beliefs (see no. 76 and its references). Timothy Wagstaff quotes Blount's opinion that some religionists "Worship *God* just as the *Indians* do the *Devil,* not as they love him, but because they are afraid of him." In the Busy-Body No. 3, Franklin echoes the same passage from Blount: "(like the Worship paid by Indians to the Devil) rather thro' Fear of the Harm thou may'st do to them, than out of Gratitude for the Favours they have receiv'd" (*P* 1:121). *Conclusion*—by Franklin.

9. **Abigail Twitterfield replies to the Sin of Barrenness.** In *New England Courant,* 8 July 1723, p. 1 *Length:* 587 words. *Previous attributions:* Suggested by *P* 1:53; Granger agreed 38n.

This reply by "Abigail Twitterfield" in the name of nine childless married women to their minister's sermon (evidently an actual sermon) satirizes the minister's "manner of Ratiocination" and advises them to "deliver nothing but the plain substantial Truths of the Gospel." Both the criticism of the logic and the advice about the proper subject matter of sermons are typical of BF (cf. *Autobiography,* 77–78). The reminder "that Four of our Reverend Pastors in this Town are deny'd the Blessing of Children" is extremely effective. The author's self-mocking humor (reinforced by the *"P.S."*) is characteristic of Franklin (see no. 2 and its references). *Conclusion*—by Franklin.

10. **Bridget Bifrons on Lecture Day Visiting.** In *New England Courant,* 19 August 1723, pp. 1–2. *Length:* 915 words. *Previous attribution:* Suggested by *P* 1:53; Granger agreed 38n.

This essay consists of a letter by "Bridget Bifrons," a quotation from Littleton's *Dictionary,* and a comment on Bridget's letter by the editor, "Bifrons." The essay must have been written by a Couranteer, and the neat reversal in the editor's opening comment suggests Franklin's authorship: "My Couzen *Bridget* I am afraid is coming into an Error which I have observ'd to be too common in the World, namely, to *make Religion of every Thing;* the natural Consequence of which is to *make Nothing of Religion."* The form of the rhetorical chiasmus and the contents are similar to Franklin's statement in the Busy-Body No. 1, *"what is every Body's Business is no Body's Business"* (*P* 1:115). The mocking of the jeremiad (*"agreeable to the good old Way, in this [once flourishing and religious] Country"*) also seems typical of Franklin—and of Nathaniel Gardner.

But despite its occasional satire of hypocrisy, the essay is basically religious. The quotation from *Proverbs* 7:13–15, and the exclamation and preaching tone in the conclusion ("Good God! That ever hearing a Prayer and a S[e]rmon, eating a Dinner, sitting at a Tea Table, and slandering all our Friends and Acquaintance; should be accounted one continued Act of Devotion") are uncharacteristic of Franklin. One might argue that Franklin was trying to counter the *New England Courant*'s reputation for irreligion and that in satirizing religious hypocrisy, he actually was satirizing the usual religion of the day. But, more likely, Nathaniel Gardner or James Franklin wrote it. *Conclusion*—not by Franklin.

11. **Suppressed Addition to Busy-Body No. 8.** In the first edition of the *American Weekly Mercury*, 27 March 1729, p. 3. *Length:* 874 words. *Previous attribution:* Lemay 1965.

Lemay fully spells out the external and internal evidence for the attribution. *Conclusion*—by Franklin.

12. **Burlesque Ballad Criticism.** In *Pennsylvania Gazette*, 16 December 1729, pp. 1–2. Reprinted in *New York Weekly Journal*, 22 November and 6 December 1736. *Length:* 1,523 words. *Previous attribution:* McMaster 70.

This fine burlesque by Henry Baker (1698–1774) originally appeared in No. 19 of his *Universal Spectator*, 15 February 1728/9. *Conclusion*—not by Franklin.

13. **The Trial and Reprieve of Prouse and Mitchel.** In *Pennsylvania Gazette*, 23 December 1729, p. 4, and 20 January 1729/30, p. 3. *Length:* 1,088 words. *No previous attribution.*

The *Pennsylvania Gazette* of 23 December 1729 reported that James Prouse and James Mitchel had been tried in Philadelphia at a Court of Oyer and Terminer for burglary, found guilty, and sentenced to death. The trial was of unusual interest because Mitchel claimed to know nothing of the burglary and because Prouse, after the verdict had been given but before the sentence was passed, asked nothing for himself but said mercy should be shown Mitchel because Mitchel was innocent. The Court nevertheless sentenced them both to be hung, but directed Mitchel to appeal to the governor for clemency. The *Gazette* of 13 January noted the execution would take place the following day. The *Gazette* of 20 January presented a long, vivid, and absolutely clear story of what happened. But the report is most striking because the author uses the occasion to judge the basic qualities of human nature: "The Concern that appeared in every Face while these

Criminals were leading to Execution, and the Joy that diffused it self thro' the whole Multitude, so visible in their Countenances upon the mention of a Reprieve, seems to be a pleasing Instance, and no small Argument of the general laudable Humanity even of our common People, who were unanimous in their loud Acclamations of *God bless the Governor for his Mercy.*" Further, the author, in telling of the preparations for the execution of Prouse and Mitchel, attempts to make the reader vicariously go through the same emotions that the crowd present on "Wednesday the 14th Instant" experienced. This author studies behavior and human emotions with a scientist's objectivity. We know that Franklin was interested in the Hobbes-Locke opposition over the natural state of man (*P* 2:185) and that he wrote philosophical essays on the Shaftesbury-Mandeville quarrel over the question of man's selfishness (*P* 2:15–21; cf. no. 48 below and its references). This reporter had similar interests. Besides, Franklin was at this time probably still writing all the local news for the *Gazette*. He evidently hired his first employee, Thomas Whitmarsh, sometime during the latter part of 1729 [*P* 1:205n].) Whitmarsh first appears in Franklin's account books in April 1730 (Eddy 14).

Further, it is typical of Franklin's attempts to dwell on positive rather than negative aspects of human nature that he analyzed the crowd's behavior on this occasion but only briefly reported (evidently at second-hand) in this same issue of the *Gazette* (20 January, p. 4) an account of a black man being burned alive at the stake for murder. Later, he merely reported that Susquehanna Indians slowly tortured a Cawtawba Indian to death (4 February, pp. 3–4), and then followed that account with a report about some warriors who refused to take part in the torture (5 March, p. 4; for Franklin's deliberate philosophy of optimism, see no. 19 and its references). *Conclusion*—by Franklin.

14. **News Note Jeu d'Esprit on "a gallant Duel."** In *Pennsylvania Gazette*, 10 February 1729/30, p. 2. *Length:* 70 words. *No previous attribution.*

Two ironic news notes appeared under the heading "Philadelphia, Feb. 10." The first said: "Saturday last, about nine o'Clock in the Morning two young *Hibernian* Gentlemen met on *Society Hill*, and fought a gallant Duel before a Number of Spectators not very usual on such Occasions. The Cause of their Quarrel is it seems unknown; and as they were parted without much Difficulty, and neither of them received any considerable Hurt, it is generally looked upon to be only a Piece of *Theatrical Representation*." The irony in the description of these cowardly braggarts (an early American appearance of the *miles gloriosus* type) reveals Franklin's pen. Since the following news note is obviously by Franklin (reprinted in *P* 1:184), I would expect the first one to be even if it did not reveal Franklin's humor. Not only are such ironic news-note jokes characteristic of Franklin (e.g., *P* 1:165, 184, 217(2), 218–19, 220, 271, 274, and 2:132; cf. nos. 34, 35, 41, 64, and 70), but he may have been still writing all the local contents of the paper (see no. 13, just above). In any case, he was probably the only person who felt free enough with the contents of the paper to write jeu d'espirit. *Conclusion*—by Franklin.

15. **The Letter of the Drum.** In *Pennsylvania Gazette*, 23 April 1730, pp. 3–4. *Length:* 1,243 words. *Previous attributions:* Suggested by Aldridge 1950, 565–66; Lemay 1967, 210, agreed.

Aldridge points out that this letter and the follow-up "were written as part of a particular propaganda campaign against religious superstition" (564) and that they satirize "the cupidity and bibulousness of clergymen" (565). He says that "the style . . . reveals Franklin's perspicuousness and idiomatic vigor" and that, typical of Franklin (565), the author uses proverbs as proof.

I might add that this author's satire of the ministry is similar to Franklin's satire in "Silence Dogood No. 4" (*P* 1:14–18) and to numerous other passages in his writings (e.g., *Autobiography,* 76–78, 97, 107, 148, and 197–98; *P* 1:354; 2:169, 250, 321, 328; 3:447; 10:272; 11:450; 21:246, and so on; see also Aldridge 1967a, passim). And Benjamin Rush records Franklin's saying that "there were three classes of people who did not care how little they got for their money, viz. school boys, sermon hearers, and sea passengers" (Rush 76). Reference to the tune "The Scots Traveller" associates superstition with Scotland, as Franklin does in "Busy-Body No. 5" (*P* 1:128–29). Both the satire of superstition and the pretense that the piece describes an actual, local happening anticipate Franklin's hoax of six months later, "A Witch Trial at Mount Holly."

The situational humor of the "Letter of the Drum" and its excellent detail ("seized violently and forcibly by the great Toe, and in great Danger of being pulled out of Bed") anticipate comparable situational humor and details in "A Witch Trial at Mount Holly." The statement that the two ministers felt a weight pressing upon them heavier "than the *Night-Mare*" is nonsensical in itself and looks forward to the "Witch Trial's" anecdote of the weighing on scales of the suspected witch against the Bible. The speaker's absurd use of "corking pins" to secure his bed curtains against ghosts is matched in "A Witch Trial at Mount Holly" by the committee's searching "the Women to see if they had any Thing of Weight about them, particularly Pins" (*P* 1:182). The persona is presented as a fool (cf. the references in no. 2, above), and the story uses a framework technique, anticipating the same structure in "the Way to Wealth" (*P* 7:340–50). Even the rhetorical devices in the "Letter of the Drum" are characteristic of Franklin. Compare the sly opening undercutting of the clergyman as a "Gentleman whose Veracity few People presume to call in Question" with the paralipses used in *P* 1:43, 198, 243, and so forth. *Conclusion*—by Franklin. (Cf. no. 16.)

16. **Philoclerus on that odd Letter of the Drum.** Dated "Burlington, April 27, 1730." In *Pennsylvania Gazette,* 7 May 1730, p. 3. *Length:* 1,302 words. *Previous attributions:* Suggested by Aldridge 1950, 563–66; Lemay 1967, 210, agreed.

Aldridge points out that the two letters (nos. 15 and 16) could be "parts of a literary hoax" (563), and noted that the style of this letter was "as clear and terse as the original account" (565).

Philoclerus defends Franklin's "prudent Management of the NewsPaper" against the possible charge of publishing anticlerical deistic propaganda. At the same time, the author explains some of the "Wit and Humour" in the earlier letter—for example, that the former writer depreciated "the Holy Scriptures by insinuating that the story of the Drummer of Tedsworth is a better attested One than that of Saul and the Witch of *Endor.*" I suspect that only Franklin would want to defend his newspaper and that only the author of the earlier piece would want to explain its satire (cf. the similar procedure in no. 38, below). Besides explaining (and thus adding to) the earlier satire and defending the *Gazette,* the letter seriously argues against attacking religion. As his writings make clear, Franklin was of two minds about satirizing religion. In *Poor Richard* for 1751, he wrote: "Talking against Religion is unchaining a Tyger; The Beast let loose may worry his Deliverer" (*P* 4:96). In a famous essay in letter form (we can be relatively certain it was put into letter form merely for dramatic purposes, since it expands a paragraph in *Poor Richard* that he wrote less than a year earlier—*P* 7:293–95; cf. 7:82), Franklin argued against publishing religious satires that might weaken the religious opinions of others; and in the *Autobiography,* he confesses that he was sorry that he had converted several friends to deism—a belief that, although it might be true, "was not very useful" (*Autobiography,* 59). On the other hand, nothing could be more complacently sacrilegious than his letter to David Hume of 19 May 1762 (*P* 10:82–84).

Philoclerus's defense of religion has two points. First, he claims religion and the clergy support "Virtue and Morality, without which no Society could long subsist." Franklin makes the same utilitarian argument in the "letter" cited above (*P* 7:294–95). Although he said in his *Autobiography* that "Revelation has indeed no weight with me," he added that he "entertain'd an Opinion, that tho' certain Actions might not be bad *because* they were forbidden by it, or good *because* it commanded them; yet probably those Actions might be forbidden *because* they were bad for us, or commanded *because* they were beneficial to us, in their own Natures, all the Circumstances of things considered" (59). Second, Philoclerus argues that it is "highly probable" that Spirits exist, though "we are very ignorant of their Natures," and he gives evidence from Newtonian optics and Lockean sensationalism of their "probable" existence. One finds no suggestion of specifically Christian belief (i.e., belief in the divinity of Christ) in this argument, nor are such suggestions found in Franklin's religious statements: see the "Articles of Belief and Acts of Religion" (*P* 1:101–9, esp. 102) and see the letter to Ezra Stiles, 9 March 1790 (Smyth 10:83–85).

Philoclerus says, "if there were no Truth in Religion, or the Salvation of Men's Souls not worth regarding, yet, in consideration of the inestimable Service done to Mankind by the Clergy, as they are the Teachers and Supporters of Virtue and Morality, without which no society could long subsist, prudent Men should be very cautious how they say or write any thing that might bring them into Contempt, and thereby weaken their Hands and render their Labours ineffectual." The pragmatism underlying this argument is typical of Franklin (see Spiller; and Rossiter 267–71)—but not too exceptional in the eighteenth century. What is extraordinary is the second clause, "or the Salvation of Men's Souls not worth regarding." One can interpret this simply to mean that the question of whether or not men have souls is not worth considering; but the explicit statement is that *even if* men have souls, the "Salvation" of the soul may not be "worth regarding." This is an extraordinary shift in eighteenth-century religious debate, completely undercutting the religionist's attempt to prove that men possess souls. Few thinkers would be capable of such shifts, but Franklin certainly was (cf. the passage in no. 57 comparing God to a skilled clockmaker gone mad).

Furthermore, the note of indifference to and even disdain for mankind (even if men are immortal) is characteristic of Franklin. In his *Dissertation*, Franklin commented on mankind's pride: "Mankind naturally and generally love to be flatter'd: Whatever sooths our Pride, and tends to exalt our Species above the rest of Creation, we are pleased with and easily believe, when ungrateful Truths shall be with the utmost Indignation rejected. 'What! bring ourselves down to an Equality with the Beasts of the Field! with the *meanest* part of Creation! 'Tis insufferable!' But, (to use a Piece of *common* Sense) our *Geese* are but *Geese* tho' we may think 'em *Swans;* and Truth will be Truth tho' it sometimes prove mortifying and distasteful" (*P* 1:71). The youthful Franklin also directly stated, "I imagine it great Vanity in me to suppose, that the *Supremely Perfect,* does in the least regard such an inconsiderable Nothing as Man" (*P* 1:102). Later in his "Speech of Miss Polly Baker," Franklin satirizes Polly Baker as a representative person. As I observed elsewhere, "Her obtuse blindness to her real situation, her passionate conviction of the justice of her own position, her belief in her absurd and wishful logic, and especially, her supreme vanity—all characterize human nature, as Franklin saw it" (Lemay 1976, 112). Franklin's disdain for human nature perhaps appears most clearly in his anecdote to John Adams about philosophers who happily abandon their thoughts to "knaw a morsel of a damn'd Hogs Arse" (Cappon 2:399).

Philoclerus's complete openness to various religious or metaphysical systems is also extraordinary. But such openness (and nonbelief) is typical of Franklin, who at various times seems to accept the possibility of metempsychosis (*Autobiography,* 4); of Platonic idealism (*P* 1:4); of hierarchic degrees of spirits (*P* 1:102–3); of men's minds existing after death (*P* 1:213); of deism (*Autobiography,* 58–59, 76, 92); of Pyrrhonism (*P* 2:202 n. 5; cf. no. 36 and its references); of atheism (*P* 1:58–71; cf. Aldridge 1967a, 17–24); and of such extraordinary beliefs as "this World is the true Hell or Place of Punishment for the Spirits who had transgress'd in a better State" (*P* 17:315; and see Aldridge 1967a, passim). As several scholars have perceived, Franklin applied what could be described as an "experimental method" to his beliefs and to his writings (Spiller, Levin, Baender, and Aldridge 1967a, 15).

The author's concluding remark that Franklin's printing this letter will prove his friendship to religion is, in effect, a kind of editorial disclaimer, absolving Franklin from responsibility as a printer for the obvious anticlerical and religious satire in the earlier letter and for the implied religious satire in this one. It is comparable to the defense Franklin makes in his "Apology for Printers" (caused by a slur on the clergy) when he wrote: "That if I have much Malice against the Clergy, and withal much Sense; 'tis strange I never write or talk against the clergy my self. Some have observed that 'tis a fruitful Topic, and the easiest to be witty upon of all others" (*P* 1:198; cf. no. 3, above). Here Franklin absolves himself from the charge of satirizing the clergy—at the very time he adds to the satire. But the Philoclerus letter mainly does defend ministers and religion, for Franklin knew that no one should be at war with his own society. He tells us that one reason he left Boston was that the good people of the town were beginning to point him out with horror as an atheist or infidel (*Autobiography*, 20). Poor Richard wrote, "You will be careful, if you are wise; / How you touch Men's Religion, or Credit, or Eyes" (*P* 2:337). Franklin advised his imaginary correspondent who would satirize religion that "he that spits in the wind, spits in his own face" (*P* 7:294). And indeed, the editorial disclaimer in itself indicates Franklin's authorship (see no. 32 and its references).

Finally, the pseudonym Philoclerus is ideal for the specific purposes of this essay. It shows a splendid appreciation of the uses of persona (cf. Franklin's "An Edict by the King of Prussia," *P* 20:413–19; see Lemay 1972, 227–32; and Ziff); and at the same time, it recalls personae that Franklin knew or used in his *New England Courant* days: Silence Dogood's boarder was "Clericus" (*P* 1:14–18), and "Johannes Clericus" signed a piece in the *Courant* for 19 February 1721/2. *Conclusion*—by Franklin. (Cf. no. 15.)

17. News Note Jeu d'Esprit on an unlucky She-Wrestler. In *Pennsylvania Gazette*, 23 July 1730, p. 4. *Length:* 46 words. *No previous attribution.*

"We have here an unlucky She-Wrestler who has lately thrown a young Weaver, and broke his leg, so that tis thought he will not be able to tread the Treadles these two Months. In the mean Time, however, he may employ himself in winding Quills." The ironic concluding comment is typical of Franklin's news-note jeu d'esprit (cf. no. 14). *Conclusion*—by Franklin.

18. Poem on the Rats and the Cheese; a Fable. In *Pennsylvania Gazette*, 24 September 1730, p. 3. *Length:* 42 lines of iambic tetrameter. *Previous attributions:* Wainwright; Davy 49; Aldridge 1962, 78; Lemay 1969, no. 161.

The editorial on Governor Belcher's speech, pointing out that "he has brought with him those very Instructions that occasion'd the Difference between Governor *Burnet* and that People" is printed in the *Papers* (1:176) but this accompanying fable is not. Nicholas B. Wainwright suggested that the poem may "have been written . . . by him and first read at a Junto meeting" (84n). Davy independently attributed it to Franklin and added that Bernard Mandeville's "The Grumbling Hive" inspired it (49). Franklin met Mandeville in London in 1725 and obviously knew his writings (*Autobiography*, 44, and no. 48, below). The poem reveals a disgust for avarice typical of Franklin ("The Love of Money is not a Thing of certain Measure, so as that it may be easily filled and satisfied. Avarice is infinite."—*P* 18:124; cf. *P* 3:317–18, 474–75, 479–80; 7:14; 17:314–15; etc.) and has a note of contempt for mankind that Franklin sometimes betrayed (*P* 11:101; Smyth 8:451–52; and cf. no. 16). Franklin, of course, wrote poetry throughout his life (see no. 1 and its references). On the other hand, Franklin may have read this poem elsewhere and judged it appropriate for the occasion. *Conclusion*—probably by Franklin.

19. "**RULES** *and* **Maxims** *for promoting matrimonial Happiness.*" In *Pennsylvania Gazette*, 8 October 1730, pp. 1–2. *Length:* 1,075 words. *Previous attribution:* Suggested by McMaster 79.

The opening statement that "the happy State of Matrimony is, undoubtedly, the surest and most lasting Foundation of Comfort and Love" is echoed by Franklin's "Reply to a Piece of Advice" of 4 March 1734/5 (*P* 2:21–26); by his bagatelle ("Old Mistresses Apologue") of 25 June 1745 comparing a bachelor to "the odd Half of a Pair of Scissars" (*P* 3:30); and by his letter of 9 August 1768 congratulating John Alleyne on his marriage (*P* 15:182–85). The purpose of the "Reply to a Piece of Advice" was to defend matrimony from a hackneyed satire on women written by a local poet (*P* 2:21–22n; Lemay 1969, no. 355). The "Rules," like the "Reply" and Franklin's "I sing my plain Country Joan" (*P* 2:352–54), have a similar object. This author's use of a proverb as proof ("*Good Wives* usually make *Good Husbands*") is typical of Franklin. No doubt the proverb appealed to Franklin in part for its sexual pun. Franklin later used a variant ("Good wives and good plantations are made by good husbands") in *Poor Richard* for 1736 (*P* 2:141). In the introduction the author says that he is addressing women rather than men not because "I suppose their Sex more faulty than the other, and most to want Advice, for I assure them, upon my Honour, I believe the quite contrary; but the Reason is, because I esteem them better disposed to receive and practice it, and therefore am willing to begin, where I may promise myself the best Success." Thus, like Franklin, the author seems to be a protofeminist.

The author's first rule echoes the proverb. The second advocates constancy (see no. 56 and its references) and recommends avoiding any "Inclination to play the Tyrant." So Franklin, in his "Reply to a Piece of Advice," satirized the poet's statement that "every Woman is a Tyrant" by observing that "perhaps his Aversion to a Wife arises from observing how his Mamma treated his Daddy." But he commented that in general "there are in the World infinitely more He-Tyrants than She-Ones" (*P* 2:22, 23). The third rule, *Sincerity*, appears as no. 7 in Franklin's list of virtues (*Autobiography*, 150, cf. 114) and is recommended elsewhere in his writings (e.g., *P* 7:80). Just as this author recommends treating husbands "with *Affection* and *Re*-

spect," so Franklin recommends to John Alleyne: "Treat your Wife always with Respect. It will procure Respect to you, not only from her, but from all that observe it" (*P* 15:184–85). The fourth rule says not to be "over sanguine before Marriage, nor promise your self Felicity without Alloy, for that's impossible to be attain'd in this present State of Things." Franklin's advice to keep your eyes wide open before marriage and half-shut afterwards (*P* 2:194) contains a similar cynical note, as does his proverb "The Golden Age never was the present Age" (*P* 3:453). And the advice to try to amend "*humane Frailty*" by "*Cheerfulness* and Good-nature" anticipates Franklin's general philosophy of optimism in the *Autobiography* (Lemay 1978, 30–32), in his fable of "The Handsome and Deformed Leg" (Smyth 8:162–64), in his parable on Fast Day sermons and the origin of Thanksgiving Day (Smyth 10:116–17), and in his satire of lugubrious religious meditations (no. 58 below; see Aldridge 1964).

The fifth rule, to "put your Shoulders to the Yoke" and work to overcome misfortunes, is typical of Franklin. He uses the same moral (echoing Aesop's fable of "Hercules and the Wagoneer") in pictoral form in his woodcut for *Plain Truth*, 1747 (see *P* 3:190 and xiv; cf. no. 55, below). The sixth rule, to "Resolve every Morning to be *good-natur'd* and CHEERFUL," again echoes the general Franklinian philosophy of conduct and optimism, and finds an analogue in Poor Richard's proverb "If you would have Guests merry with your cheer, Be so yourself, or so at least appear" (*P* 1:358; cf. 2:448). The seventh rule, which advises against disputes, anticipates Franklin's observation in the *Autobiography* about "disputing, contradicting and confuting People" who "get Victory sometimes, but they never get Good Will, which would be of more use to them" (133).

The eighth rule advises the wife to identify with the husband and "share and sooth his Cares." Franklin's praise of his wife in the *Autobiography* (144–45) and his celebration of his "Companion delightfull and dear" in stanza 3 of "I sing my plain Country Joan" (*P* 2:353) both echo the rule. But this and the next three "Rules and Maxims" contain eighteenth-century attitudes toward marriage and women that are not especially feminist. The most blatant, the ninth rule, says, "Read frequently with due Attention the Matrimonial Service; and take care in doing so, not to overlook the Word *Obey*." Franklin similarly wrote in his "Reply to a Piece of Advice": "I scarce ever knew a Man who knew how to command in a proper Manner, but his Wife knew as well how to show a becoming Obedience" (*P* 2:23). We lose historical perspective by expecting Franklin or anyone else in the eighteenth century to be as consistently sensitive in his attitudes toward feminism as someone living in the late twentieth century. The point is that Franklin, like this author, is, in comparison to his contemporaries and to the general zeitgeist of his times, a feminist. The author turns the table on the sexist chauvinism appearing in a few rules ("*Address'd to all* Widows, Wives, *and* Spinsters") in the essay's conclusion. There the speaker surprises us (as Franklin so often does with a humorous or ironic turn when ending an essay) by saying that the rules, "with a very little alteration, are as proper for Husbands as Wives." That is what one expects of the Franklin who, as a teenager, wrote a series of essays arguing that women's abilities were equal to men's and that women too should have the advantage of education. Although he said he took this position "perhaps a little for Dispute sake" (*Autobiography*, 13), in fact he maintained the same opinions on women's equality in papers published later (*P* 2:204; see also 23:297). He believed that women had "some reason to be displeas'd with" the Freemasons because women were not admitted to the Society (*P* 2:204). One subject of satire in "The Speech of Miss Polly Baker" is the double standard of morality for men and women. In his old age, Franklin wrote the "Petition of the Left Hand" (Smyth 10:125–26), a parable on the equality of women. And he directly stated that "there should be no distinction" between the sexes in the laws of inheritance (Smyth 9:357; cf. 8:455–56; and see Wages on Franklin's feminine personae).

The twelfth rule, on behavior, is standard eighteenth-century advice, but the thirteenth, on having a "due Regard to his Income and Circumstances in all your Expences and Desires," is characteristic. Franklin devotes his Anthony Afterwit sketch (*P* 1:237–40) to the moral and praises his wife, Deborah, for these qualities in the *Autobiography* (144–45). The note about the force of "Necessity" anticipates a favorite Poor Richard proverb, *"it is hard for an empty Sack to stand upright"* (*Autobiography* 94; *P* 2:248).

The fourteenth and last rule, which advises self-examination of one's conduct, anticipates the *Autobiography*'s advice on "daily Examination" and on the Pythagorian regimen (78–89). The advice that the "best Attonement" for past errors is to correct them in the future is typical of Franklin's pragmatic attitudes (see *P* 2:18). The speaker concludes with Creech's translation of the epigraph from Horace. The democratic aesthetic that makes the epigraph available characterizes Franklin (cf. nos. 4 and 21), as does the egalitarian author's satiric reference to the supposedly different tastes of the "unlearned" and "learned" readers (cf. no. 72, below). Finally, the structuring device of "Rules and Maxims" is a favorite of Franklin (see no. 3 and its references).

Franklin's biography strengthens this attribution. When he returned to America in 1726, he wrote that since he was entering a new scene of life, he would "make some resolutions and form some scheme of action, that, henceforth, I may live in all respects like a rational creature" (*P* 1:99–100). The "Rules" appeared just over a month after Franklin and Deborah Read were married in a common-law agreement (*Autobiography,* 71). Evidently Franklin was attempting to set forth "resolutions" and a "scheme of action" whereby he and Deborah stood the best chance for happiness. The attempt, as part 2 of his *Autobiography* also attests, was characteristic. *Conclusion*—by Franklin.

20. **On Conversation.** In *Pennsylvania Gazette,* 15 October 1730, pp. 1–2. Reprinted in *P* 1:177–81. *Length:* 964 words. *Previous attributions: P* 1:177–81; rejected by Aldridge 1960, 209.

Alfred Owen Aldridge found that Franklin reprinted "On Conversation" from Henry Baker's *Universal Spectator* of 11 October 1729. *Conclusion*—not by Franklin.

21. **News Report on the Aurora Borealis.** In *Pennsylvania Gazette,* 29 October 1730, p. 4. *Length:* 149 words. *No previous attribution.*

Franklin's interest in the aurora borealis, which came to fruition in his 1778 paper "Aurora Borealis: Suppositions and Conjectures toward forming an Hypothesis for its Explanation" (Smyth 7:209–15), was evidently aroused by the display written up in this notice. The reporter begins his news account: "Last Thursday Evening there was seen throughout this Province in the N. East, a very bright Appearance of the *Aurora Borealis,* or Northern Twilight." Giving an English paraphrase ("Northern Twilight") of the Latin name ("Aurora Borealis") is characteristic of Franklin (see no. 19). The reporter then explains the reason for the name, gives a brief history of the most striking occurrences of the aurora borealis in England and Europe, and concludes: "But a sufficient Number of Observations have not yet been made by the Curious." The reporter has used the best scientific source, the *Philosophical Transactions,* for his information. Two weeks later, 12 November 1730, pp. 3–4, the *Gazette* reprinted news items about the same display of the aurora borealis from Newport, Boston, and New Hampshire.

Over six years later, when the *Gazette* of 6 January 1736/7, p. 3, reported another display of the aurora borealis, the reporter commented: "It was more red and luminous than that which we saw here about Six Years ago." This note is evidently by the same reporter who described the earlier appearance, and now he prints the extract from the *Philosophical Transactions* that he had earlier paraphrased. The later description is reprinted in *P* 2:185–86. *Conclusion*—by Franklin.

22. **Why the earliest New Englanders came to America.** In *Pennsylvania Gazette*, 5 November 1730, p. 3. *Length:* 72 words. *Previous attributions:* Aldridge 1962, 78–79; Lemay 1969, no. 167.

Franklin is the logical and obvious author for this editorial defense of Americans, which was inspired by verses (Lemay 1969, nos. 164–67) on the Belcher salary issue (see above, no. 18). Aldridge (79) points out that "Franklin repeated this sentiment almost verbally" (*P* 12:414; cf. *P* 5:447, 451; 6:264, 299; 8:350–51). *Conclusion*—by Franklin.

23. **On Swearing.** In *Pennsylvania Gazette*, 12 November 1730, pp. 1–2. *Length:* 1,282 words. *Previous attribution:* McMaster 78.

The author's discrimination between "well-bred People" and the "*Common People*" is unlike Franklin (cf. nos. 72 and 73 below). The strident tone and name-calling ("the meerest *Ideots*") are also both uncharacteristic. And although the Addisonian subject matter was not unusual for Franklin, this particular vice was not liable to upset him as much as it seems to have upset the author, whose position must have seemed too strong even for an eighteenth-century audience. The borrowed foreign-observer device that concludes the letter is quite well done and may explain why McMaster attributed the essay to Franklin. *Conclusion*—not by Franklin.

24. **The Lying of Shopkeepers.** In *Pennsylvania Gazette*, 19 November 1730, pp. 1–2. *Length:* 1,005 words. *Previous attributions:* Printed by Duane 2:493–94; attributed by McMaster 70; and Aldridge 1960, 210.

Although no internal evidence shows that this is a local essay (it is the first of a two-part series—see no. 25), the subject matter, opinions, techniques, and style all suggest Franklin. The arguments that "Truth, Diligence and Probity" are the best way to succeed in business and that "Character raises a Credit which supplies the Want of Fortune," are favorite themes in the *Autobiography* (119, 158; cf. 89). The ability to create witty *sententiae* also bespeaks Franklin's authorship. The author not only uses proverbs but is willing to revise them, as Franklin does throughout *Poor Richard:* "Example works more than Precept" (cf. Wilson 233), and "who will *lie* will *swear*" (cf. Wilson 792). The writer burlesques the periphrasis *historical* for *lying*, reminding one of Franklin's amusement at similar circumlocutions (cf. "The Drinker's Dictionary," *P* 2:173–78). The author's satire of false reasoning (paragraph 1) and his appeal to classical examples (paragraphs 4 and 6), although common in the eighteenth century, are also typical of Franklin (e.g., his remarks on hospitality in *A Narrative of the Late Massacres*, *P* 11:56–63). And yet there is almost too much historical quotation in the two paragraphs. The diction is sometimes surprisingly learned when a simple word would do as well: "yet there are too many, who will endeavor to deceive, and, backing their Falsities with *Asseverations,* pawn their Salvation to raise their Price" (my italics). On the other hand, the diction is precise, and the sounds in *falsities* and *Salvation* might well make one want to use the word *Asseverations* to reinforce the *s* and *v* consonance and the *a* and *i* assonance. But the religious appeal is also not especially Franklinian, though he certainly used it for special purposes (cf. no. 85).

If this essay stood alone, I would conclude that it was "probably by Franklin," but the companion piece (no. 25) is entirely Franklinian. *Conclusion*—by Franklin. (Cf. no. 25.)

25. Betty Diligent and Mercator on the Lying of Shopkeepers.

In *Pennsylvania Gazette,* 3 December 1730, p. 1. *Length:* 379 words. *Previous attributions:* Printed by Duane 2:494; attributed by McMaster 70; and Aldridge 1960, 209–10.

Aldridge believes that these "two humorous essays on lying . . . reflect the techniques of Franklin's ironical character sketches." I agree. Although one letter pretends to be from a shopkeeper ("Betty Diligent") and the other from a wholesale dealer ("Mercator"), they so nicely complement one another that they are evidently by the same author. Further, they follow a prefatory epigraph from the Apocrypha (Ecclesiasticus 27:2) and a prefatory editorial note—either of which makes the editor's cooperation essential. Although the prefatory editorial notes as well as the two letters could have been copied from some other periodical, the essay's dramatic ironies bespeak Franklin's authorship. The self-deluding narrator, "Betty Diligent," says: "the Blame of all the Lying properly belongs to the Customers that come to buy; because if the Shopkeepers strain the Truth a little now and then, they are forced to do it in their own Defence." The ironic rhetoric here echoes Silence Dogood's statement (although not her salacious puns) on the causes of men's sins: "and when you have once reformed the Women, you will find it a much easier task to reform the Men, because Women are the prime Causes of a great many Male Enormities" (*P* 1:19). The rhetoric also anticipates Franklin's ironic portrayal of the self-deluding Polly Baker as she concludes her speech (Lemay 1976, 99–100, 112–13).

Finally, the incredibly pessimistic and black worldview of lying and conniving by customers, shopkeepers, and wholesale merchants—in short, by everybody—that emerges from this two-part series is extraordinary in the eighteenth century, but it characterizes some aspects of the beliefs and worldview of the private Franklin (e.g., "He that best understands the World, least likes it" and "none of us are [happy] while in this Life"—*P* 4:405; 11:253). Taken together, these pessimistic essays may even shed some light upon the reason why Franklin, falling seriously ill while he was a shopkeeper working for Thomas Denham, resigned himself to death and was rather disappointed to find himself recovering (*Autobiography*, 52). They may also shed some light upon his giving up shopkeeping and returning to printing while Denham was gravely ill (Roach 136–37). The essays also tend to explain his diction when he condemned England and Holland during the Revolution as "shopkeeping" nations (Smyth 7:7; 8:292; cf. *P* 15:78). And they may partially explain his later statement that "*Commerce . . .* is generally *Cheating*" (*P* 16:109; see McCoy 613–14). *Conclusion*—by Franklin. (Cf. no. 24.)

26. **An ironic Comment on Astrology.** In *Pennsylvania Gazette*, 8 December 1730, p. 2. *Length:* 87 words. *Previous attribution:* Aldridge 1962, 78.

After reporting the "vehement Drought" throughout Europe and the "Northern Parts of America" last summer, the editor ironically comments: "It is not observed that any *Almanack-maker* in the World foretold this Universal dry Weather." Franklin similarly mocked astrology throughout the *Poor Richard* almanacs. *Conclusion*—by Franklin.

27. **Compassion and Regard for the Sick.** In *Pennsylvania Gazette*, 25 March 1731, pp. 1–2. *Length:* 776 words. *Previous attributions:* Cook 101; Aldridge 1962, 80–81; 1965, 56; and 1967, 84–85.

Aldridge 1962 and 1967 definitively presented reasons for the attribution. *Conclusion*—by Franklin.

28. **The Conduct of Common Life.** In *Pennsylvania Gazette*, 1 April 1731, pp. 1–3. *Length:* 1,696 words. *Previous attribution:* Cook 101–2.

Cook believes that this essay and number 20 have "the same philosophy" as Poor Richard, but "on the deeper values in life" (101).

Although this essay contains no internal evidence of being local, much of the content and the style is typical of Franklin. Several references to man's underlying vanity (e.g., he "is so far from envying his Neighbor's Excellence, that he rather pities or despises him for want of that ample Portion he thinks has been administered to himself") recall Franklin's ironic statements: Poor Richard writes "To show the Strength, and Infamy of Pride, / By all 'tis follow'd, and by all deny'd" (*P* 3:101; cf. *Autobiography*, 2, 90–91). The author's self-mockery on his lack of order ("according to a frequent Custom among Writers on such Subjects, I shall" write "without any Order, but that with which they ["Remarks"] come into my Mind") has a humorous Franklin touch.

The doctrine "that a good Reputation is the most infallible Means of Success in our Aims and Endeavours, that the Uncertainty of Worldly Things admits of" is typical of Franklin, advocated in *Poor Richard* and in the *Autobiography*, for example, "no Qualities were so likely to make a poor Man's Fortune as those of Probity and Integrity" (89). The arguments that a "good Reputation . . . may be obtained" and that a "great Reputation is not so desireable as a good One" both anticipate Poor Richard's advice: "Strive to be the *greatest* Man in your Country, and you may be disappointed; Strive to be the *best*, and you may succeed: He may well win the race that runs by himself" (*P* 3:102). The recommendation of "Sincerity and Punctuality" is similar to the praise of sincerity in the *Autobiography* (59, 79, 88). The advice "to treasure up" criticisms upon one's "Behaviour" and to "attend to such Reflections" anticipates Franklin's adding humility to his list of virtues after being criticized for his pride (*Autobiography*, 89–90; also *P* 8:128–29). On the other hand, vanity and reputation are major subjects in the eighteenth century, and it is surprising that this essay contains no verbal echoes on these subjects from Franklin's other writings.

Further, several elements in the essay are uncharacteristic of Franklin. The reasoning proceeds by dichotomization (in a Ramistic way) and Franklin generally avoids this procedure (which he no doubt identified with the Puritan preachers he heard as a boy) in favor of Cartesian logic. The author refers to "the meanest and most ignorant People" and to the various "Stations" of life. Although common in the eighteenth century, such epithets were despised by the egalitarian Franklin (cf. no. 72 and its references). Finally, the author undercuts his own argument by granting that "a high Reputation is very often the Act of Fortune as much as the Effect of Merit." Franklin would probably agree that this opinion was true, but since it undercuts the essay's thesis, the opinion is not useful (cf. *Autobiography*, 59). Although Franklin often maintains contrary positions in philosophical issues, he does so in separate essays, usually making as strong a case as possible for the chosen position in a single essay. *Conclusion*—not by Franklin.

29. English Officials for America. In *Pennsylvania Gazette*, 27 May 1731, p. 3. *Length:* 29 words. *No previous attribution.*
The news report implicitly chafes at the second-class treatment of Americans: "We hear from *North-Carolina*, that Governor *Burrington* is arrived there, accompanied by several Gentlemen, who are to have the chief Places of Profit and Trust in that Government." The underlying tenor of this note satirizes both the English policy toward America and the English colonial officials who enjoy the official English patronage. Of course the note reflects Franklin's proto-nationalistic American attitudes (cf. *P* 2:453; 3:13; 4:130–33, 233; 5:444; 8:310, 340–56; and nos. 30 and 38, below). *Conclusion*—by Franklin.

30. The Effects of the Molasses Bill. In *Pennsylvania Gazette*, 17 June 1731, p. 4. *Length:* 73 words. *No previous attribution.*
On page 3, Franklin reprinted a notice from a London newspaper of 27 March that the Sugar Islands trade was soon to "come under the Consideration of Parliament." Then on page 4, under the Philadelphia dateline, the *Gazette* reported: "By way of Boston there is Advice, That a Bill for prohibiting the Importation of Rum, Sugar, and Mellasses from the French and Dutch Plantations into the Northern Colonies in America, has passed both Houses of Parliament, pursuant to a Petition from the Island of Barbadoes. What Effect this will have, as to raising or falling the Prices of those Commodities and our Flour, &c., is left to the Judicious to consider." To this author's unusual use of *falling*, compare Franklin's uncommon use of *fall:* "sudden great Demand for Bills in the Colonies may, at any time, advance the Exchange; and a sudden great Demand abroad for their Commodities may *fall* the Exchange" (no. 74 below, my italics; see also nos. 6, 73 [and its references], and 96, for Franklin's coinages and interest in unusual words).
The following week (24 June, p. 4) Franklin reported from the *New York Gazette* that the bill was likely to pass in the House of Commons, despite the protests of the agents from Massachusettes, Rhode Island, and New Jersey, and despite publications against the bill. On 1 July, page 1, Franklin reprinted an essay from the *Whitehall Evening Post* of 10 April, arguing against the bill because it would raise the price of sugar in England. In that same issue, page 4, Frank-

lin reported that the bill had passed the House of Commons, but that the merchants trading to the Northern Colonies had petitioned for a hearing on the bill before the House of Lords and succeeded in postponing the hearing until Parliament was prorogued. He warned, however, that the bill was sure to be introduced in the next session of Parliament. On 8 July, page 1, he printed "The Case of the British Sugar-Colonies" against the New England trade with the French West Indies. The following week (15 July, p. 1), he featured the New England agents' reply, "The Case of the British Northern Colonies." In this usage, the "Northern Colonies" included the mainland colonies from Nova Scotia through South Carolina. On 22 July, page 1, Franklin reprinted an assessment of the West Indies trade that had originally appeared in the *Free Briton* and that opposed the bill, calling it a "*Navigation Act* for the Benefit of the French."

A new stage of the Molasses Act quarrel began in November, when Governor Patrick Gordon called together the Assembly because the Sugar Islands were "preparing to renew . . . their Attack against the Trade of these Northern Colonies." When Gordon explained how it affected Pennsylvania, he echoed the concern the *Pennsylvania Gazette* had voiced. Gordon said that although "we are not . . . so deeply concerned as some others [New England], yet if they are abridged of vending their Flour in those Channels, and confined only to such as this Province has generally traffick'd in, it will in the Consequence no less nearly affect our Trade in that Commodity, than it will theirs" (*Pennsylvania Gazette*, 27 November, p. 1). In 1732 news and rumors concerning the bill appeared in the *Gazette* for 27 April, page 4; 11 May, page 4; and 8 June, pages 2–3, where news of other bills restricting American trade and manufacturing also were featured. On 31 July, pages 1–2, Franklin reprinted an attack on the trade in New England and an excellent refutation of the attack. Franklin continued to feature news of the bill: reprinted essays and further news items appeared on 28 December, page 1; and in 1733 on 12 April, page 2; 10 May, page 2; 28 June, page 4; and 12 July, page 3. Franklin printed the official Molasses Bill, 14 and 21 September.

The commentator who wrote the note on the Molasses Act shrewdly foresaw that Pennsylvania's great export, flour, must be affected by the act. Thus the news comment anticipated (and probably caused) Governor Patrick Gordon's comments to the Pennsylvania Assembly quoted above. Franklin's *Pennsylvania Gazette*, first alarmed the mainland colonists about the consequences of the impending Molasses Act and kept up a continuous stream of notices and discussions concerning this and other mercantile acts (e.g., 8 June, p. 3; 31 July, pp. 1–2; and 28 December, 1732, p. 1). Although the *Gazette* reprinted both sides of the economic arguments, its editorial position against the act was clearer than that of any other American paper. *Conclusion*—by Franklin.

31. **Death Rates in Boston.** In *Pennsylvania Gazette*, 26 August 1731, p. 2. *Length:* 400 words. *Previous attribution:* Aldridge 1949a, 27 n.5.

Aldridge definitively set forth reasons for the attribution. *Conclusion*—by Franklin.

32. **Apollo and Daphne, A Dialogue.** In *Pennsylvania Gazette*, 4 November 1731, p. 2. *Length:* Eight lines of alternating iambic tetrameter and trimeter. *Previous attribution:* Lemay 1969, no. 195.

The prefatory editorial disclaimer typically indicates Franklin's authorship (see *P* 1:122, 195; 2:28; Aldridge 1964, 204–9; and cf. nos. 39 and 58). The content of the mildly salacious poem anticipates Franklin's letter to Joseph Priestley of 7 June 1782 on mankind making love at night (Smyth 8:451–52). And Franklin wrote poetry on occasion throughout his life (see no. 1 and its references). *Conclusion*—by Franklin.

33. **Hints on Fairs.** In *Pennsylvania Gazette*, 27 November 1731, pp. 2–3. *Length:* 415 words. *No previous attribution.*

The editors of the *Papers* (1:211–12) print a draft in Franklin's hand of a "Petition to the Pennsylvania Assembly regarding Fairs" similar to these "Hints," noting that the Hints "probably suggested" Franklin's draft. Since the language, style, and content are almost identical, it appears to me that Franklin was trying to influence public opinion by publishing the "hints" before submitting a petition on the subject to the Pennsylvania Assembly. His *Autobiography* testifies that before Franklin attempted to enact a new proposal, he usually tried "to prepare the Minds of the People by writing on the Subject in the Newspapers" (122). *Conclusion*—by Franklin.

34. **News Note Jeu d'Esprit on a Lion.** In *Pennsylvania Gazette*, 25 January 1731/2, p. 2. *Length:* 12 words. *Previous attribution:* Aldridge 1960, 78.

After reprinting a news note from the *Boston News Letter,* 3 January 1731/2, on the death of a lion, the *Gazette* wryly commented, "Like other Kings, his Death was often reported, long before it happened." In the same spirit, at the end of Poor Richard's "Catalogue of the principal Kings and Princes in Europe with the Time of their Births and Ages," Franklin printed an entry for *"Poor Richard,* an

American Prince, without Subjects, his Wife being Viceroy over him, [Born] 23 Oct 1684, [age] 49" (*P* 1:310). *Conclusion*—by Franklin.

35. News Note Jeu d'Esprit on a Burnt-Offering. In *Pennsylvania Gazette*, 15 February 1731/2, p. 2. *Length:* 78 words. *No previous attribution.*

A news note tells of a man living "near Sahaukan," who bit off "a large Piece" of his wife's tongue and threw it into the fire *"for a Burnt-Offering."* Although this could describe an actual incident, I suspect Franklin created the savage anecdote. It anticipates the verses on a similar subject in *Poor Richard* for June 1736 (*P* 2:139). *Conclusion*—by Franklin.

36. Marcus burlesques Portius. In *Pennsylvania Gazette*, 30 March 1732, p. 1. *Length:* 1,041 words. *Previous attributions:* Suggested by Cook 97–98; and by Aldridge 1950, 566.

When Portius, writing in Andrew Bradford's *American Weekly Mercury* for 23 March 1731/2, attacked infidelity and the "*Blasphemers* and revilers of *Establishments*," he was, as contemporaries knew, pointing at Franklin and Andrew Hamilton. In reply, this essay appeared, signed Marcus, ostensibly continuing the attack on infidelity—but really mocking the style, redundancy, and absurd logic of Portius. Marcus's essay on "the prodigious Growth of Infidelity" is a *reductio ad absurdum*. Marcus, an incredibly obtuse narrator, writes: "Scepticism infests almost every Conversation; and one continually meets with People, otherwise seemingly of tolerable Sense, who openly declare, that they know not but as much may be said against any Opinion as for it: Some profess they know only this, That they know nothing; and there are others who assert, that even this cannot certainly be known." The last clause applies the techniques of the tall tale to the Pyrrhonist position (which appears in Shaftesbury's *Characteristics*, III, i, among other sources Franklin knew), carrying on the argument beyond the point of absurdity. The seeming nonsense really masks a brilliant attack on Pyrrhonism. It reveals a verbal ability, reasoning power, and interest in philosophical issues typical of Franklin. Franklin implicitly advocated a Pyrrhonist position in the draft of a letter to his parents, 13 April 1738 (*P* 2:202, n. 5), in the "Speech of Miss Polly Baker" (Lemay 1975, 104 and notes 23–25), and in a letter of late 1759 to Mary Stevenson ("all our Knowledge is so imperfect"—*P* 8:456). But like all other religious and metaphysical systems, Pyrrhonism too seems to have been, on occasion, grist for his satire (cf. no. 2 and its references).

Next Marcus writes a mock appreciation of Portius's essay: "Often have they [the unbelievers] been attack'd with great Strength and Judgment . . . but never so effectually as in the last Weeks Mercury; *Portius* has afforded a Blow that staggers even the stoutest of 'em; and needs only to be well follow'd, to cause their entire Overthrow." And so Marcus will "add my Force to his" in "Five Hundred several Propositions . . . each of which shall be clear to the Understanding, convincing to the Judgment, undeniable by the most perverse Sceptic, and against which the least Shadow of an argument can not be raised." Franklin similarly overpraised the elegy on Mehitabel Kittle in his seventh Dogood essay (*P* 1:23–26; cf. nos. 66 and 78). Marcus "proves" his claims with five brief paragraphs that are grotesquely illogical and redundant. They splendidly parody the weak reasoning and repetitiousness of Portius. Marcus ends by congratulating himself upon his performance and advising the reader to "preserve this Paper carefully" because it contains "irrefragable Truths" that "may hereafter serve as first Principles indisputable, from which to prove and demonstrate Truths more abstruse and remote." The absurdly vain persona anticipates other of Franklin's personae such as Polly Baker and Poor Richard (cf. no. 2 above and its references).

Franklin was the logical person to reply to Portius's attack. Discussing Hamilton's patronage in the *Autobiography,* Franklin wrote and then crossed out: "I too was at times of some small Service to him" (65). I cannot help but speculate that the "small Service" Franklin could do for Hamilton was to defend him in the *Gazette.* Contemporaries too evidently thought he wrote it. An anonymous reply (probably by Portius) to Marcus in the *American Weekly Mercury* for 13 April 1732 mentions that the real Marcus was famous for his "Skill in Punning," thus identifying one of Franklin's personal characteristics (cf. *Autobiography,* 47 and 80; *P* 1:197; 7:246; 12:201, etc.; and see below, no. 40). Furthermore, Marcus evidently wrote five more pieces (nos. 38, 39, 40, 42, and 43) on religion, all to some degree inspired by the continuing attacks by Prosit and other *Mercury* writers upon Franklin, Hamilton, and the editorial policies of the *Pennsylvania Gazette.*

In discussing this controversy, Anna Janney DeArmond (84n) wrote that the series was related to the Reverend Jacob Henderson's quarrel with Daniel Dulany: "Its connection with the episode of the Maryland clergy is suggested not only by its general subject matter but also by two specific facts: a letter [in the *Mercury,* 13 April 1732] from 'T.E.' in "New-Town, in Maryland' attacked both Marcus and an enemy of the Reverend Mr. Henderson (who was mentioned by name); a little later 'Marcus Verus' referred to 'T.E.'" (*Mercury,* 11 May 1732). To these bits of information, I might add that this issue (30

March) of the *Gazette* carried an advertisement of Franklin's reprint of William Bowman's "*The Traditions of the Clergy Destructive of Religion with a Dedication to the Reverend* Mr. [Jacob] Henderson *by* Athanasius Wildfire.*"* (The underlying reason for the Maryland clergy quarrel to flare up at just this time was that the Maryland Tobacco Act of 1730—which lowered the clergy's salary—expired on 31 March 1732.)

But the *Pennsylvania Gazette* essays herein claimed as Franklin's have nothing to do with the local Maryland quarrel over ministers' salaries. To be sure, the *Mercury* opponent once (11 May 1732) referred to the quarrel (presumably because he associated it with the opposition between traditional Christianity and deism), but it is really irrelevant to his purposes. Of course the pieces by "T. E." (for "The Extinguisher," i.e., the person who will put out the fire of "Athanasius Wildfire") directly concern the Maryland quarrel, but they have nothing to do with the attack on Hamilton and Franklin. Neither Daniel Dulany nor Jacob Henderson, the two leading contenders in the Maryland quarrel, took any part in the Pennsylvania newspaper controversy. (Cf. Dulany's *A Letter to the Reverend Mr. Jacob Henderson* [Annapolis: Parks, 1732], Evans 39989; and *The Rev. Mr. Jacob Henderson's Fifth Letter to Daniel Dulany* [?Philadelphia:?Bradford], 1732, Evans 3551). For the contexts of the Maryland quarrel, see Lemay 1972, 121, and its references. *Conclusion*—by Franklin. (Cf. nos. 38, 39, 40, 42 and 43).

37. **Simplicity.** In *Pennsylvania Gazette*, 13 April 1732, pp. 1–2. *Length:* 1,396 words. *No previous attribution.*

The author begins: "There is in Humane Nature a certain charming Quality, innate and original to it, which is called SIMPLICITY." He claims that simplicity existed in the "first Ages of the World" and opposes it to "*Artifice* . . . and Craft," which are "The Tinsel Habits and false Elegance . . . worn to cover the Deformity of Vice and Knavery." In the beginning, he claims, "Simplicity was the Dress and Language of the World, as Nature was its Law." Poor Richard in 1756 set up the same oppositions and used similar diction when he wrote: "By the Word *Simplicity,* is not always meant *Folly* or *Ignorance;* but often, pure and upright Nature, free from Artifice, Craft or deceitful Ornament" (*P* 6:328).

The author maintains that "Simplicity of Speech and Manners is the highest Happiness as well as the greatest Ornament in Life; whereas nothing is so tiresome to one's self, as well as so odious to others, as Disguise and Affectation." As his deliberately cultivated appearance of simplicity in France (see Franklin to Emma Thompson, 8 February

1777; *P* 23:298) proves, Franklin had just this appreciation of the charms of simplicity. John Adams commented that Franklin "was master of that infantine simplicity which the French call naivete, which never fails to charm" (C. F. Adams 1:663–64). Further, the praise of simplicity as "the homespun Dress of Honesty" echoes Franklin's description in Busy-Body No. 3 of the virtuous "Cato" who "appear'd in the plainest Country Garb; his Great Coat was coarse and looked old and thread-bare; his Linnen was homespun; his Beard perhaps of Seven Days Growth, his Shoes thick and heavy, and every Part of his Dress corresponding" (*P* 1:119; cf. the obituary of James Merrewether, *P* 2:359–60).

Both Franklin's praise of the virtuous American farmer Cato and this author's praise of simplicity are tinged with primitivism: "What Relief do we find in the simple and unaffected Dialogues of uncorrupted Peasants, after the tiresome Grimace of the Town!" And yet this author could not allow himself to fall into the stereotype of believing that one must "go into the Country in search of this amiable Complexion of Mind, Simplicity." Egalitarianism and virtue are the fundamental qualities underlying this writer's apparent primitivism. He maintains that in the city as well as the country, "Men of the truest Genius and highest Characters in the Conduct of the World" possess simplicity. Franklin similarly asserted that *"there was never a truly Great Man that was not at the same Time truly Virtuous"* (*P* 1:121).

The author also possesses Franklin's aphoristic ability. He says, "None but Fools are Knaves, for wise Men cannot help being honest." In addition to the aphoristic style, the sentiment and the diction are Franklin's. His son William Franklin, writing on 26 May 1808 to Jonathan Williams, recalled one of his father's favorite sayings: "All Knaves were Fools; for if they were not Fools they would not be Knaves" (Jonathan Williams manuscripts, Lilly Library, Bloomington, Indiana). The opinions in this essay are similar to those in Franklin's "Man of Sense" essay (*P* 2:15–19). Indeed, this work has the same oppositions as that essay (virtue being identified with true knowledge, which leads to general happiness, whereas vice can be identified with sophistication and is not incompatible with the specific knowledge of subjects). Franklin writes, "In proportion as a Man is vicious he loses the Favour of God and Man, and brings upon himself many Inconveniences. . . . Virtue is really the true Interest of all Men" (*P* 2:17).

Just as this author says "that Wisdom and Vertue are the same Thing," so Poor Richard says, "Virtue and Sense are one; and, trust me, he Who has not Virtue is not truly wise" (*P* 3:6). This author also anticipates Franklin when he says, "for the future, we shall resolve to be what we would seem, which is the only sure way not to be afraid to seem what we really are." Poor Richard advised, "What you would seem to be, be really" (*P* 2:396; cf. 1:67; 4:357; 7:191; 8:131, 308; 9:76–7; etc.). Franklin was acutely conscious of the possible dichotomy between appearance and reality: he said in the *Autobiography*, "I took care not only to be in *Reality* Industrious and frugal, but to avoid all *Appearances* of the Contrary" (68; cf. rule 8 in no. 89, below; and Jesse Bier on the theme of appearance and reality in the *Autobiography*).

Although the author is obviously acquainted with the eighteenth century's frequent praise of simplicity (see Havens) he gives the term several of Franklin's distinctive interpretations. Since, however, the term *simplicity* in the eighteenth century primarily referred to aesthetic qualities, I should point out that Franklin voiced the same preferences for simplicity in his writings on aesthetics. In "On Literary Style," he wrote that "with all true Judges, the simplest Stile is the most beautiful," and advocated that writing should "be *smooth, clear, and short*" (*P* 1:329). Writing of music and of songs, he characteristically expressed his preference for the "simple Beauty" of the old Scotch songs, opposing them to the more complicated arias of the moderns: "And, indeed, there is so much simple Beauty in so many of them, that it is my Opinion they will never die, but in all ages find a Number of Admirers among those whose Taste is not debauch'd by Art" (*P* 10:385; cf. 11:539–43; 12:162–64). *Conclusion*—by Franklin.

38. *"This is the Practice at home": a second Satire on Portius.* In *Pennsylvania Gazette*, 20 April 1732, p. 1. *Length:* 770 words. *Previous attributions:* Suggested by Cook 99 and Aldridge 1950, 566.

In the *American Weekly Mercury* for 13 April, a writer (evidently Portius) said he "found it hard to understand *Marcus's* Discourse" (no. 36, above) and asked him to clarify his meaning. The speaker in this reply is not Marcus but a relatively straightforward and dispassionate commentator. The speaker defends Marcus and the *Pennsylvania Gazette* from the possible charge of being irreligious by claiming that Portius's defense of Christianity in the *Mercury* (23 March, the essay that "Marcus," no. 36, burlesques) is "so lamely and wretchedly perform'd, that suspicious People are apt to think they are only Sham Defences, made purposely by the crafty Infidels themselves, thereby artfully to insinuate that the Cause of Christianity is not really capable of better." Franklin used the same argument in defending the Reverend Samuel Hemphill in 1735: he claimed that the Presbyterian Synod's logic was so bad that "one would imagine these Men were jesting about this Affair, or that they really wrote with a

Design to burlesque Christianity" (*P* 2:121). This author next claims that ridiculing such performances actually serves religion, "and therefore the Paper of *Marcus*, which I suppose had no other View, is tolerable if not commendable." Thus, the author manages to defend both Marcus and the *Pennsylvania Gazette* from the charge of satirizing religion (cf. no. 16, above). Franklin, of course, would want to do just that.

The second paragraph calls "one of these Scribblers" (evidently Portius) a plagiarist whose "bad connexion and Arrangement of the Parts" reveals his inability to write or to think as well as his source (cf. the passage on imitation in no. 52, below). The third and longest paragraph characterizes his opponent (Portius) as an Englishman who assumes superiority over "a People, who, living in a remote Corner of the Earth [America], must of necessity be extreamly weak and ignorant." The Englishman "believes we can have had no Opportunity to learn good Manners, and therefore is continually instructing us?" (The author of this attack on English condescension to Americans prefaced the essay with a whining, repeated epigraph: *"This is the Practice at home. This is the Practice at home."*) Franklin chafed at English condescension throughout his life, as his "Rattlesnakes for Felons" satire (*P* 4:130–33; cf. 8:340–56; and Crane, 1950, passim) and "Information to Those who would remove to America" (Smyth 8:603–14) attest (see also no. 29, above). In 1745, he mentioned to William Strahan his annoyance at Pope's slur on America as "ape and monkey lands," and in 1753, he even suggested to Cadwallader Colden that an anti-American prejudice existed in science: "I see it is not without Reluctance that the Europeans will allow that they can possibly receive any Instruction from us Americans" (*P* 3:13; 4:463).

The author's use of a concluding anecdote is typical of Franklin. As he wrote his daughter on 26 January 1784, "You know every Thing makes me recollect some story" (Smyth 9:168; see also *Autobiography*, index, s.v. "anecdotes"; cf. no. 41 and Aldridge 1967b, 54–55). Further, the earthy meiosis in the Orwellian anecdote of the English pigs who "think they have more Sense and Merit than the rest of my Pigs" is Franklinesque (cf. *P* 13:184; Lopez 22–26; and Van Doren 111, 154).

After the end of this persona's reply, a brief paragraph by Marcus complements the main piece. Marcus's rejoinder is set off from the main letter by spacing and typography (it is in italic type), but the typographic lines on the page indicate that Marcus's rejoinder belongs with this satire. The contents and format of the two replies suggest that they are by the same author (and the *Mercury* opponent also thought they were identical—see no. 39), and the expert use of heading, spacing, and typography also suggests that the printer, Franklin, took special care with the format of these two pieces. *Conclusion*—by Franklin. (Cf. nos. 36, 39, 40, 42, and 43.)

39. **Prosit satirizes Prosit.** In *Pennsylvania Gazette*, 4 May 1732, p. 1. *Length:* 774 words. *Previous attribution:* Suggested by Aldridge 1950, 566.

In the *American Weekly Mercury* of 27 April, a writer who signed himself Prosit attacked the author of the second satire on Portius (no. 38). The *Mercury* Prosit addressed the author of the second satire as Marcus-Porcus, thus saying that he believed that Marcus (the author of no. 36) and the anonymous writer who told the tale of the farmer's pigs (in no. 38; thus the name Porcus) were really the same person. Now Marcus-Porcus (to use the *Mercury* writer's name for the *Gazette* satirist) adopts the pseudonym Prosit and pretends to be the *Mercury* Prosit. Actually, the *Gazette* Prosit is burlesquing the *Mercury* Prosit. (That may seem confusing, and at least one scholar has not realized that the *Gazette* Prosit is satirizing the *Mercury* Prosit, but the identities are clear if one keeps in mind that in this quarrel the *Gazette* author(s) wrote only for the *Gazette* and the *Mercury* author(s) wrote only for the *Mercury*. Of course, one would hardly expect otherwise if the editor of the *Gazette* were himself a writer in the controversy.)

As in no. 38, the format suggests that the *Gazette*'s editor took great care with the reply. Appearing first, a brief poem (perhaps reprinted from some English periodical) on the "*charming Pow'r of Self-Opinion*" evidently scorns the *Mercury* Prosit, even though it is separated by a printer's line from the following essay. Then comes Franklin's editorial statement apologizing for printing the essay: "*I do not love to have the Gazette fill'd with these* Controversies about Religion, *yet I cannot refuse to insert the following Piece, as it appears to be written in his own Vindication, by a Gentleman who has not been very tenderly used in my Papers.*" Herein Franklin pretends not to understand that the following letter signed Prosit really satirizes the *Mercury* Prosit. Franklin, of course, knew better. And the editorial disclaimer is itself a mark of Franklin's authorship (cf. no. 32). Since a common publishers' protocol forbade allowing another author to assume someone else's pseudonym (Crane 1950, xxi, xxvii, xxix, 54–55), Franklin declared himself a partisan merely by allowing this author to print under the name "Prosit." Further, few writers would dare to adopt another's pseudonym to satirize him. But Franklin definitely would dare, and he did so elsewhere (*P* 13:54–58).

The opening paragraph (after cleverly saying that all critics censure

Prosit's writings) says that Prosit is now writing in the *Gazette* "because the Witlings have of late taken much Pains to decry the *Mercury*, and hinder its being so universally read as it ought to be." This attack on the *Mercury* (and praise of the *Gazette*) directly presents Franklin's interest (cf. *P* 1:249–50).

The second paragraph points out that Prosit uses "a Figure in Rhetorick [occupatio] by which the Orator seems not to do what he is then doing." The expert appreciation of rhetoric also suggests Franklin's authorship (see Jorgenson; Lemay 1976, 100–106; and no. 72). The concluding sentence in the paragraph parodies the vanity of Prosit and his condescension to Americans, thus providing a link with the second satire on Portius (no. 38). In the third paragraph, this author attempts to defend his "former" mixed metaphors in the *Mercury*, thereby, of course, calling attention to and lampooning the *Mercury* Prosit's style.

Prosit says that he will write nothing more in the *Mercury* and that if anything appears there which pretends to be by him, "*it will be only a Contrivance of my Enemies, to render me more ridiculous.*" This statement anticipates Poor Richard's prediction of the death of Titan Leeds (*P* 1:311) and particularly Poor Richard's reply to Leeds that Leeds's later writings only prove that he is really dead (*P* 2:3–4).

The masterful use of a series of personae (all evidently by the same writer) and the extraordinary cooperation of the printer in arranging the format of this and the previous essay (no. 36) both also suggest Franklin's authorship. *Conclusion*—by Franklin. (Cf. nos. 36, 38, 40, 42, and 43.)

40. **A glorious Passage in Persius.** In *Pennsylvania Gazette*, 25 May 1732, pp. 1–2. *Length:* 830 words. *No previous attribution.*

Since the publication of the *Gazette* Prosit essay (no. 39) on 4 May, two attacks on the *Gazette* Prosit (no. 39) had appeared in the *Mercury*. On 11 May, Marcus Verus in the *Mercury* wrote, "it is granted by them [the *Gazette* author(s)] that *Prosit* has not been very tenderly, *i.e.*, rudely used in some former Gazettes," thus citing Franklin's editorial note of 4 May as coming from a writer of the *Gazette* satires. (Of course this identification could have been made carelessly or inadvertently by Marcus Verus.) And on 18 May, "S.H." in the *Mercury* evidently had Franklin in mind when he condemned "Satyrical and Witty Gentlemen, who Pride themselves in being Ludicrous upon every subject" (see no. 36 and its references).

This essay on a passage in Persius continues the anticlerical satire. Persius was a favorite classical author of Franklin, other passages from Persius appearing as the epigraphs for "Busy-Body No. 5" and for

The Nature and Necessity of a Paper Currency (*P* 1:127 and 139). The lines from Persius recommend virtue ("a sincere and generous Heart, deeply imbued with the most lively Sentiments of Justice and Honour") as the highest religion—a sentiment, of course, of Franklin (see the references on virtue in no. 37). The lines also condemn offerings to the gods of gold and material gifts and thus, by implication, condemn supporting ministers (cf. Franklin's satire where *"Pecunia"* beckons to the theology students [*P* 1:17]). As a writer in the following week's *American Weekly Mercury* (1 June 1732) pointed out, the essay tended to "throw a slur upon *Priests of all Denominations.*" Franklin was frequently anticlerical (see no. 15 and its references). The same *American Weekly Mercury* writer claimed that the piece reflected Matthew Tindal's deistic tract, *Christianity as Old as the Creation* (1730).

The heightened rhetoric of this essay is evidently a deliberate tour-de-force, and the author says in his follow-up piece (no. 42) that the declamatory style is most proper for "the Pulpit and the Bar." Franklin attacked the usual preaching style in "On Literary Style" (*P* 1:328–31) and, on an underlying level, in both "The Speech of Miss Polly Baker" and "The Way to Wealth" (Lemay 1972, 216–17; cf. Jorgenson and Mott, cxiv–cxlii). Franklin used a variety of styles in his essays (e.g., *P* 6:114–24, 124–28; 9:342–47; 17:220–27). He seriously (and splendidly) used the high declamatory style of his *Narrative of the Late Massacres* (*P* 11:42–69), and, of course, he used a religious declamatory style in his "Proclamation for a General Fast" (*P* 3:226–29; cf. Aldridge 1967, 147–49).

The subject matter and techniques (and the two follow-up essays, nos. 42 and 43), all point to Franklin's authorship. The two follow-up essays also show that this is the fourth in the series of six essays defending Hamilton and Franklin from the attacks by author(s) in the *American Weekly Mercury. Conclusion*—by Franklin. (cf. nos. 36, 38, 39, 42, and 43.)

41. **A Quaker Lady on a Lover's Threat.** In *Pennsylvania Gazette*, 25 May 1732, p. 3. *Length:* 196 words. *No previous attribution.*

This skit appears in the news section and opens with a reference to the *Gazette* news reports of the previous week (18 May, p. 3) when, according to this author, two persons killed themselves "one by hanging, and the other by drowning; both, as 'tis said, with this single View, to slip the matrimonial Noose." The ironic pun in hanging oneself "to slip the matrimonial Noose" seems typical of Franklin. So too does this author's freedom with the facts. Although the news report of 18 May attributed William Young's drowning himself to "some

Difference with his Wife and being disguised in Liquor," the report of William Whitisin's hanging himself said, "he was seen a little in Drink on Horseback not long before, but no Body can tell what induc'd him to destroy himself." According to the news reports, the moral would be that drunkenness led to the deaths; this author, however, changes the facts in order to create a tone of ironic humor for the story's main anecdote. Franklin similarly creates anecdotes and misrepresents facts to make a point (Lemay 1967, 201; 1972, 238; see also no. 38 and its references).

"I can now give thee an Account of a third, who last Firstday Night undertook to break his own Neck, by leaping head foremost off the steepest part of the *Bank* into *Water-street,* in case I would not consent to marry him the Week following." The Quaker lady makes fun of the supposed threat and concludes with a poem (by the English poet William Walsh [Lemay 1969, no. 222]).

Although the mock account is enjoyable, enlivened by the local references, an opening ironic joke, and the persona's amused tone, the piece is stereotyped wit, evidently written as filler, as the reprinted old poem suggests. Nevertheless, the piece bespeaks Franklin's pen—and who else could write such filler? *Conclusion*—by Franklin.

42. **A Discourse on Argumentations from California or the Moon.** In *Pennsylvania Gazette,* 1 June 1732, pp. 1–2. *Length:* 1,006 words. *No previous attribution.*

The persona claims to be an "oldish Man" who has "lived long in this Country" and who is pleased with the "*Wit* and *bright Geniuses*" of Pennsylvania. The ambivalent voice underlying this passage seems typical of Franklin's complex persona: expressing patriotic pride in the achievements of the colonists and yet mocking the provincial idea that "*Wit* and *bright Geniuses*" abound more in Pennsylvania than elsewhere. The parenthetical clause about "our Young (tho' in the Eyes of a great Part of the World insignificant) Colony" is also typical of Franklin's undercutting man's vanity—while no doubt satirizing the point of view that would consider America more "insignificant" than, say, England (see the patriotic note and references in no. 29).

The author also writes a deliberate "Digression" about logic, based on Locke's notions of the association of ideas. Franklin, of course, was often especially concerned with logic—and deliberately used digressions in a similar manner (*Autobiography,* 10). The thought about "how small a *Dot* our Globe is, in respect to those innumerable vast Bodies which are in and out of Ken around us" recalls Franklin's statements that "this little Ball on which we move" is insignificant in comparison to "that Space that is every Way infinite . . . fill'd with

Suns like ours, each with a Chorus of Worlds for ever moving round him" (*P* 1:102; cf. 7:91). And the self-mocking words "in and out of Ken" show Franklin's earmark (cf. no. 2). The thought that *"Fables"* and other wise writings may come from California or "from our neighbouring Globes, especially the Moon" anticipates the delightful fancy that Franklin employed in "The Ephemera" (Smyth 7:206–9).

The essayist claims that such "an Import of the Erudition, Wit, and learned Debates of the Inhabitants" (of California and the moon) will greatly improve "our Arts, Morality, and Religion." The implied criticism here ties in with the earlier satire on Prosit (supposedly by Prosit—no. 39) wherein the foolishly proud author says, "considering the little Time I have been in the Country, it cannot be suppos'd they [the Americans] have gain'd much knowledge of the polite Arts." Ostensibly the present writer is satirizing the strange qualities of the "Arts, Morality, and Religion" of Marcus. Then the author slyly makes clear that he is mocking the *American Weekly Mercury* writer: "Nay, may it not be presum'd we have already, and that of late, some valuable Specimens published of their manner of Disputing; all that's wanting is our Ability to understand, either *what they mean, or what they say.*" Thus this author allies himself with the writer of nos. 36, 38, and 39. And the author gives the Library Company a plug (as we would expect of Franklin) when he refers to the "Volumes and Tracts" in the recently formed library.

The author anticipates Franklin's fancy in "The Elysian Fields" (Smyth 7:204–6) when he wonders if "Lunative Learning" will reveal whether "the Defunct obtain" any satisfaction in seeing the living assume their names *"Marcus, Portius, Verus."* The pseudonyms refer to the earlier essays (nos. 36, 38, and 39) and suggest that the same self-mocking author is responsible for this essay as well as all the earlier ones. He appeals to the people as a source of value ("the honest homespun Coats and leather Jackets are resolved to laugh us down") in a manner characteristic of Franklin (cf. the "Leather Apron Man," *P* 1:9; and the pseudonym "Homespun" *P* 13:7–8; see also the egalitarianism of nos. 37 and 72 and the latter's references). And his concluding note, saying that he fears if he goes on too long, his piece will be divided "with the Note *To be continued in our next,*" nicely contrasts with the following essay (no. 43) in the same issue of the *Gazette,* thereby suggesting that the same person wrote both.

A further reason to attribute the essay to Franklin occurs in the Postscript. There the author gives a religious justification and interpretation of the *"Encomium . . . upon those Lines of Persius"* (no. 38). He says that the lines *"show that God has made noble Impressions on the Mind of Man through all . . . Ages."* Thus he defends the religiousness of the essay and, indirectly, Franklin for publishing it. Franklin earlier used the *consensus gentium* argument in his Junto lecture entitled "On the Providence of God in the Government of the World" (*P* 1:265; cf. Aldridge 1967a, 34–35). The author then speculates whether the "truly benevolent, extensive and salutary Precepts of the Gospel," if *"now newly brought to us from China,"* would receive the ecstatic *"Encomiums"* of *"the Wits of our Age."* Although the essay seems at first to praise religion, it really advances a deistic position, for such writings *"from China, or some remote Country"* would be praised not for their truths as revealed religion, but for their system of morality. And that, of course, is Franklin's position regarding the Bible and the teachings of Christ (Smyth 10:83–86). Indeed, Franklin later printed two excerpts from the "the Morals of Confucius" in the *Gazette,* 3 November 1737 and 21 March 1737/8 and cited Confucius (not Christ) in a letter to the great revivalist George Whitefield (*P* 3:383). *Conclusion*—by Franklin. (Cf. nos. 36, 38, 39, 40, and 42.)

43. **On Declamation.** In *Pennsylvania Gazette,* 1 June 1732, pp. 2–3. *Length:* 1,415 words. *No previous attribution.*

This essay is by the anonymous author of the praise on some lines of Persius (no. 40) and defends that brief piece against some supposed criticisms. Actually, however, it again (like nos. 36 and 38) burlesques Portius: "From the Moment, therefore, he [an author] is made sensible of his Inability to instruct or please, he ought to quit a ridiculous Endeavour, from which his reader can derive no Benefit, nor himself any Reputation." The charges that this author says have been brought against his Persius essay do not include anticlericism and anti-Christianity (charges that appear in the *American Weekly Mercury* of this same date). The author may have simply wanted to ignore these obvious criticisms; but the more probable reason for omitting them is that he knew the other essay (no. 42) in this same issue of the *Pennsylvania Gazette,* defended him from them.

The same person apparently wrote both no. 42 and no. 43. This author's statement that the words *"To be continued in our next"* were omitted by the printer from the bottom of no. 40 contrasts too aptly to be coincidental with the other author's expressed fear of having his essay "divided, with the Note *To be continued in our next"* (no. 42). Evidently Franklin was providing his reader with proof that, as he said one year earlier in his "Apology for Printers," *"So many Men so many Minds"* (*P* 1:194; cf. Franklin on the "Diversity of Opinions," *P* 1:51). This author says that "the Proper Theatre for Declamation seems indeed to be the Pulpit and the Bar." Similarly, Franklin, in his essay "On Literary Style," said that preachers and lawyers could be allowed to amplify (*P* 1:330). Once again, the author seems to be satirizing the lawyer Portius. The satire is reinforced by the mock advertisement in the same issue (1 June) of the *Pennsylvania Gazette*, for "An Essay upon the Nonsense of the Pulpit" and "An Essay upon the Nonsense of the BAR" by *Timothy Scrubb* (*P* 1:272–73).

The writer goes on to argue that different styles are suitable for different occasions; Franklin, in his essay on literary style, said, "that is best wrote, which is best adapted to the Purpose of the Writer" (*P* 1:331). This author satirizes "the Way of Writing which some people are pleased to call *easy*." And he quotes Wycherley's saying that *"These Fellows call easy Writing that which any Body may easily write."* The writer's point is that one can only attain the true easy style ("Showing no trace of effort; smooth, flowing"—*OED* 4b) by great effort, re-writing, and practice. Franklin had just this appreciation of the true easy style (which he defined as *"smooth, clear,* and *short"*), saying that it was much easier "to offer Rules than to practise them" (*P* 1:329, 331). To justify the occasional use of the declamatory style, the author cites "the *Moral Painter,* described by my Lord *Shaftesbury* in his Characteristicks," a work that Franklin knew well (see nos. 13 and 48 and the latter's references).

Although the essayist does not, in some details, appear to be Franklin, that is the effect that Franklin would have desired if he wrote it. And the mocking voice underlying this author's previous essay (no. 40) reinforces the conclusion that this piece is meant in great part to burlesque Portius.

In view of the evidence that the same author is responsible for Timothy Scrubb's burlesque advertisement in this issue (*P* 1:272–73), for the accompanying essay (no. 42), and for the series of four earlier essays, it is difficult to believe that anyone other than Franklin wrote it. Evidently Andrew Bradford thought so, for in the *American Weekly Mercury* of 8 June 1732 he refused to print a letter to T. Scrub because it was "too full of personal Invectives. . . . Most People think that *Scrub,* be who he will, has sufficiently exposed *himself* and the *Publisher of the Gazette* by his rude and rediculous Advertisements, and by the incoherent Jargon of his two last Nonsensical Discoveries" (i.e., nos. 42 and 43). *Conclusion*—by Franklin. (Cf. nos. 36, 38, 39, 40, and 42.)

44. **Philanthropos on helping young Men.** In *Pennsylvania Gazette*, 26 June 1732, pp. 1–2. *Length:* 848 words. *Previous attributions:* Suggested by Cook 102; advocated by Aldridge 1960, 209; 1965, 57.

In reviewing volume 1 of *The Papers of Benjamin Franklin*, Alfred Owen Aldridge suggested that this essay expands a passage in the standing queries of the Junto: "Do you know of any deserving young beginner lately set up, whom it lies in the power of the Junto anyway to encourage?" (*P* 1:258). He also noted its similarity in theme to a codicil in Franklin's will (Smyth 10:503-7). But the topic is not uncommon; the diction is imprecise ("Men who have natural Abilities and Hearts"—did others [before modern transplants] have unnatural hearts?); the structure is loose and rambling; and the whole piece is rather tedious. In addition, the author is too religious—and even sounds like a minister ("many Gentlemen whose *Works of Piety and Charity are going up continually for a Memorial before God*"). In fact, the essay originally appeared in the *New England Courant* for 11 June 1772, pp. 1-2, following "Silence Dogood No. 6." Although Franklin could have written another essay for that same issue of the *Courant*, the internal evidence says otherwise. *Conclusion*—not by Franklin.

45. Belinda on a too-bashful Suitor. In *Pennsylvania Gazette*, 26 June 1732, p. 2. *Length:* 689 words. *Previous attribution:* Aldridge 1962, 80.

This essay by James Franklin (W. C. Ford 352) first appeared in the *New England Courant*, 19 March 1721/2; and a poetic version appeared in the *Courant* for 3 December 1722 (Lemay 1969, no. 32). *Conclusion*—not by Franklin.

46. Praise for William Penn. In *Pennsylvania Gazette*, 14 August 1732, p. 3. *Length:* 556 words (including Andrew Hamilton's brief speech). *No previous attribution.*

The praise for William Penn occurs in a news report of the arrival of Pennsylvania's proprietor Thomas Penn in Philadelphia. As the editor, Franklin was the logical person to write up the important event, and the concluding sentence, praising William Penn, reveals Franklin's Whiggish principles (*P* 1:13; Smyth 10:130-31; cf. no. 73): "The universal Joy and Satisfaction which appeared on this Occasion, seems a just Tribute to a worthy Son of the Great and Good Mr. PENN, whose Memory must ever remain dear to all those who set a just Value on the ample Privileges and Liberties granted by him, and at this Time fully enjoyed by all the Inhabitants of this flourishing Colony." Franklin no doubt was attempting indirectly to influence Thomas Penn by his praise. Later, Franklin celebrated William Penn in similar terms in *Poor Richard* for 1748: "WILLIAM PENN, the great founder of this Province; who prudently and benevolently sought success to himself by no other means, than securing the *liberty,* and endeavouring the *happiness* of his people" (*P* 3:259). A notice (though without the Whiggish praise for William Penn) of John Penn's 1734 arrival in America appears in the *Papers* (1:381). *Conclusion*—by Franklin.

47. Censure or Backbiting. In *Pennsylvania Gazette,* 7 September 1732, pp. 1–2. *Length:* 1,332 words. *No previous attribution.*

This local essay replies to "*An* ESSAY *on* ENVY, *Philosophical and Political*" by CIVICUS in the *American Weekly Mercury* of 31 August and 7 September. In the following issue of the *Gazette* (12 September), Franklin, writing as Alice Addertongue, even points out that this essay on Censure "was published very seasonably to reprove the Impertinence of a Writer in the foregoing Thursdays *Mercury*" (*P* 1:243–44). The subject matter, techniques, and style of the essay are all characteristic of Franklin. Even the definition of scandal as "*Censure or Backbiting*" suggests Franklin's authorship, for he coupled the two words in his letter to Jared Eliot, 12 September 1751: "This Fondness for ourselves, rather than Malevolence to others, I take to be the general Source of *Censure and Backbiting*" (*P* 4:195; my italics).

When the author says that censure is a "Virtue," he anticipates Franklin's revision of a proverb in the following issue of the *Gazette,* where Alice Addertongue writes, "*Scandal,* like other Virtues, is in part its own Reward" (*P* 1:245). He claims he will prove that scandal is a virtue "by shewing its Usefulnes, and the great Good it does to Society," thus anticipating Franklin's praise of vanity at the beginning of the *Autobiography:* "being persuaded that it is often productive of Good to the Possessor and to others that are within his Sphere of Action" (2). Indeed, Franklin's turning the tables upon the usual attitudes toward vanity ("it would not be quite absurd if a Man were to thank God for his Vanity among the other Comforts of Life") echoes both the techniques and the substance of this author's praise of scandal: "All Divines have condemn'd it, all Religions have forbid it, all Writers of Morality have endeavour'd to discountenance it, and all Men hate it at all Times, except only when they have Occasion to make use of it."

The essayist gives four "advantages" of "*Censure or Backbiting.*" First, censure "is frequently the Means of preventing powerful, politick, ill-designing Men, from growing too popular" by exposing them or by forcing them "to enter into a Course of true Virtue, without which real Grandeur is not to be attained." The idea of "a Course of true Virtue" suggests a deliberate, systematic method of attaining virtue—similar to Franklin's scheme of thirteen virtues, which he methodically presented as "a Course compleat in Thirteen Weeks, and four Courses in a Year" (*Autobiography*, 82). And the statement that "real Grandeur is not to be attained without "true Virtue" anticipates the argument in Franklin's "A Man of Sense" essay (*P* 2:15–19).

The second argument is that the fear of censure "assists our otherwise weak Resolutions of living virtuously." The pessimistic attitude toward human nature (see no. 16 and its references), the suggested hypocrisy of some religious people (see no. 15 and its references), and the sexual joke (see no. 79 and its references) are all typical of Franklin: "This [the fear of censure] preserves the Integrity of the Wavering, the Honesty of the Covetous, the Sanctity of some of the Religious, and the Chastity of all Virgins." Third, censure helps "a Man to *the Knowledge of himself*," for our Friends are not "sincere or rash enough to acquaint us freely with our Faults," although enemies will do so. The author thus advocates the usefulness of enemies—a seeming contradiction that Franklin often advanced (e.g., *P* 11:318; 14:72–73; Smyth 8:306). As Poor Richard said, "Love your Enemies, for they tell you your Faults" (*P* 6:321). And the antitheses of the following clauses seem characteristic of Franklin's prose style: "we now hear of many Things said *of* us, that we shall never hear said *to* us; (for out of Goodwill to us, or Illwill to those that have spoken ill of us, every one is willing enough to tell us how we are censured by others)."

Especially Franklinian is the satire on Providence and on human nature in the statement "Providence . . . has given every Man a natural Inclination to backbite his Neighbour." Compare Franklin's implied satire of Providence in the *Autobiography:* "And indeed if it be the Design of Providence to extirpate these Savages in order to make room for Cultivators of the Earth, it seems not improbable that Rum may be the appointed Means" (121; cf. the satire of the First Cause in nos. 50 and 57, and the former's references).

The fourth proof of the usefulness of "the common Practice of *Backbiting*, is, that it helps exceedingly to a thorough *Knowledge of Mankind*, a Science the most useful of all Sciences." The underlying satire on human nature (herein humans are implicitly defined as those animals that enjoy condemning everyone else) echoes Franklin's sentiment in Busy-Body No. 1: "But as most People delight in Censure when they themselves are not the Objects of it, if any are offended at my publickly exposing their private Vices, I promise they shall have the Satisfaction, in a very little Time, of seeing their good Friends and Neighbours in the same Circumstances" (*P* 1:115). When concluding, the essayist uses the declamatory style in a way that anticipates the conclusion of "The Speech of Miss Polly Baker" (*P* 3:124). His aphoristic abilities ("all that deserve Censure . . . hate the Censorious") also are typical of Franklin. And finally, the author's self-conscious turn in the conclusion is characteristic of Franklin's ironic personae (cf. no. 2 and its references).

In addition to the internal evidence, there is some external evidence. Alice Addertongue's skit in the following issue of the *Pennsylvania Gazette* continues this essay. Not only does Franklin as Alice Addertongue several times refer to the previous essay on censure (*P* 1:243–44), but the body of Alice Addertongue's essay contrasts the boredom of a tea-table conversation restricted to praising other people with the vivacious interest aroused by a conversation detailing scandal. Finally, Alice Addertongue's maxims *"there are none without their Faults"* and "the worst that is said of us is only half what *might* be said, if all our Faults were seen" (*P* 1:246, 248) defend censure and condemn human nature in exactly this essayist's manner. *Conclusion*—by Franklin.

48. **"Y.Z." on the Benevolence as well as Selfishness of Man.** In *Pennsylvania Gazette*, 30 November 1732, p. 1. *Length:* 1,011 words. *No previous attribution.*

This essay poses the Hobbes vs. Locke, Mandeville vs. Shaftesbury quarrel concerning the basic nature of man (cf. no. 13, above). Mandeville's position (which may be viewed as a revision of Hobbes) is presented in the opening statement: "that Man is a Creature altogether selfish, and that all our Actions have at Bottom a view to private Interest." Shaftesbury's position (which may be viewed as a revision of Locke) is presented in the second paragraph: "A late ingenious Author . . . conceives that we have a certain internal *Moral Sense*, which tastes the Beauty of a rational benevolent Action, and the Deformity of an ill-natured cruel one."

The author then argues "the Fact is certain, that we do approve and disapprove of Actions which cannot in the least influence our present Affairs." And he offers as proof the reader's own feelings (his *"moral Sense* of Tasting") upon reading the enclosed short story, translated from the French. Franklin also urged the benevolence of most (but not all) men in his news account of Prouse and Mitchel (no. 13) and in his praise of brave men at fires (no. 54), and in both reports tried, by his narrative account, to make the reader experience (and thus unwittingly testify to) the reality of benevolence. Thus both news reports are nonphilosophical versions of this essay.

We know that Franklin read Hobbes and Locke (*P* 2:185), Mandeville and Shaftesbury (*Autobiography,* 44; *P* 1:58; Jorgenson and

Mott, cxvii–cxxviii; Aldridge 1949b; 156–58; 1965, 58–74, and especially 1967 [see the index]); that he was interested in the quarrel on the nature of man (e.g., *P* 2:15–21, 185); and that he discussed such topics in the Junto (*P* 1:262–69). Indeed, the Hobbes-Locke opposition is probably the major intellectual quarrel of the eighteenth century and the underlying subject of Part 2 of the *Autobiography* (Lemay 1967, 203).

The author says that he has "translated" the story from the French. Franklin "in 1733 . . . made myself so much a Master of the French as to be able to read the Books with Ease" (*Autobiography*, 97). If this author really translated the French short story and if Franklin did not begin to study French until 1733, then he cannot be the author. But dates in the *Autobiography* are sometimes only approximations. He tells about learning French, Italian (making an amusing anecdote of it by the story of his chess and Italian competition), and Spanish as a prelude to suggesting that these modern languages be taught before Latin. In fact, the *Autobiography*'s dates inadvertently suggest that he went through these three languages and then took up Italian—all in 1733. But the precise date is inconsequential to Franklin and to the story of the *Autobiography*. I suspect, however, that he remembered the date as 1733 because he and his chess opponent "beat one another into" Italian during that year (97). This passage occurs in Part 3 of the *Autobiography*, written in 1788. It covers the topic "Learn French and German" in the outline of the *Autobiography* (203). He wrote the outline in 1771 and does not mention learning German in the *Autobiography* itself. But if the outline's sequence of languages is correct (no doubt it merely says something of my own background that it seems to me it should be correct), then Franklin attained proficiency in French before 1732; for he expertly translated "The Palatines Appeal" from the German early in February 1732 (*P* 1:226–29). Indeed, the very fact that we know Franklin was frequently translating French throughout this period strengthens the attribution.

The unostentatious way the opinions of Mandeville and Shaftesbury are referred to (neither author is named), the excellent brief characterizations of their positions, and the brilliance of the author's arguments—all point to Franklin. *Conclusion*—by Franklin.

49. Chatterbox on the Family of Boxes. Dated "Nest of boxes, January 3, 1732/3." In *Pennsylvania Gazette*, 11 January 1732/3, pp. 1–2; reprinted in *South Carolina Gazette*, 14 April 1733. *Length:* 756 words. *Previous attributions:* McMaster 78; suggested by *P* 1:319n; argued by Aldridge 1962, 80.

The editors of the *Papers* note that this piece imitated Isaac Bickerstaff's essay on the family of Staffs in the *Tatler,* No. 11, and add: "The editors recognize the possibility that BF was the author, but cannot find sufficient evidence, internal or otherwise, to justify including it here" (*P* 1:319n). Aldridge points out that the dating indicates it is a local essay. He finds it significant that the essay appeared in the same issue that contained Franklin's essay on slippery sidewalks (*P* 1:318–19). He also notes that Bradford's *American Weekly Mercury* imitated it the following week (25 January, by "Cassettie") and three months later (12 April, by "Mack"). Most convincing, Aldridge says that "style also points to Franklin, particularly a distinction between talk and action in human conduct: 'a man of Words and not of Deeds, has always been a contemptible Character; *Sandbox* has the same Opinion of a Man of *Deeds* who is not a Man of Words.'" Aldridge points out that on 16 September 1758 Franklin cited the same saying in a letter to his sister: "A Man of Words and not of Deeds, / Is like a Garden full of Weeds" (*P* 8:155).

In addition, I might note that the surprising reference to "*Paper-Money* the Conqueror" suggests Franklin's authorship (see *P* 1:139–57; and no. 74 below). The definition of *Tinderbox* as "a Tradesman" who "rises before day, and has by the single Force of Industry, got so much Money in a little time, that People think he has found a Treasure" anticipates many of Poor Richard's prudential statements on the rewards of industry (e.g., *P* 3:304–8), and the ironic remark about finding a treasure echoes Franklin's satire on treasure-hunting in Busy-Body No. 8 (*P* 1:135–39). The characterization of *Sandbox* as a scrivener who is "a prodigious Lover of Circumlocution and Tautology" anticipates Franklin's association of lawyers and amplification (*P* 1:330; 2:146–49; cf. no. 43, above). The scurrilous note (cf. nos. 52 and 79 and the latter's references), the originality of the expression *Lickbehind! Lickbehind!*" (for an ass-kisser), the humor of the whole piece, and its fertility of invention (while at the same time imitating an existing form)—all seem typical of Franklin.

Finally, Franklin's former apprentice Thomas Whitmarsh, who was at this time his partner in Charleston, South Carolina, evidently (like Andrew Bradford) believed Franklin was the author, for he reprinted this piece in the *South Carolina Gazette,* 14 April 1733. Although Whitmarsh of course reprinted numerous pieces from various papers, he especially tended to flatter Franklin by reprinting his writings (cf. *P* 1:199n; and nos. 58 and 62 below). *Conclusion*—by Franklin.

50. **On Drunkenness.** In *Pennsylvania Gazette,* 1 February 1732/3, pp. 1–2. *Length:* 1,572 words. *No previous attribution.*

This local essay is in three parts, with the format suggesting that the printer took special care in presenting it. Part 1, a letter addressed "*To the Printer of the* GAZETTE," begins with a compliment to the printer because of "the short Caution you gave in one of your late Papers" against women drinking (*Pennsylvania Gazette,* 7 December 1732, p. 2; in *P* 1:278). The second part, an essay that begins with a reference to the letter, points out "that this Kind of Intemperance is by far more frequent among the Men." Thus the writer of the second part obviously speaks in the persona of *"the Printer of the* GAZETTE" (and this author's reference to "the four unfortunate Wretches, who within these few Weeks have died suddenly in this County," also proves that the essay is local). Part 3 merely presents a quotation from Dr. John Allen's *Synopsis of Physick.*

The *Autobiography* testifies that Franklin opposed the London printers' "detestable Custom" of constantly drinking beer and that he tried in vain to reform them (46). His character sketches of his early friends John Collins and Hugh Meredith attribute their failures to drinking (*Autobiography,* 32–33, 53, 56, 64, 65). He devoted Silence Dogood No. 12 to the subject and later, about 1732, made notes in his commonplace book on temperance (*P* 1:263, 271). One of the "standing queries" for the Junto began, "What unhappy effects of intemperance have you lately observed or heard?" (*P* 1:257).

Of course, recommendations of temperance are commonplace. What distinguishes this essay as Franklin's (beside the local references and the device of a long editorial comment on the letter) are the three religious references made with Franklin's characteristic freedom (cf. no. 85, below, and its references)—but absolutely atypical of the usual writers against drinking, the ministers. First, the author of the letter undercuts religious services when he writes that some women drink "as if Drinking Rum were part of their Religious Worship, they never fail their constant daily Sacrifice." Second, in the long editorial comment, the author implicitly satirizes the nature of a God capable of inflicting original sin upon mankind when he condemns pregnant mothers who drink: "what Crimes have their unhappy Offspring committed, that they are condemn'd to bring Misery into the World with them, to be born with the Seeds of many future Diseases in their Constitution." Elsewhere, Franklin directly attacked the idea of original sin as "absurd in it self" and said that a God who could punish mankind for original sin must be "unjust and cruel" (*P* 2:114; cf. 12: 360–61). And Franklin cleverly satirized original sin (and the nature of a God who could punish mankind for original sin) in "The Speech of Miss Polly Baker" (Lemay 1975, 112; cf. no. 47 above). Third, this author also undercuts the idea of miracles when he says that it would be "a modern Miracle" if there were "*A Smith,* or indeed any other Tradesman, *in our Town"* who never went to the tavern except for business.

Franklin reinforced this essay by printing a follow-up news note in this issue of the paper, p. 2, on a local "Servant Maid," who, "having drank a large Quantity of Rum, died in a few Hours." *Conclusion*—by Franklin.

51. **A Meditation on a Quart Mugg.** In *Pennsylvania Gazette*, 19 July 1733, p. 1. *Length:* 708 words. *Previous attributions:* McMaster 70–72; Cook 95; Smyth 2:198; Jorgenson and Mott 170–72; Davy 47; and Lemay 1967, 187.

Authorities from the time of McMaster (1887) to the editors of the *Papers* considered this a "characteristic" Franklin essay. The editors, however, judged the essay "not sufficiently characteristic of Franklin's style to be attributed to him" (*P* 1:328). But the essay *parodies* the common religous essays on the cares of life. Naturally the author imitates the style of the religious meditation, so if the piece is to be successful, it cannot be in Franklin's usual style.

And the parody is typical of Franklin. The choice of a quart mug as the subject, which of course is synonymous with taverns and drinking, itself undercuts the genre of the religious meditation. Franklin uses the same ironic juxtaposition in the *Autobiography*. He replies to the Reverend Charles Beatty's complaint that the soldiers were not generally attending his "Prayers and Exhortations" with the suggestion that Beatty serve as "Steward of the Rum" and "deal it out" immediately after prayers. Franklin ironically comments "never were Prayers more generally and more punctually attended" (148). The pun in the essay's opening that makes the "Bar" both the court of justice and the tavern is typical of Franklin. Typical too is the author's implied satire on the courts of law for favoring the rich: "Sad Spectacle, and Emblem of human Penury, oppress'd by arbitrary Power." As Poor Richard said, "*Laws* like to *cobwebs* catch small Flies, / Great ones break thro' before your eyes" (*P* 1:356; cf. Lemay 1976, 119 n. 36).

The ability to write such a parody (cf. *P* 4:114–24, 124–28; 9:342–47; 17:220–27), the use of Swift's "Meditation upon a Broom-Stick" as a model (cf. Davy 156–62; and Jorgenson and Mott 531 n.27), and the satire both of religion and pessimism—all indicate Franklin's authorship. For a similar parody, which Alfred Owen Aldridge has definitively shown to be Franklin's, see no. 58. *Conclusion*—by Franklin.

52. **"Blackamore" on Molatto Gentlemen.** In *Pennsylvania Gazzette*, 30 August 1733, p. 1. *Length:* 663 words. *No previous attribution.*

The vehicle of the metaphor, which concerns the relations between blacks, mulattoes, and whites, strongly suggests an American origin. The use of a proverb (Wilson 41) as the epigraph suggests Franklin's authorship. This author's ability to write good *sententiae* ("'tis the Curse of *Imitation,* that it almost always either under-does or over-does") is typical of Franklin, as is the sentiment (cf. Franklin on plagiarism, no. 38 above). The scurrilous note too is common in Franklin: "we below cannot help considering him as a Monkey that climbs a Tree, the higher he goes, the more he shows his Arse" (cf. no. 79 and its references). The statement that "there are perhaps *Molattoes* in Religion, in Politicks, in Love, and in several other Things" anticipates the various applications of those who give *"too much for their whistles"* (Smyth 7:416).

Although the essay contains many elements of class consciousness, these reflect eighteenth-century realities, whereas the essay primarily satirizes those persons who condescend to others (cf. no. 72). A person who condescends is defined as a *"Molatto Gentleman."* One may at first find the term *Molatto* used in this context to be racist (but of course eighteenth-century America—like the rest of the world—was racist), but Franklin undercuts even this typical twentieth-century criticism by his choice of the ironic pseudonym Blackamore. The posture of the persona, who calls himself "an ordinary Mechanick" and who at the end of the piece claims to be a "Blackamore," is typical of Franklin's democratic identifications and of his final ironic turns upon the personae (cf. no. 2). *Conclusion*—by Franklin.

53. Poem by Pennsylvanus against Party-Malice. In *Pennsylvania Gazette,* 28 September 1733, pp. 1–3. *Length:* 208 lines of iambic pentameter. *Previous attribution:* Suggested by Lemay 1969, no. 272.

Franklin used the same pseudonym only three months later (no. 54, definitively attributed to Franklin by Aldridge 1960, 209). Franklin was certainly capable of writing the poem, as his occasional poetry demonstrates (see no. 1 and its references). And the poem, in effect, favors Andrew Hamilton, Franklin's friend and patron. Most of the sentiments in the poem (e.g., praise of reason and truth) are commonplaces, but a couple are unusual, though characteristic of Franklin. The poet advises that in order to know a candidate's "intrinsick Worth," one should list all his virtues and also list all his faults. Then if one subtracts "the Lesser from the Great," "Arithmetick must bring the Ballance forth." Franklin advocated using such a system of *"Moral* or *Prudential Algebra"* in letters to Joseph Priestley and to Jonathan Wililliams, Jr. (*P* 19:300; Smyth 7:281–82). The poet also says that if one person were found to be "clear from Crimes, and fill'd with Sense," that person would be certain to be "defam'd" after he were praised. This echoes Alice Addertongue's way of finding out someone's faults—by praising her: "If you know any thing of Humane Nature, you perceive that this naturally introduces a Conversation turning upon all her Failings, past, present, and to come" (*P* 1:246).

One unusual note in the poem is the frank statement of class identifications and jealousies (lines 35–46, 199–202): poor against rich, learned against illiterates. The poet points out that "Fortune, unconstant, will have her Smiles bestow, / To sink the High, and elevate the Low" (lines 51–52). Franklin voiced this commonplace frequently, most notably in his "Appeal for the Hospital": "We are in this World mutual Hosts to each other; the Circumstances and Fortunes of Men and Families are continually changing; in the Course of a few Years we have seen the Rich become Poor, and the Poor Rich; the Children of the Wealthy languishing in Want and Misery, and those of their Servants lifted into Estates, and abounding in the good Things of this Life" (*P* 4:148; cf. 3:330). But in this case, the poet is implicitly arguing for the essential equality of man. Nevertheless, the poet recognizes an opposition between the classes and says that "High for High, and Low for Low, will fight" (line 53). The sentiment is uncommon in the early eighteenth century. Franklin, however, took account of such class antagonisms and occasionally used them in his *Nature and Necessity of a Paper-Currency* (*P* 1:139–57), in *Plain Truth* (*P* 3:180–204), and in the "Busy-Body No. 4" (see also Lemay 1965, 309). In "Busy-Body No. 4" he directly stated, "There are a Set of Great Names in the Province, who are the common Objects of Popular Dislike" (*P* 1:122).

Lemay 1969, no. 272, pointed out that the poem appeared while Franklin was on a visit to Boston. Franklin, however, frequently published his possibly contentious writings beneath editorial disclaimers (see above, no. 32); and since he sometimes resorted to publishing his own controversial compositions in other papers (*P* 3:135–40; cf. no. 79, below), he might well leave behind a political piece to be published while he was away. Indeed, in the summer of 1753 when he visited Boston, Franklin evidently left a political piece behind in Philadelphia to be published while he was away and even had another printer, James Chattin, bring it out (*P* 4:513).

In a personal letter of 9 January 1985 Professor David S. Shields wrote me that he agreed that Franklin may have written this poem, pointing out the similarity between it and Poor Richard's "Advice to Youth" of 1749, particularly the verses for October, which advise: "Shun Party-Wranglings, mix not in Debate / With Bigots in Religion or the State" (*P* 3:346). I see too that this poet quotes (with some changes) Pope's lines, "May they, with Pleasure own their Errors past, / And make, each Year, a Critick on the last" (cf. *Essay on Criticism*, lines 570–71). Poor Richard's verses for March 1749 paraphrase the same lines from Pope ("and while thy Frailties last, / Still let each following Day correct the last" [*P* 3:337]), and of course a well-known passage in the *Autobiography* (78–83) attempts to apply the advice to Franklin's life. Despite all these similarities, I am not absolutely convinced that Franklin wrote the poem, although I still suspect that he did. *Conclusion*—probably by Franklin.

54. **Pennsylvanus on brave Men at Fires.** In *Pennsylvania Gazette*, 20 December 1733, p. 1. *Length:* 999 words. *Previous attributions:* Aldridge 1960, 209; 1965, 57.

Aldridge points out that Pennsylvanus is "followed by another *Gazette* essay in 1735 known to be Franklin's [*P* 2:12–15] and reflects a concern expressed in his *Autobiography*."

In addition, one might note that the author uses the occasion to argue that the heroism displayed by men at a fire proves the existence of abstract virtue in some men: "Some of the chiefest in Authority, and numbers of good Housekeepers, are ever ready, not only to direct but to labour, and are not seen to shun Parts or Places the most hazardous; and Others who having scarce a Coat in the World besides that on their Backs, will venture that, and their Limbs, in saving of Goods surrounded with Fire, and rending off flaming Shingles. They do it not for Sake of Reward of Money or Fame: There is no Provision of either made for them. But they have a Reward in themselves, and they love one another." The absolutely clear and deceptively simple style, the underlying egalitarianism, and the consciousness of philosophic questions implied by men's actions are all characteristic of Franklin (cf. nos. 13 and 48).

When the author says that specific examples of "Virtue" cannot be "prais'd without Danger of Envy and Calumny rising against her," he echoes Franklin's opinion of "Humane Nature" (ironic pun intended; *P* 1:246). Like Franklin, this author relies for proof upon a proverb ("Virtue will be its own Reward")—and it was one Franklin used in the same Alice Addertongue essay just cited: "*Scandal*, like other Virtues, is in part its own Reward" (*P* 1:245). The author's attention to practical necessity (e.g., firefighters must have "Buckets and Ladders; without which the Business could not be done") is typical of Franklin. And the author ends with an anecdote and an implied moral—stylistic devices that also suggest Franklin's authorship (see no. 38 and its references).

A further bit of evidence suggesting that Franklin wrote it turns up in a brief news report (evidently by Franklin) of an actual fire. The report, 20 May 1736, p. 3, recapitulates this essay when it praises "the Diligence, Courage and Resolution of some active Men" (*P* 2:158) who prevented a fire from spreading. Indeed, it may be significant that whereas Franklin reported in 1730 the "Thieving" at fires (*P* 1:186), he had by 1733 evidently resolved to emphasize (and thus, presumably, encourage) praiseworthy actions, rather than crimes, that occurred at fires (cf. *P* 1:272, 377; 2:132, 158, etc.). On the other hand, one might argue that Philadelphians were growing braver and more honest at fires; if so, one might suspect that Franklin's reporting and this essay were partly responsible. *Conclusion*—by Franklin.

55. "Queries" urging establishing a Pennsylvania Militia. In *Pennsylvania Gazette*, 6 March 1733/4, p. 4. *Length:* 598 words. *Previous attributions:* Aldridge 1962, 79; 1965, 77.

Aldridge (1962, 79) notes that "many years before writing his antipacifist tract *Plain Truth* [1747], Franklin used the news columns of the *Gazette* to publicize the dangers to Philadelphia threatened by the French." Besides pointing out that the same attitudes and positions underlie both the 1734 "Queries" and the 1747 pamphlet, Aldridge noted that one query was substantially repeated in *Plain Truth*: compare this author's statement, "Whether 500 disciplined Men well armed, are not able to beat an unarm'd, unheeded, undisciplined, and affrighted Mob of 5000?" with Franklin's, "knowing that 600 Men, armed and disciplined, would be an Over-match perhaps for 60,000, unarmed, undisciplined, and off their Guard" (*P* 3:193).

In addition, three other echoes of the "Queries" appear in *Plain Truth*. The author of the "Queries" cites Judges 18 as a case comparable to Pennsylvania. Franklin cited the same biblical comparison in *Plain Truth* (*P* 3:192–93, 202). The author asked "whether the ancient Story of the Man, who sat down and prayed his God to lift his *Cart out* of the Mire, hath not a very good Moral?" Franklin used a woodcut illustrating this Aesop fable on the verso of the title page of *Plain Truth* (*P* 3:190, xiv). Third, the author of the "Queries" concludes by asking "whether, if it were known that we fortifyed and exercised ourselves, it would not contribute towards discouraging any Enemy from attacking us?" Franklin concludes *Plain Truth* with the same argument, "The very Fame of our Strength and Readiness would be a Means of Discouraging our Enemies," driving it home with a sententia: "The Way to secure Peace is to be prepared for War" (*P* 3:203).

I might also point out that the querist adopts specialized forms of Quaker diction, thus implicitly arguing that not all Quakers are against defensive warfare (cf. Franklin's *Autobiography*, 109, 111–16; and no. 86, below). Franklin used Quaker diction in "Martha Careful and Caelia Shortface" (*P* 1:112–13); "Advice to a Pretty Creature" (*P* 1:129), and in the news filler (no. 41) above. The form too of this piece, a set of ironic queries, was later used by Franklin (*P* 6:418–20; 8:164–88). *Conclusion*—by Franklin.

56. **On Constancy.** In *Pennsylvania Gazette*, 4 April 1734, p. 1. *Length:* 1,043 words. *No previous attribution.*

Although no internal evidence proves that the essay is local, the opinions are Franklin's. The praise of constancy has similarities to Franklin's "Art of Virtue" (*P* 9:104–5) and to his "Project of arriving at moral Perfection" (*Autobiography*, 78–88). The author's observation that "Men of Wit and Learning, in Spite of their excellent natural and acquir'd Qualifications" have sometimes "been ruined for want of CONSTANCY" anticipates Franklin's statement in the *Autobiography*, that "one Man of tolerable Abilities may work great Changes and accomplish great Affairs among Mankind, if he first forms a good Plan, and, cutting off all Amusements or other Employments that would divert his Attention, makes the Execution of that same Plan his sole Study and Business" (93). The author says, "Without Steadiness or Perseverance no Virtue can long subsist." Franklin, writing to his sister Jane Mecom about her son, uses the same diction: "without some share of steadiness and perseverance, he can succeed no where" (*P* 4:385; cf. Smyth 8:372; and Adams 3:186, quoting Franklin).

The essayist says, "A Man who has no End in View, no Design to Pursue, is like an irresolute Master for a Ship at Sea, that can fix upon no one Port to steer her to, and consequently can call not one Wind favourable to his Wishes." Not only is the writing absolutely clear and seemingly simple, but the comparisons are extraordinarily apt, as well as suggestive for how to live a happy and satisfying life. Further, Franklin, like this author, associated a ship voyage with a plan in life. He recalls in his *Autobiography* that on his return to America in 1726, he kept a journal while on board ship. "Perhaps the most important Part" of the journal was "the *Plan* . . . which I formed at Sea, for regulating my future Conduct in Life" (51–52). The surviving portion of Franklin's plan determines upon "a regular design in life" and attributes his previous "confused variety of different scenes" to the lack of such a plan (*P* 1:99).

Perhaps most telling, this writer chooses an epigraph from Lucan and praises Cato and Charles XII of Sweden for their constancy. Franklin, in *Poor Richard* for 1756, also quotes Lucan and links Cato and Charles XII together (*P* 6:329–30). Finally, the essayist compares

Charles II of England with Oliver Cromwell, judging the latter a greater man. Franklin never praises Charles II but he twice memorializes Oliver Cromwell in *Poor Richard* (*P* 3:251–52, 342). *Conclusion*—by Franklin.

57. **The Death of Infants.** In *Pennsylvania Gazette*, 20 June 1734, p. 1. *Length:* 826 words. *No previous attribution.*

The references to England and to Europe suggest that this essay was written in the colonies. The author begins by citing William Petty (an author Franklin cited elsewhere—e.g., *P* 1:35, 140–41) and the European bills of mortality. As his "Observations Concerning the Increase of Mankind" (*P* 4:225–34) shows, Franklin was interested in the bills of mortality (cf. no. 31 above) and he frequently printed them in the *Pennsylvania Gazette* (e.g., 3 February 1729/30, p. 4; 7 May 1730, p. 2; 21 May 1730, p. 3; 29 December 1730, p. 2; 5 January 1731, p. 1; and 26 August 1731, p. 2).

The author discusses "Arguments, to prove a *Future State*" and Franklin had done so (directly and indirectly) in his *Dissertation on Liberty and Necessity* (*P* 1:57–71) and in his Junto lecture "On the Providence of God in the Government of the World" (*P* 1:264–69). The author refers to the biblical *Dives* and *Lazarus* in a loose way typical of Franklin's free biblical allusions (cf. the references in no. 86). The author says that injustices that occur in this life raise "in us a violent Presumption that there is another State of Retribution, where the Just and the Unjust will be equally punished or rewarded." Franklin recorded in his *Autobiography* that he always believed "'that God will certainly reward Virtue and punish Vice either here or hereafter'" (92). The author refers to death as "sleep" and so does Franklin (*P* 1:65; cf. Aldridge 1964, 206–7).

The writer says, "Should an able and expert Artificer employ all his Time and his Skill in contriving and framing an exquisite Piece of *Clock-work*, which, when he had brought it to the utmost Perfection Wit and Art were capable of, and just set it a-going, he should suddenly dash it to pieces; would not every wise Man naturally infer, that his intense Application had disturb'd his Brain and impair'd his Reason?" Franklin earlier wrote, "It is as if an ingenious Artificer, having fram'd a curious Machine or Clock, and put its many intricate Wheels and Powers in such a Dependance on one another, that the whole might move in the most exact Order and Regularity, had nevertheless plac'd in it several other Wheels endu'd with an independent *Self-Motion* . . . and these would every now and then be moving wrong, disordering the true Movement" (*P* 1:62–63). The author's concluding clause in that quotation, which compares God to a skilled clockmaker gone mad, is extraordinary in the eighteenth century—but almost what we might expect from Franklin (cf. the passage on "the Salvation of Men's souls not worth regarding," no. 16). Just as this writer uses the physico-theological arguments to describe "an Infant, that curious Engine of Divine Workmanship," so Franklin used the physico-theological arguments both in his "Articles of Belief and Acts of Religion" (*P* 1:107–9) and in his Junto lecture "On the Providence of God in the Government of the World" (the passage beginning "That he must be a Being of infinite Wisdom, appears in his admirable Order and Disposition of Things . . ." [*P* 1:265]).

The essayist says, "the Notion of Annihilation has in it something so shocking and absurd, Reason should despise it." Franklin writes: "when I see nothing annihilated, not even a Drop of Water wasted, I cannot suspect the Annihilation of Souls" (Smyth 9: 334). The author continues: "rather let us believe, that when they drop this earthly Vehicle they assume an Aetherial one, and become the Inhabitants of some more glorious Region." Franklin writes: "it is the will of God and Nature that these mortal bodies be laid aside, when the soul is to enter real life; 'tis rather an embrio state, a preparation for living; a man is not completely born until he be dead: Why then should we grieve that a new child is born among the immortals?" (*P* 6:406–7). The writer speculates, "May they not help to people that infinite Number of *Starry* and *Planetary* Worlds that roll above us." In his "Articles of Belief and Religion," Franklin calls to mind the "System of Planets, beyond the visible fix'd Stars" and the "Space that is in every Way infinite" but "Fill'd with Suns like ours, each with a Chorus of Worlds for ever moving round him" (*P* 1:102). This author also asks if departed infants may "not become our better *Genii*, our Guardian Angels," and Franklin, in the *Autobiography*, refers to "some guardian Angel" (59) that guided him.

This author's gamut of possible religious comforts (lacking only a specifically Christian one) seems typical of Franklin. Writing in the *Autobiography* (where he wanted to present himself as possessing reasonably acceptable beliefs), he says: "And this Persuasion [of the excellence of morality], with the kind hand of Providence, or some guardian Angel, or accidental favourable Circumstances and Situations, or all together, preserved me . . . without any *wilful* gross Immorality or Injustice that might have been expected from my Want of Religion" (59). Just as Franklin allows one or another or all of these "causes" to be responsible for the course of his life, so does the author admit a large variety of possibilities, even while satirizing the nature of God—if a God is responsible for the death of infants.

Like Franklin, the author has the ability to create aphoristic sententiae: "When Nature gave us Tears, she gave us leave to weep." He tells us that the concluding four-line epitaph was "taken from a Tombstone in a little obscure village in *England*." Perhaps so, but it splendidly turns the tables on the previous thoughts in the essay:

>Read this and weep—but not for me;
>Lament thy longer Misery;
>My Life was short, my Grief the less;
>Blame not my Hast to Happiness!

Suddenly this life, as Franklin sometimes directly said (*P* 1:64), is regarded as a continuous course of misery. One suspects that the epitaph too is Franklin's creation. Poor Richard's verses on Thracian infants are quite similar (*P* 2:166).

Finally, there may be a biographical consideration. This author quotes Sir William Petty's observation that half of the infants who "are born in this World, die, before they arrive to the age of *Sixteen*." The Franklins' first child, Francis Folger Franklin, was not yet two years old. A sickly child, he was not inoculated because Franklin wanted him to be entirely well before inoculation (*P* 2:154). Perhaps his concern for his son (who died at age four of smallpox) inspired this essay. *Conclusion*—by Franklin.

58. **Parody of and Reply to a melancholy religious Meditation.** In *Pennsylvania Gazette,* 8 August 1734, pp. 2–3. *Length:* 920 words. *Previous attributions:* Aldridge 1964, 204–9; 1965, 51; 1967, 67–68.

Aldridge (1964) definitively set forth the reasons for the attribution. I might just add that the editorial disclaimer preceding the piece is typical of Franklin (see above, no. 32) and that the statement "The World is a very good World" is almost exactly repeated in Franklin's letter to Jane Mecom of 1 March 1766 ("the World is a pretty good sort of a World"—*P* 13:188). The same thematic contrast (between pessimism and optimism) and pragmatic underlying philosophy (it is better for oneself and everyone else to be—or at least to attempt to be—optimistic) occur commonly in Franklin's writings (see rule 4 in no. 19 above, and its references). And Franklin's partner reprinted the piece in the *South Carolina Gazette* for 25 January 1734/5 (cf. no. 49 and its references). *Conclusion*—by Franklin.

59. **Note on a Thunderstorm.** In *Pennsylvania Gazette,* 25 September 1734, p. 3. *Length:* 105 words. *No previous attribution.*

Franklin formulated his theory of the movement of northeast storms in 1743 (*P* 3:149, 392–93n, 463–65; 9:110–12), but this news note reveals he was interested in the question at least nine year earlier: "Sunday last between 7 and 8 in the Evening we had the most terrible Gust of Wind and Rain accompanied with Thunder and Lightning, that can be remembered in these Parts. . . . The Violence of it did not continue long, but the Storm was of wide Extent, for we have heard of it from *Conestogoe,* from the Mouth of the Bay, and from *New-York:* At *Conestogoe* it was about half an hour before it arrived here, but in the Bay it was at near Midnight." Franklin's authorship is strongly suggested by the reporter's detailed notes concerning *when* as well as *where* the storm struck. Such information later enabled Franklin to theorize that northeast storms came up from the South. *Conclusion*—by Franklin.

60. **Report on the Murder of a Daughter.** In *Pennsylvania Gazette*, 24 October 1734, p. 3. *Length:* 408 words. *No previous attribution.*

This news story touches upon several themes found in Franklin's writings. The writer reports the trial in Philadelphia of a man and his second wife, "for the Murder of a Daughter which he had by a former Wife, (a Girl of about 14 Years of Age) by turning her out of Doors, and thereby exposing her to such Hardships, as afterwards produced grievous Sickness and Lameness." After they were convicted of manslaughter, the judge told them that "if they were not perfectly stupified, the inward Reflection upon their own enormous Crimes, must be more terrible and shocking to them, than the Punishment they were to undergo: For that they had not only acted contrary to the particular Laws of all Nations, but had even broken the Universal Law of Nature; since there are no Creatures known, how savage, wild, and fierce soever, that have not implanted in them a natural Love and Care of their tender Offspring, and that will not even hazard Life in its Protection and Defence." In "The Speech of Miss Polly Baker," Franklin similarly moves from a discussion of particular laws to the law of nature and uses similar arguments to justify having children.

The reporter next gives his opinion: "But this is not the only Instance the present Age has afforded, of the incomprehensible Insensibility *Dram-drinking* is capable of producing" (cf. "On Drunkenness," no. 50). And then the reporter shows that despite the acts of barbarism recounted in the story, the man was not without some humane feelings: "They were sentenced to be burnt in the Hand, which was accordingly executed in Court, upon them both, but first upon the Man, who offer'd to receive another Burning if so be his Wife might be excused; but was told the Law would not allow it."

The clear style, interest in natural law, disgust for drunkenness, concern for reporting the man's gesture of compassion (cf. nos. 13 and 48 and the latter's references) as well as his earlier barbarities, and anticipations of some themes and details from Polly Baker—all suggest that Franklin wrote it. *Conclusion*—by Franklin.

61. **Exaggerating Body Counts in Battle Reports.** In *Pennsylvania Gazette*, 19 December 1734, p. 2. *Length:* 88 words. *No previous attribution.*

The editorial headnote explains that *"there is nothing more partial than the Accounts given of Battles, all of them lessening or magnifying the Loss or Gain on either Side, just as the Writers are affected."* The underlying relativistic thought of this passage (that authors' opinions created the world that they saw) occurs elsewhere in Franklin. Poor Richard says, "Historians relate, not so much what is done, as what they would have believed," and "It's the easiest Thing in the World for a Man to deceive himself" (*P* 2:220; 3:63). Franklin expressed the same view in an earlier editorial note, 23 October 1729, when he printed four paragraphs on the peace with Spain from four different papers—two from government papers, one from a Whig paper, and one from a Tory paper: "When the Reader has allowed for these Distinctions, he will be better able to form his Judgment on the Affair" (*P* 1:165; cf. no. 78, below). The example in Franklin's pessimistic letter to Joseph Priestley of 7 June 1782 is also pertinent: "Men I find to be a Sort of Beings very badly constructed, as they are generally more easily provok'd than reconcil'd, more disposed to do Mischief to each other than to make Reparation, much more easily deceiv'd than undeceiv'd, and having more Pride and even Pleasure in killing than in begetting one another; for without a Blush they assemble in great armies at NoonDay to destroy, and *when they have kill'd as many as they can, they exaggerate the Number to augment the fancied Glory*" (Smyth 8:451–52, my italics). The editorial headnote is evidently unique to the *Gazette*. *Conclusion*—by Franklin.

62. **Veridicus on a pertinacious Obstinacy in Opinion.** In *Pennsylvania Gazette*, 27 March 1735, p. 1. *Length:* 945 words. *No previous attribution.*

The general subject of keeping an open mind was a favorite of Franklin. A statement in the *Autobiography* encapsulates the argument of this essay: "If you wish Information and Improvement from the Knowledge of others and yet at the time express your self as firmly fix'd in your present Opinions, modest sensible Men, who do not love Disputation, will probably leave you undisturb'd in the Possession of your Error" (16, cf. 90). Franklin also generalized that "these disputing, contradicting and confuting People are generally unfortunate in their Affairs" (133).

Veridicus says "in our present fallible Condition . . . a Love of Truth and Goodness is not more essential to an honest Man than a Readiness to change his Mind and Practice, upon Conviction that he is in the wrong." Franklin used some of the same words when he voiced the same opinion: "In the present weak State of humane Nature, surrounded as we are on all sides with Ignorance and Error, it little becomes poor fallible Man to be so positive and dogmatical in his Opinions" (*P* 2:33, cf. 203; 8:456–57). The author's concern with religion and his freedom of speculation both suggest Franklin's authorship. Veridicus hypothesizes that a series of gradations exists in the afterlife: "possibly those who are arrived at a better State, may get clear of all their Mistakes, as well as their ill Habits immediately, and yet be capable of an endless Improvement in Knowledge, by having their Minds extended still to discover further Objects and new Relations of Things which they had no Notions of before." The suggestion that bad habits as well as ignorance might continue in an afterlife is extraordinary—but typical of Franklin's original habit of mind (cf. Prickett on his irony and originality); and the series of gradations of angels implicitly espoused by this writer was explicitly set forth in Franklin's "Articles of Belief" (*P* 1:102; on the "Great Chain of Being" in Franklin's thought, see Pitt 156–65, Stourzh 5–10, and Aldridge 1964, 204–5, and 1967a, 64–68).

The author says: "*Prevailing Opinions* insensibly gain the Possession of our Minds, and have commonly the advantage of being Firstcomers: and yet are very often no better than *prevailing Falshoods, directly the Reverse of Truth.*" Poor Richard said: "Philosophy as well as Foppery often changes Fashion" (*P* 4:404; cf. no. 8 and its references). Although the last sentiment is common among eighteenth-century intellectuals, Veridicus's observation on human psychology that follows has Franklin's earmark: "A Man can hardly forbear wishing those Things to be true and right, which he apprehends would be for his Conveniency to find so." As Franklin said, "we are very apt to believe what we wish to be true" (*P* 1:95), and "So convenient a thing it is to be a *reasonable Creature,* since it enables one to find or make a Reason for every thing one has a mind to do" (*Autobiography,* 35).

The writer says, unless we "*lie open to Conviction . . . Reason* would be given us in vain, *Study* and *Converse* wou'd be useless and unprofitable Things." Franklin wrote: "And as the chief Ends of Conversation are to *inform,* or to be *informed,* to *please* or *persuade,* I wish well meaning sensible Men would not lessen their Power of doing Good by a Positive assuming Manner that seldom fails to disgust, tends to create Opposition, and to defeat every one of those Purposes for which Speech was given us, to wit, giving or receiving Information, or Pleasure" (*Autobiography*, 16). The author satirizes those who "arrive to an Opinion of Infallibility." Infallibility was a favorite object of scorn for Franklin who, in his speech at the end of the Constitutional Convention urging the adoption of the Constitution, said: "But, though many private Persons think almost as highly of their own infallibility as of that of their Sect, few express it so naturally as a certain French Lady, who, in a little dispute with her sister, said, 'But I meet with nobody but myself that is *always* in the right'" (Smyth 9:607). Similarly, Franklin praised the Dunkards for being the "singular Instance in the History of Mankind" of a Sect that did not suppose "itself in Possession of all Truth" and drove home his satire with the parable of a man in a fog (*Autobiography*, 115–16). (David Levin's influential reading of the *Autobiography* and David Seed's apt characterization of the man in a fog parable [396] both find that an essential meaning of the *Autobiography* complements this essay.) Finally, Franklin's partner reprinted the essay in the *South Carolina Gazette* 1 June 1734 (cf. no. 49 and its references). *Conclusion*—by Franklin.

63. Statistics on Trade in Colonial Ports. In *Pennsylvania Gazette*, 8 April 1736, pp. 3–4. *Length:* 222 words. *No previous attribution.*

After a list of the "Vessels Entered and cleared" from Philadelphia for the past year, an editorial note said: "Here follows an Account we have received from *South-Carolina* of the Entries and Clearances in one Year at the Port of *CharlesTown*, which may enable the curious Reader to make a Comparison in some Respects of the Trade of that Place with this." Following the detailed Charleston report, another editorial note gave the 1730 totals for Philadelphia, "by which the Encrease of our Trade may be observed." The article then gave the totals for New York and Massachusetts, Rhode Island and New Hampshire. Such economic data interested Franklin (cf. *P* 2:302–3; and no. 30, above) and, as the editor of the *Gazette*, he is the logical author. *Conclusion*—by Franklin.

64. Report of a Sea Monster. In *Pennsylvania Gazette*, 29 April 1736, p. 3. *Length:* 89 words. *No previous attribution.*

Under the Philadelphia dateline, the *Gazette* reports: "From Bermuda, they write, that a Sea Monster has lately been seen there, the upper part of whose Body was in the Shape and about the Bigness of a Boy of 12 Years old, with long black Hair; the lower Part resembled a Fish. He was first seen on shore, and taking to the Water, was pursu'd by People in a Boat, who intended to strike him with a Fishgig; but approaching him, the human Likeness surpris'd them into Compassion, and they had not the Power to do it." Perhaps the report did come from Bermuda, but the clear style and stress on human compassion (cf. nos. 48 and 60) seem suspiciously like Franklin. *Conclusion*—probably by Franklin.

65. **David's Lamentation.** In *Pennsylvania Gazette,* 22 September 1737, pp. 1–2. *Length:* 692 words, plus 69 lines of verse. *Previous attribution:* McMaster 85–86.

The author's praise for the Hebrews in opposition to the Greeks and Romans, his literal acceptance of (at least portions of) the Bible, his self-satisfaction ("I have seen it several times in an *English* Dress, but none of them have given me any more Satisfaction, than perhaps I shall give to those who read mine"), his ability to translate Hebrew, and the subject matter itself—all testify that Franklin was not the author. *Conclusion*—not by Franklin.

66. **Philomath on the Talents requisite in an Almanac Writer.** In *Pennsylvania Gazette,* 20 October 1737, p. 1. *Length:* 1,052 words. *Previous attributions:* Kellogg 285; Davy 61–62; Aldridge 1962, 79–80; Goldberg 85–87; Aldridge 1965, 65.

This local essay, dated "Sept. 27, 1737," satirizes Titan Leeds's 1736 almanac. Kellogg, Davy, Goldberg, and Aldridge all point out that it continues the war with Leeds's almanac that Franklin waged in *Poor Richard* from 1733 on. Aldridge (1962, 79) says: "Like Alexander Pope's brilliant discussion of a 'Receipt to make an Epic Poem' (*Guardian* 78), which Franklin had previously imitated in No. VII of the Dogood Papers, the mock discourse makes an ironical application of precepts of neoclassical criticism which had gained universal acceptance" (cf. nos. 36 and 78). After discussing this essay's contents, Aldridge concludes: "This piece could have served as a preface to *Poor Richard,* and not one of its prefaces has any better claim to be included in the Franklin canon."

I might just add that the self-satire on the obtuse persona is Franklinian (cf. no. 2 and its references), and that Philomath's opening reference to almanacs as *"Labours of the Learned"* parallels *The Way to Wealth*'s opening reference to almanac writers as "learned Authors" (*P* 7:340). *Conclusion*—by Franklin.

67. **The Origin of the English Constitution.** In *Pennsylvania Gazette*, 30 March 1738, pp. 1–2. *Length:* 2,002 words. *Previous attribution:* Suggested by Aldridge 1965, 106.

Aldridge says, "Franklin may have written this important essay himself, and, if he did not, he was indebted to its author for the ideas on population which later gave him world-wide fame as a political philosopher." The key statements occur in the first paragraph on page 2:

> No nation ever sent forth colonies but with an eye to her own advantage. The view of *Britain* in planting and protecting so many settlements, at so great an expence, on this side of the globe, was to extend her trade and vend her manufactures. These we consume in proportion to the number of our inhabitants. Now it is an allowed maxim, that wherever Liberty shines, there people will naturally flock to bask themselves in it's Beams. The great acquisitions we have made from *Germany* and other parts of *Europe*, which we annually drain of their people, is a pregnant proof of the fore-going observation. For In a modest computation, the Province has trebled her inhabitants within these last 20 years; while our neighbours of *M———d*, harrassed by a petty-Tyranny and an ignorant vicious Clergy, daily decrease in their numbers.

Thus, this author says that Pennsylvania has tripled in population in twenty years because of emigration from Germany and other parts of Europe; and he attributes the emigration to liberty.

Franklin, in "Observations Concerning the Increase of Mankind," says that the population in the colonies doubles every twenty years because a greater proportion of people marry in America than in Europe and because they marry younger in America than in Europe. Franklin attributes these facts to the higher standard of living in the colonies: "When Families can be easily supported, more Persons marry, and earlier in Life" (*P* 4:227). Both Franklin's figures and his explanation for the causes of the expanded population are entirely different. Nevertheless, this author does connect the expansion of the colonial population with Britain's trade and manufacture. And so does Franklin in his "Observations": "But in Proportion to the Increase of the Colonies, a vast Demand is growing for British Manufactures" (*P* 4:229).

The author, however, evidently thinks other parts of the colonies are declining in population. He says that Britain was at "great . . . expence" to settle the colonies—a position that Franklin would have objected to even in 1738 (cf. no. 22) and one that he later directly refuted (*P* 8:350). Further, most of this essay's subject matter (including the long discussion on the origin of the English constitution and the sustained high praise for William Penn and the Charter of Pennsylvania) was not of great interest to Franklin and not relevant to the essay's main purpose. More telling, the comparatively poor structure, the self-indulgent extraordinary length, and weak conclusion are entirely unlike Franklin's careful attention to "Method in the Arrangement of Thoughts" (*Autobiography,* 14).

Finally, the essayist's style and mannerisms are peculiar and self-indulgent. His use of italic swash capitals and various other unusual types actually hinder the reader. He occasionally writes extremely awkward sentences, like the one at the bottom of page 1, column 1, beginning, "They invaded *England."* Although he paraphrases Algernon Sidney's maxim on liberty, he weakens it so that it is not memorable. All in all, the author writes an old-fashioned, baroque prose, much more like Cotton Mather's, James Logan's, or John Webbe's than Franklin's. *Conclusion*—not by Franklin.

68. "A.B." writes "Dear Ned" on Pennsylvania Politics. In *Pennsylvania Gazette,* 4 May, 6 July, and 12 October 1738; and 29 March and 5 April, 1739. *Length:* Five long essays, the first having 2,257 words. *Previous attributions:* Davy 52–55, 161; Lemay 1967, 196.

Davy thought the author was a clever satirist and pointed out that he was influenced by Swift (161). Davy identified the "Grand Maitre" in the essay as the proprietor, the "Petit Maitre" as the governor, and the machine as the legislature of Pennsylvania (54). Davy therefore believed Franklin to be the author. Lemay (1968), giving no additional reasons, followed Davy. But the satire in the first (and best) essay is rather mechanical, depending mainly for its effects upon simple identifications of the machine and the "Grand" and "Petit Maitre." The identifications must have been obvious to contemporary readers. Since George Thomas, deputy governor of Pennsylvania, did not arrive in Pennsylvania until 1 June 1738, he could not be the "Petit Maitre." Instead, if we accept Davy's scheme, James Logan, as the president of the council, would have been acting governor of Pennsylvania and thus he was the "Petit Maitre" in "Dear Ned's" satire. It does not make sense that Franklin would attack his good friend and patron, Logan. Further, if Davy were right in his identifications, then the third "inconstant Wheel" who ran the "stupendous Machine" would have to be the speaker of the house, Andrew Hamilton, Franklin's other major friend and patron.

In view of these difficulties, I consulted Professor Alan Tully of the University of British Columbia. In a letter dated 1 August 1983 Professor Tully informed me that he believed James Logan was the "Grand Maitre"; Speaker Andrew Hamilton was the "Petit Maitre";

and Jeremiah Langhorne was the third "inconstant Wheel." Professor Tully's identifications of the figures in the satiric allegory make consistent good sense, and I think he is right. Professor Tully further suggests that Robert Charles (d. 1770) was the author. At any rate, the historical facts make it clear that the author was not Benjamin Franklin, who had recently (15 October 1736) been appointed clerk of the assembly (the "Machine" in the satiric allegory) and who was the friend and disciple of both Logan and Hamilton. *Conclusion*—not by Franklin.

69. **News Note on the Compassion of Captain Croak.** In *Pennsylvania Gazette*, 10 August 1738, p. 3. *Length:* 428 words. *No previous attribution.*

After describing the circumstances leading to the saving of sixty-one persons from a sinking ship, the reporter commented:

> *As it was running a Risque, which few others have cared to do, it was therefore a more remarkable Act of Humanity, in the Commander of the* Rose, *to take so many additional Mouths on Board, when he had only Provisions for his own Company. This is such an Instance of a laudable Compassion, that it is to be wished it may not be more admired than imitated on the like Occasions.*

The style suggests Franklin's authorship, for example, the synecdoche *Mouths* for *persons* in a context concerning the food so many additional persons would consume. Both the praise for the virtue of compassion (cf. no. 48) and the attempt to do good by inspiring others in a similar situation to be compassionate (cf. no. 54) are typical of Franklin. *Conclusion*—by Franklin.

70. **News Note Jeu d'Esprit on Octuplets.** In *Pennsylvania Gazette*, 24 November 1738, p. 1. *Length:* 31 words. *No previous attribution.*

In the middle of a column of filler reprinted "*From the* LONDON-MAGAZINE *for* August, 1738" appeared the following sentence, which is not in the original: "*Aug.* 5. We hear that the Wife of a Peasant in the District of *Boisleduc* was brought to Bed of eight Children, seven Girls and one Boy, who were all living." The believe-it-or-not addition must have been made by a bored typesetter with a sense of humor who felt free with the contents of the paper. *Conclusion*—by Franklin.

71. **The New Jersey House of Representatives' Address to Governor Lewis Morris, Monday, 28 April 1740.** In *Votes and Proceedings*

of the New Jersey Assembly begun and held at Burlington April 10, 1740 . . . (Philadelphia: B. Franklin, 1740), pp. 20–23. Evans no. 4569; Miller no. 199. *Length:* 1,234 words. *No previous attribution.*

In the outline for his *Autobiography*, Franklin jotted down "Writing for Jersey Assembly" (205). John Jay recorded a conversation with Franklin on 19 July 1783 that gives fuller details:

> Dr. Franklin told me that not long after the elder Lewis Morris . . . came to the Government of New Jersey, he involved himself in a Dispute with the assembly of that Province. The Doctor (who was then a printer in Ph[iladelphi]a) went to Burlington while the Assembly was sitting there, and were engaged in the Dispute with their Governor. The House had referred his message to a Committee, consisting of some of their principal Members. Jos. Cooper was one of them. But tho they were Men of good understanding and respectable, yet there was not one among them capable of writing a proper answer to the Message, and Cooper who was acquainted with the Doctor prevailed upon him to undertake it. He did and went thro the Business much to their Satisfaction. In Consideration of the Aid he gave them in that way and afterwards, they made him their Printer (Morris 1980, 2:713).

During Morris's governorship, the assembly met alternatively at Perth Amboy (convenient to New York) and at Burlington (convenient to Philadelphia). The first session of the New Jersey assembly after Morris became governor in 1738 met at Perth Amboy, beginning on 27 October 1738. None of the House of Assembly's speeches to the governor was interesting or remarkable; Joseph Cooper was not on the committee to reply to the governor's address (see the *Votes and Proceedings* . . . [Evans no. 4283] 9, 10); and the New York printer, John Peter Zenger, was awarded the printing contract by the House of Representatives and mentioned (in preference to other printers) later in the *Votes and Proceedings* (title page, 10, 45, 55, and 56). All extant evidence testifies that Franklin was not present at Perth Amboy and did not write an address from the House to the governor during this session.

The second session of the assembly met at Burlington on Thursday, 10 April 1740. On 16 April Governor Morris attacked the representatives in a blistering speech. On Friday, 18 April 1740 the House appointed a committee consisting of "Mr. [Mahlon] Stacy, Col. [Thomas] Farmar, Mr. Richard Smith of Burlington, Mr. [Joseph] Cooper, Mr. [Aaron] Leaming, and Mr. [John] Low" to draw up the reply. And on the same day, the House "Ordered, That Benjamin Franklin do print his Excellency's Speech, and the Minutes and Votes of This House (Evans no. 4569, p. 13). If Franklin had not already gone to Burlington in an effort to secure the printing of the *Votes and Proceedings,* he would now have journeyed there in order to make arrangements with the speaker of the house, Colonel Andrew Johnston, for the prompt and safe transferral every week of the manuscripts to Philadelphia and of the printed votes back to Burlington. (C. William Miller, no. 199, comments: "These votes for the spring and summer sessions of the New Jersey Assembly appear to have been printed weekly.")

On Friday, 25 April 1740, "Mr. [Mahlon] Stacy Reported from the Committee appointed to draw up an Address to his Excellency, That they had drawn up an Address, which he presented to the House, and the same was read. Ordered to be engrossed" (17). Although nearly all committee addresses were revised and amended in the House (acting as a committee of the whole), before being engrossed (i.e., before the official, fair copy was prepared), this address evidently won the instant and entire approval of the House. In diction, logic, and especially in its tone of humorous superiority, it is the one extraordinary literary speech prepared by a committee of the New Jersey legislature during the administration of Governor Morris. By cleverly adopting phrases and clauses from the lambasting speech that Morris delivered on 16 April, the reply turns the tables on Morris—thoroughly ridiculing his address and turning all his arguments against him. Although individuals and committees of colonial New Jersey produced many notable speeches (e.g., Nevill, Spicer, and no. 80, below), no other that I have read is as funny (if one knows Morris's angry speech), as devastating, or as well written as this one. It required a master's hand.

All the facts of this speech dovetail with the reminiscence recorded by Jay. First, it was early in Governor Lewis Morris's administration (he was appointed in 1738 and died in 1746). Second, this assembly met in Burlington. Third, Joseph Cooper served on the committee appointed to prepare the reply. (It was the only time while Morris was governor that Cooper served on the committee to reply to the governor.) And fourth, Franklin thereafter (for several years) printed the New Jersey business. (Although Franklin earlier printed occasional business for New Jersey [Evans nos. 3693, 3801, and 4392], only after this session did his imprint read, "Printer to the King's Most Excellent Majesty for the Province of New Jersey" [see Evans nos. 5014, 5252, 5254, 5818, 5819, and 6200].) *Conclusion*—by Franklin (Cf. no. 80.)

72. **Obadiah Plainman defends the Meaner Sort.** In *Pennsylvania Gazette,* 5 May 1740, pp. 1–2. *Length:* 1,053 words. *Previous attribution:* Suggested by Aldridge 1967a, 111–12.

Aldridge 1967a, 111–12, says: "It is possible that Obadiah Plainman was Franklin's pseudonym. Obadiah was at any rate pro-Whitefield. He defended the accuracy and objectivity of the original news story and satirized the proprietors of the Assembly for their arrogant assumption that the best people in Philadelphia were the patrons of the Assembly."

On 1 May 1740, page 3, Franklin printed a brief news item in the *Pennsylvania Gazette:* "Since Mr. *Whitefield's* Preaching here, the Dancing School, Assembly and Concert Room have been shut up, as inconsistent with the Doctrine of the Gospel: And though the Gentlemen concern'd caus'd the Door to be broke open again, we are inform'd that no Company came the last Assembly Night." The leaders of the dancing school objected to the news report's insinuation that they closed their club because of Whitefield's opposition (in fact, the season was over) and replied with a letter attacking George Whitefield and William Seward. Franklin printed a prefatory note to the letter (*P* 2:257–59) explaining why he was printing it—but his prefatory note (which states "I think there is a good deal of Difference between a *Vindication* and an *Invective*") makes it obvious that he believes the "gentlemen" concerned in the assembly reacted too severely.

Obadiah Plainman wrote to the dancing assembly "gentlemen" on 15 May that he could not discover in that news paragraph of 1 May "the least injurious Reflection on the Characters of the Gentlemen concerned." Thus he begins with a defense of Franklin's news report, but he also complains that the "gentlemen" also "must needs tell *us* incoherent Stories of Mr. *Whitefield* and Mr. *Seward,* and, under Pretence of a Vindication, foist into the News-paper Invectives against those two Gentlemen." The sentiment echoes Franklin's editorial statement of the preceding week.

Obadiah Plainman particularly chafed at the gentlemen's discrimination between the "BETTER SORT" and the "meaner Sort." Franklin objected to such characterizations throughout his life. In his early essay "On Titles of Honor" (*P* 1:51–52), Franklin mocked William Penn's logic concerning hats, but he reinforced Penn's underlying democratic argument with his hope that all people "will continue to treat one another handsomely." And he echoed Penn's diction and egalitarian argument (honor "properly ascends, and not descends") in his letter to Sarah Franklin Bache, 26 January 1784, satirizing the Society of the Cincinnati (Smyth 9: 161–68). His early writings even occasionally betray a hostility to the "Great Names in the Province" (*P* 1:122; cf. *P* 3:197, 198, 200; 11:296–97; and nos. 4 and 11, above). In 1729, he wrote that "*Labouring and Handicrafts Men . . . are the chief Strength and Support of a People*" (*P* 1:144). In 1737, Franklin added an editorial comment to an essay in the *Pennsylvania Gazette* saying: "A PECUNIARY Gratification is offered to any of the learned or unlearned, who shall *Mathematically* prove, that a Man's having a Property in a Tract of Land, more or less, is thereby entitled to any Advantage, *in point of understanding,* over another Fellow, who has no other Estate, than 'THE AIR—*to breath in,* THE EARTH—*to walk upon,* and ALL THE RIVERS OF THE WORLD—*to drink of* " (*P* 2:189).

Poor Richard frequently advocates egalitarianism and ridicules the idea of aristocracy. In July 1734 Poor Richard advised, "Don't value a man for the Quality he is of, but for the Qualities he possesses" (*P* 1:355). In April 1738 Franklin published a brief poem expanding the old radical proverb "When Adam delved and Eve span / Who was then the gentleman?" (*P* 2:193); October 1739: "Let our Fathers and Grandfathers be valued for *their* Goodness, ourselves for our own"; March 1745: "All blood is alike ancient"; December 1750: " 'Tis a Shame that your Family is an Honour to you! You ought to be an Honour to your Family"; and November 1751: "It is an amusing Speculation to look back, and compute what Numbers of Men and Women among the Ancients, clubb'd their Endeavours to the Production of a single Modern. [After showing that 1,048,576 ancestors would take one back only to the Norman Conquest, Franklin concluded] the Pretension of such Purity of Blood in ancient Families is a mere Joke" (*P* 2:223; 3:5, 454; 4:97–98).

The one note Franklin made concerning the topic "My Character" in the outline of the *Autobiography* concerned social relations: "Costs me nothing to be civil to inferiors, a good deal to be submissive to superiors" (205). Although this quotation demonstrates Franklin's consciousness of the social realities of the eighteenth century, it also reveals his personal and philosophical resentment of any "submissiveness." Just as Obadiah Plainman chafed at the common distinction between the "better Sort" and the "meaner Sort," so Franklin resented even the connotations of the diction distinguishing the *upper* from the *lower* house of the legislature (Smyth 10:60). He pretended late in life to the French and English that all Americans were naturally democrats, like "the Porter, who, being told he had with his Burthen jostled the Great Czar Peter . . . '*Poh!*' says he, '*we are all Czars here*' " (Smyth 8:503). Indeed, the most romantic strain in Franklin's character was his egalitarianism. From his early character of "Cato" (*P* 1:119–20) and his obituary of the "obscure" James Merrewether who, despite "an unpromising Appearance," was "one of the honestest, best, and wisest Men in Philadelphia" (*P* 2:359–60), to his espousal of a former galley slave "whose rustic and poor appearance" belied his "character" as a *"veritable philosophe"* (Smyth 8:565), Franklin loved the idea of the common man.

Plainman points out that the gentleman "appealed to the *Mob* as *Judges*" while at the same time scorning the "meaner Sort." He says that "in this (and so it is in many other Cases) the Words are to receive their Construction from the *known* Mind of the Speaker." Similarly, Franklin wrote, "Such is the Imperfection of our Language, and perhaps of all other Languages that notwithstanding we are furnish'd with Dictionaries innumerable, we cannot precisely know the import of Words, unless we know of what Party the Man is that uses them" (*P* 11:277; cf. no. 78 below). The commonman pose of the pseudonym itself, "Obadiah Plainman" (cf. Franklin's pseudonym "Homespun," *P* 13:7–8, 44–49; cf. nos. 52 and 73), suggests Franklin's authorship. And the assertion in his editorial note of 8 May (*P* 2:257–58) that a rebuttal to the gentleman would be forthcoming supplies an external bit of evidence that Franklin was Plainman.

Two replies to Obadiah Plainman appeared the following week, one in the *Mercury* for 22 May, signed *Tom Trueman*, and an anonymous reply in the *Gazette* of the same date. The latter is obviously by the author of the 8 May essay that Plainman found objectionable. The anonymous *Pennsylvania Gazette* author gave four hints about Obadiah Plainman's identity. First, he accused Plainman of imagining himself "the Prince and Leader of a Set of People" called the "meaner sort." Franklin's contemporaries widely recognized this aspect of his character. The *American Weekly Mercury* criticized him on 6 January 1735/6, for "running violently on the side of the Populace." And Thomas Penn wrote in 1748 that Franklin "is a Sort of Tribune of the People" (*P* 3:186).

Second, the anonymous *Gazette* author calls Plainman "only a temporizing Convert, drawn in with Regard to your Worldly Gain." Tom Trueman's essay against *Plainman* (who said in his reply of 29 May that both essays were by the same person) made a similar charge: "I shall never get one Farthing" by defending Whitefield "which is what you know Somebody can't say." All contemporaries knew that Franklin was Whitefield's American publisher. On 15 November 1739 Franklin had advertised: "*The* Rev. Mr. *Whitefield* having given me Copies of his Journals and Sermons, with Leave to print the same; I propose to publish them with all Expedition." C. William Miller noted that Franklin's printing of the journals and sermons of Whitefield "must have been one of his first large business ventures and certainly a lucrative one" (Miller no. 180). Tom Trueman in the *Mercury* added: "It cannot be said with any Truth that I ever sneer'd either at the Man [Whitefield] or his Doctrine, as the worthy Author of the Letter I am answering has done more than once where he thought it wou'd not hurt his Interest." Since Franklin made no secret of finding "some of the Dogmas" of Protestantism "unintelligible, others doubtful" (*Autobiography*, 76), this charge too probably pointed at the deistic Franklin.

Third, the anonymous *Gazette* author of 22 May defends his use of the "better Sort" by supposing "that a curious Stranger, hearing we had a Library Company in Town, should ask of what People the Society was composed?" According to this writer, "a better answer could not be given, than that they were of the *better Sort* of People." Since Franklin was known as the primary projector and founder of the Library Company, this stroke also was probably aimed at him. Fourth, the anonymous writer concludes by directly identifying Plainman as the editor of the *Pennsylvania Gazette:* "I shall dismiss you with this Piece of Advice, that the next Time you make Extracts out of other Men's Works, *viz.* those of the Party-Writers in *England,* introduce them a little more *apropos,* for at present your Paper is but a miserable Piece of Patch-Work." The totality of these hints could point at no one but Franklin, but the contemporary author could have been wrong in his attribution. Obadiah Plainman's opponent, however, was evidently Richard Peters. William Seward says that "the chief Speaker" for the Dancing Assembly party (a group which included the proprietor, Thomas Penn) was "Mr. P———," a "Person who opposed Mr. *Whitefield* in the Pulpit, and was formerly a Clergyman, but cast off the Gown for Secular Employment" (Seward 22). Certainly Peters, a former clergyman who opposed Whitefield and currently served as secretary of the provincial land office, was an extremely knowledgeable contemporary.

Finally, an anecdote that William Temple Franklin recorded in his edition of Franklin's *Memoirs* sheds light on both this and the following essay.

> In Philadelphia, where there are no noblesse, but the inhabitants are all either merchants or mechanics, the merchants, many years since, set up an assembly for dancing, and desiring to make a distinction, and to assume a rank above the mechanics, they at first proposed this among the rules for regulating the assembly, "that no mechanic or mechanic's wife or daughter should be admitted on any terms." These rules being shown by a manager to Dr. Franklin for his opinion, he remarked, that one of them excluded *God Almighty.* "How so?" said the manager. "Because," replied the Doctor, "he is notoriously the greatest mechanic in the universe; having, as the Scripture testifies, made all things, and that by weight and measure." The intended new gentlemen became ashamed of their rule, and struck it out (2:298).

Although some details of the anecdote may be apocryphal, it shows that Franklin had spoken decades later to his grandson about the dancing assembly. The anecdote thus suggests both that the dancing assembly was or had been memorable to him and that he chafed at its aristocratic airs. *Conclusion*—by Franklin. (Cf. no. 73.)

73. **Obadiah Plainman to Tom Trueman.** In *Pennsylvania Gazette*, 29 May 1740, pp. 1–2. *Length:* 1,805 words. *Previous attribution:* Suggested by Aldridge 1967a, 111–12.

Obadiah Plainman herein replies to the two articles against him, one in the *Mercury* of 22 May and the other in the *Gazette* of that date. He says that "from the near Conformity they bear to one another in Sentiment, Reasoning, and *Similes*, I am apt to conclude they were wrote by the same Hand," and so he simply calls his adversary (who was evidently Richard Peters—see above, no. 72) "*Tommy* Trueman." Plainman characterizes himself as "a poor ordinary Mechanick of this City, obliged to work hard for the Maintenance of myself, my Wife, and several small Children." Such characterization was typical of Franklin's personae—and of his identification with the ordinary person. In fact, he had only one child in 1740, William (born c. 1731), since Francis Folger Franklin (1732–36) had died of smallpox four years earlier and Sarah Franklin was not born until 11 September 1743. Plainman further says of himself: "When my daily Labour is over, instead of going to the Alehouse, I amuse myself with the Books of the Library Company, of which I am an *unworthy* Member." That portrait anticipates Franklin's self-portrait in the *Autobiography* when he says, "In order to secure my Credit and Character as a Tradesmen, I took care not only to be in *Reality* Industrious and frugal, but to avoid all *Appearances* of the Contrary. I drest plainly; I was seen at no Places of idle Diversion . . . a Book, indeed, sometimes debauch'd me from my Work; but that was seldom, snug, and gave no Scandal" (68). Plainman thus acknowledges that the *Gazette* author of 22 May was correct in hinting that the real Plainman belonged to the Library Company (cf. no. 72).

When Plainman uses a common word in an unusual, though readily understandable way ("I shall make Use of that Privilege to *Document* you a little") he reflects a Franklin characteristic. See, for example, his expressed preference for the possible word *uncomeatable* in his conciliating reply to David Hume's criticisms of his Americanisms (*P* 9:230); his collection of circumlocutions for being drunk (*P* 2:173–78); his puns and wordplay in the "Letter to the Royal Academy" (Lopez 22–26); and nos. 6 and 30 above. And when he tells Trueman that his request "is contrary to all Laws of Argument," he reveals Franklin's expert knowledge of logic (cf. nos. 3, 6, 36, 42, etc.). To the charge that he imagined himself "the Prince and Leader of" the "mob" or "meaner sort" of people, Plainman replied: "In my Animadversions on it ["that extraordinary Epistle"], I personated the

Public, which you charge as a Crime, tho' it is an allowed Figure in Speech, frequently used, and particularly by those great Assertors of *Public Liberty* ["*Demosthenes*' and *Ciceroes*, . . . *Sidneys* and *Trenchards*"], whose Names I mentioned at the Time." The Whiggism (see no. 46) and the thorough knowledge of rhetoric are typical of Franklin.

The most convincing detail indicating Franklin's authorship occurs in Plainman's reply to the accusation that "your Paper is but a miserable Piece of Patch-Work" put together from "Extracts out of other Men's Works." Plainman asked for proof and declared: "I have, more than once, told you, that no Man has a Right to bring an Accusation before the Publick, without bringing his *Proofs* along with it." Since "Obadiah Plainman" never appeared in the *Pennsylvania Gazette* before the essay of 15 May, and since Plainman does not there tell his opponents, even once, about how to conduct arguments in a newspaper, one must acknowledge that Plainman is here speaking as the publisher of the *Gazette*—Benjamin Franklin. And Plainman's voice here is indubitably Franklin's; compare Franklin's editorial statement prefacing the gentlemen's rejoinder, 8 May 1740: "I have often said, that if any Person thinks himself injured in a Publick News-Paper, he has a Right to have his Vindication made as publick as the Aspersion" (*P* 2:258).

Finally, Plainman does not deny that he is the printer and editor of the *Pennsylvania Gazette;* nor does he deny that he (Plainman) will profit from his association with Whitefield. If Plainman were anyone other than Franklin, he should have defended the printer from these charges. Instead, his only reply to the latter charge is to state: "As to the PERSONAL SCANDAL, in both your Letters, it is a Commodity I never deal in." Compare Franklin's statement in the *Autobiography*, "In the Conduct of my Newspaper I carefully excluded all Libelling and Personal Abuse" (94; cf. *P* 1:196). *Conclusion*—by Franklin. (Cf. no. 72.)

74. Paper Currency in the American Colonies. *General Magazine* 1 (February 1741): 117–20. *Length:* 1,650 words. *Previous attributions:* Aldridge 1962, 81; 1974, 523.

Aldridge (1962, 81) convincingly presented the reasons for attribution and located Franklin's manuscript draft of this essay at the American Philosophical Society. *Conclusion*—by Franklin.

75. Theophilus Misodaemon on the Wandering Spirit. *General Magazine* 1 (February 1741): 120–22. *Length:* 1,299 words. *Previous attribution:* Suggested by Lemay 1975, 225.

Misodaemon satirizes religious enthusiasm, the Great Awakening, and George Whitefield. Although Franklin was antienthusiastic and generally anticlerical (see no. 16 and its references), he genuinely admired George Whitefield. In 1747 he wrote to his brother John that Whitefield "is a good Man and I love him" (*P* 3:169). Deborah Franklin no doubt shared her husband's attitudes. She wrote him in 1770 news of "the Death of our verey kind Friend Mr. White Field it hurte me indeaid" (*P* 17:251). Franklin testified the next year: "I knew him intimately upwards of 30 Years: His Integrity, Disinterestedness, and indefatigable Zeal in prosecuting every good Work, I have never seen equalled, I shall never see exceeded" (*P* 18:53). Franklin even defends Whitefield in the *Autobiography* from the implication that he misappropriated the funds from the orphanage (cf. nos. 77, 83 and 84, below; and see Aldridge 1967a, 103–23). *Conclusion*—not by Franklin.

76. Letter from Theophilus, Relating to the Divine Prescience.
In *General Magazine* 1 (March 1741): 201–2. *Length:* 382 words. *No previous attribution.*

The question "*Whether God concurs with all human Actions or not?*" pretends to be posed by a philosophically inclined reader who requests "to see some Remarks upon this Subject" in future numbers of the *General Magazine*. Thus, if the piece is by Franklin, one reason for writing it was to draw forth future essays (and boost circulation) for the *General Magazine*. The reasoning is brief and brilliant. Theophilus says that some theologians discriminate between the "principal efficient Cause" and the "second Causes" of actions. But Theophilus argues that "*if God did not concur with every Action that's produc'd, then there would be an Action, and consequently some Being, independent of God, which is absurd.*" Theophilus also points out that unless all acts have been decreed from eternity, "there is no Possibility . . . of defending the Doctrine of the *Divine Prescience.*" And he concludes, "So that whoever denies God's immediate Concourse with every Action we produce, must of Consequence deny God's Foreknowledge."

The consequences of the argument are twofold: first, it denies all freedom of the will; and second, it makes God responsible for all evil in the universe. This brief metaphysical essay is, I believe, an example of the kind of logical dilemma that Franklin (as he says in the *Autobiography*, 15–16, 35–36) used to confuse his religious opponents.

The subject matter and the technique are similar to Franklin's *Dissertation on Liberty and Necessity* (1725). There he wrote "*If a Creature is made by God, it must depend upon God, and receive all its Power from Him; with which Power the Creature can do nothing contrary to the Will of God, because God is Almighty"* (*P* 1:60). And *"If the Creature is thus limited in his Actions, being able to do only such Things as God would have him to do, and not being able to refuse doing what God would have done; then he can have no such Thing as Liberty, Free-Will or Power to do or refrain an Action"* (*P* 1:61–62). Like his *Dissertation on Liberty and Necessity,* this brief "Question" really burlesques the standard definitions of the attributes of God (cf. the satire on Providence, no. 47, and the satire on the first cause, no. 50, and their references).

The Reverend Joseph Morgan attempted an "Answer to the Letter from Theophilus" in the *General Magazine* 1 (May 1741): 340–42, but it sheds no light on the identity of Theophilus. *Conclusion*—by Franklin.

77. An infallible Receipt to make a new Kind of Convert, by Esculapius. In *General Magazine and Historical Chronicle,* 1 (June 1741): 414. *Length:* 288 words. *Previous attribution:* Suggested by Mott 76; mentioned by Sappenfield 106.

Since Franklin admired Whitefield (cf. nos. 75, 83, and 84 and their references), it seems most unlikely that Franklin would call him "our great modern Mountebank." Although Franklin used the "Receipt" form in his Silence Dogood No. 7 (*P* 1:25–26), the contents and prose style of this brief piece seem uninspired. Indeed, the *ad hominem* attack alienates the reader by being too strong. It is completely unlike Franklin's usual ironic personae. *Conclusion*—not by Franklin.

78. Introduction and "Remark" on "What is True?" In *Pennsylvania Gazette,* 24 February 1742/3, pp. 1–3. *Length:* 418 words. *No previous attribution.*

In a "Dearth of News," a reader sends in an extract from the *Journal* of John Wesley at Hernhuth, Germany, followed by "*An* Extract *of the Constitution of the Church* of the Moravian *Brethren at Hernhuth.*" In his prefatory remarks, the "reader" undercuts the extracts that follow by saying, *"an Account of their Discipline will methinks well enough stand in the Place of NEWS, as there is something in it so uncommon and particular, that we have never seen or heard of any thing like it."* Like this reader, Franklin was interested in the customs and practices of the Moravians, and describes them in the *Autobiography* (145, 149–50). And Franklin also satirized opponents and literature by commenting on their extraordinary originality (see nos. 36 and 66).

But the "Remark" on *"what is true?"* at the end of the two extracts especially reveals Franklin's mind and style. The "Remark," supposedly written by "one of the Moravian Brethren in Philadelphia," begins by claiming: "The Questions, Accounts and Testimonys falling under the Consideration of Magistrates, go upon that Point; *what is true?* But Posterity likes very often, and that justly, to hear *how a Thing is true,* especially in Matters of Religion, where the Appearance of a Thing, (which however with Men exceeding often goes for the *verum physicum* and *metaphysicum*) infinitely differs from the *verum morale.*" This author's concern with appearance and reality is characteristic of Franklin. In his *Dissertation on Liberty and Necessity* (1725) Franklin says, "we can judge by nothing but Appearances, and they are very apt to deceive us" (*P* 1:67–68; cf. 1:22; 8:308; and see no. 36 and its references). Just as this author discriminates between the kinds of truth and how things are true, Franklin comments on the different ideas different writers have of the "moral Virtues" (*Autobiography,* 78–79) and he chafes under recommendations of virtue that do not show "the *Means and Manner* of obtaining Virtue" (*Autobiography,* 88–89). Further, the author has an almost Melvillean grasp of the different orders and structures of reality: legal, scientific, metaphysical, and moral—all being suggested in this one sentence. Few people in the eighteenth century had such a complex view of possibilities of reality, but Franklin did. Compare his explanation of the possible reasons for his conduct: "And this Persuasion, with the kind hand of Providence, or some guardian Angel, or accidental favourable Circumstances and Situations, or all together, preserved me . . . without any wilful gross Immorality or Injustice that might have been expected from my want of Religion" (*Autobiography,* 59).

The supposed Moravian further says, "It is therefore much the best, considering human Imperfection, that each Party describes itself as good, and as bad, as sincerely and as insincerely as they can and will, and leave it to such as are capable, to gather as much as is possible of what is true and solid, from Peoples Stile and Expressions." The combination of relativism, skepticism, disgust with "human Imperfection" and with parties for lying to themselves and others—all commonly recur in Franklin. In his preface to Joseph Galloway's *Speech,* Franklin wrote: "Such is the Imperfection of our Language, and perhaps of all other Languages, that notwithstanding we are furnish'd with Dictionaries innumerable, we cannot precisely know the import of Words, unless we know of what Party the Man is that uses them" (*P* 11:277; cf. no. 72). As I pointed out above (no. 61), Franklin explained the differing reports of government, Whig, and Tory papers by identifying their party identifications: "When the Reader has allowed for these Distinctions, he will be better able to form his Judgment on the Affair" (*P* 1:165).

Franklin's contemporaries attributed the "Remark" to him. A writer in the *Pennsylvania Journal,* 8 March 1742/3, p. 2, said that "several persons in Town and especially such as are fond of the Moravians are unwilling to believe any of them to be the Author of that Enigmatical remark, on the Extract published from Mr. Wesley's Journal." The *Journal* author said that they "rather suppose it be a Satyr of your own upon them, especially since some of the *Moravians* do now disclaim it." He cleverly added, "And as I cannot but believe you are guiltless in the case, I am willing to give you a publick opportunity of wipeing away such an Aspersion from your Character, by letting you know what is surmis'd concerning you." Evidently the *Pennsylvania Journal* writer believed Franklin wrote the "Remark" and took this rhetorically superior way of accusing him. Franklin made no reply.

The supposed circumstances of publication also suggest that the editor of the *Pennsylvania Gazette* must be the author: at the very time one reader sends in the "Extract" during a "Dearth of News" (and only an editor is likely to be much concerned with a lack of news for the paper), a member of the "Moravian Brethren" comments on "what is true" in the Extract.... Although one can imagine possibilities that may account for such an extraordinary coincidence, there is only one likely explanation. *Conclusion*—by Franklin.

79. "*An* Apology *for the young Man in Goal, and in* Shackles, *for ravishing an old Woman of 85* at Whitemarsh, *who had only one Eye, and that a red one.* In *American Weekly Mercury,* 15 September 1743, p. 4. *Length:* 20 lines of iambic pentameter. *No previous attribution.*

The poem was based upon an actual occurrence. The *Pennsylvania Gazette* for 25 August 1743, page 3, reported: "Last Sunday a young Fellow about 20 Years of Age was brought to Town from Whitemarsh and committed to Prison, being charg'd with Ravishing a poor old Woman upwards of Eighty, and injuring her so that her Life is tho't to be in Danger." This news note appeared only in the *Pennsylvania Gazette;* neither the *American Weekly Mercury* nor the *Pennsylvania Journal* mentioned it. Evidently the poet, disgusted with the youth's animality but also, to a lesser degree, with what he had heard of the old woman's behavior, wrote the poem shortly after the *Gazette* news note appeared.

When the case came to trial, the jury found mitigating circumstances. Two weeks after the poem appeared in the *Mercury,* both the *Mercury* (which had printed the poem) and the *Gazette* reported the trial's outcome. The *Gazette* for 29 September 1743, page 3, announced: "Yesterday William Coulter, a likely young Fellow of about

22 Years of Age, was tried at a Court of Oyer and Terminer, on an Indictment for ravishing a miserable old Dutch Woman of fourscore. The Jury acquitted him of the Rape, but found him guilty of an Assault." A similar notice appeared in the *Mercury* of 29 September, page 4, omitting the young man's name but adding that the trial lasted "about 4 Hours." The *Pennsylvania Gazette* took more interest in the case than the other two Philadelphia newspapers: a year and three months later, the *Gazette* of 18 December 1744, page 3, reported an event that, for those who knew the poem, must have been ironic: "We hear that the old Dutch Woman, that prosecuted the young Fellow for a Rape, some time since, is lately married."

Although it may seem surprising that Franklin would not publish the poem in his own newspaper, he did not, in fact, publish his own best hoaxes and satires in the *Gazette*. He gradually came to think the *Pennsylvania Gazette* was unsuitable for grotesque or bawdy pieces. "Old Mistresses Apologue" (*P* 3:27–31), "The Speech of Miss Polly Baker" (*P* 3:120–25), the "Verses on the Virginia Capital Fire" (*P* 3:135–40), "A Parable against Persecution" (*P* 6:114–24), and "A Parable on Brotherly Love" (*P* 6:124–28)—all circulated in manuscript copies and were first printed by others. Therefore, if this excellent, ribald, scurrilous verse had appeared in the *Gazette*, I would have some reason to doubt that he wrote it. The long descriptive title is itself unusual and anticipates Franklin's genius in entitling the Polly Baker satire: "The SPEECH of Miss POLLY BAKER, before a Court of Judicature, at Connecticut near Boston in New-England; where she was prosecuted the Fifth Time, for having a Bastard Child: Which influenced the Court to dispense with her Punishment, and induced one of her Judges to marry her the next Day" (*P* 3:123).

The savage humor and grotesque subject matter are typical of that employed by Franklin in some of his early news hoaxes and late satires (*P* 1:165, 184, 217–18, 271; 13:182–84, 240–42; 21:220–22; Smyth 7:27–29; Lopez 22–26; cf. no. 35, above). The sexual subject matter appeared earlier in the Silence Dogood essays (*P* 1:12, 37–38, and 41–42) and would recur later in "Old Mistresses Apologue" (*P* 3:27–31) and in "The Speech of Miss Polly Baker" (*P* 3:120–25). The facetious argument "Yet may thy Council urge this prudent Plea, / That by one Crime, thou hast avoided three" (ll. 9–10) recalls Franklin's facetious one/three argument in the satire on Kitelic poetry: "The latter only mentions three Qualifications of *one* Person who was deceased, which therefore could raise Grief and Compassion but for *One*. Whereas the former, *(our most excellent Poet)* gives his Reader a Sort of an Idea of the Death of *Three Persons*" (*P* 1:25). The argument "Or hadst thou sought a blooming Virgin's Rape, / Thou shouldst not from the Penalty escape" (ll. 14–15) anticipates the sixth reason for preferring an old woman to a young one in "Old Mistresses Apologue": "Because the Sin is less. The debauching a Virgin may be her Ruin, and make her for Life unhappy" (*P* 3:31). And lines 17–20 in the poem ("But when the Object is long past her Flow'r, / and brings no County-Charge, and wants no Dow'r; / Who, slighted all her Life, would fain be ravished, / Thou sholdst be pity'd for thy Love so lavish'd") anticipate the following reasons in Franklin's bagatelle "Old Mistresses Apologue": "#7. Because the Compunction is less. The having made a young Girl *miserable* may give you frequent bitter Reflections; none of which can attend the making an old Woman *happy.* 8. They are *so grateful*!!" (*P* 3:31). Thus a similarity to "Old Mistresses Apologue" exists not only in subject matter and in some details but even in the sequence of thought.

One notices too that the poet is willing to change or to supply facts to make the satire more effective. Although the old Dutch woman evidently had two eyes, and neither a "red one," the poet says she *"had only one Eye, and that a red one."* And although the first news report placed her age "upwards of Eighty" and the *Gazette's* second report placed it at "fourscore," yet the poet calls her "an old Woman of 85." Franklin, of course, similarly changed or supplied facts for his literary purposes (see no. 41 and its references).

In colonial America, only Joseph Green and, later, Robert Bolling wrote poetry that approaches the grotesque qualities of this poem. But neither Green nor Bolling ever attains this author's sureness of tone and voice. The extraordinary detachment of the underlying authorial voice; the witty, superior tone (splendidly embodied in the heroic couplet form, recalling in itself the finely balanced cadences of eighteenth-century decorum—as if the outrageous words were set to the music of a precisely controlled minuet); the disgust for the criminal—and for the animality of man (especially in the opening eight lines); the fine structure, turning, in the first word of the ninth line ("Yet") from disgust for the criminal to the burlesque "Apology" for his crime; the shifting authorial attitudes; the precise diction and inevitability of thought—all point to Franklin as the author. Lemay (1969, no. 695) judged it "excellent ribald poetry." Unless Philadelphia had some completely unknown literary genius with a flair for the grotesque as well as Franklin's habits of mind, Franklin wrote it.

After I had written the above reasons, Professor Alfred Owen Aldridge kindly read the entire manuscript, pointing out several errors and careless slips. One possible typographical error that he queried was the spelling *Goal* rather than the common eighteenth-century spelling of jail, *Gaol.* I rechecked it, found that *Goal* was in the original poem, and then recalled that Franklin characteristically used this unusual spelling (e.g., *Autobiography*, 104, line 30). *Conclusion*—by Franklin.

80. **The New Jersey House of Representatives' Address to Governor Lewis Morris, 18 April 1745.** In *The Votes and Proceedings of the General Assembly of the Province of New Jersey, the Fourth of April, 1745* . . . (Philadelphia: William Bradford, 1745), 19–23. *Length:* 2,663 words. *Previous attribution:* Suggested by Morris 1975, 15; and attributed by Morris 1980, 718, n. 9.

This speech contains sentiments similar to those known to be Franklin's, but the diction, style, and tone do not display his verbal genius. Richard B. Morris early (1949) recognized this address as a splendid statement of American democratic principles; so he naturally recalled it when he annotated John Jay's conversation with Franklin (wherein Franklin spoke of writing for the New Jersey Assembly while Lewis Morris was governor) and when he edited Jay's record of those reminiscences (1975 and 1980).

But besides the internal evidence, the four key facts that John Jay recorded about Franklin's writing for the New Jersey Assembly make one reject the attribution (see above, no. 71). First, this Assembly address was made late, rather than early, in the administration (1738–46) of Governor Lewis Morris (he died 21 May 1746). Second, this session of the assembly met at Perth Amboy (near New York), rather than Burlington (near Philadelphia). Third, the committee appointed to draft the address consisted of Richard Smith, William Cook, Robert Lawrence, John Low, and Pontius Stelle; Joseph Cooper was not on it. And fourth, Franklin, by 1745, had already done most of the printing that he ever was to do for the New Jersey colony. Although he did print three more issues of its laws (Evans nos. 5818, 5819, and 6200), William Bradford printed the *Votes and Proceedings* of the House for this session and the following ones (Evans nos. 5650, 5651, 5820, and 5821.) *Conclusion*—not by Franklin. (Cf. no. 71.)

81. **Cut of Louisburg.** In *Pennsylvania Gazette*, 6 June 1745, p. 5. *Size:* 90 × 115mm. *No previous attribution.*

The Louisburg map, as the editors of *The Papers of Benjamin Franklin* point out, "is the first news illustration to appear in the *Gazette*" (*P* 3:55 n.7). After using the cut, Franklin evidently sent it on to his partner James Parker, who printed it in his *New York Weekly Post Boy*, 10 June 1745. Wheat and Brun, *Maps and Charts Published in America before 1800*, enter the Parker reprint as no. 70 in their bibliography, but they overlook the original *Pennsylvania Gazette* printing. The cut is not reprinted in the *Papers*, C. William Miller, or Reilly.

Franklin evidently wrote the accompanying prose explanation (reprinted in *P* 3:54–56). He was a competent, though not an excellent artist and craftsman, entirely capable of producing a woodcut or wood engraving of this quality. The author of the Louisburg account apologizes for the map, "rough as it is, for want of good Engravers here." If Franklin had hired someone else to produce the cut, I doubt that he would thus impugn the work. For an earlier woodcut map generally attributed to Franklin, see Wheat and Brun no. 474; C. Miller no. 63; and Reilly no. 1774 (see also *P* 1:324, n. 9). *Conclusion*—by Franklin.

82. **Appreciation of George Whitefield.** In *Pennsylvania Gazette*, 31 July 1746, p. 3. *Length:* 328 words. *No previous attribution.*

The author has a familiar acquaintance with Whitefield, commenting that he has "an infirm Constitution, still daily declining." Since Whitefield was now staying with the Franklins when he visited Philadelphia (*Autobiography*, 106), Franklin must have known his health well. This editorial appreciation of Whitefield's preaching is certainly among the best by any contemporary, ranking, indeed, only behind Franklin's classic tribute in the *Autobiography* (103–7; cf. *P* 18:53). Briefer notes concerning Whitefield, including the follow-up appreciation of 28 August (*P* 3:97–98), are routinely included in the "Extracts from the Gazette" in *The Papers of Benjamin Franklin* (cf. 2:241, 242, 244, 282, 284–85, 288, 290, 291, etc.). Perhaps this one was excluded because of its length. *Conclusion*—by Franklin. (Cf. nos. 75, 77, and 83).

83. **George Whitefield's financial Accounts.** In *Pennsylvania Gazette*, 23 April 1747, p. 2. *Length:* 490 words. *No previous attribution.*

On 16 April 1746 Whitefield wrote Franklin, giving details of his receipts and expenditures for the Georgia orphanage. Franklin printed the letter in the *Gazette* for 22 May 1746 (*P* 3:71–74). The editors of the *Papers* note that the purpose of the accounts "was to silence rumors and asseverations, especially in New England, that the Orphan-House did not exist and that Whitefield had misappropriated the funds." In this follow-up editorial, the author prints quotations from two letters from Charleston, South Carolina, giving an account of the latest contributions Whitefield raised there. Then the author defends Whitefield's honesty: "The above Extracts will, we doubt not, at once please the Friends of the Reverend Mr. *Whitefield,* and convince every candid Reader, that his Accounts of the Disposition of the Sums of Money heretofore collected for the Use of his *Orphan House* in *Georgia* are just; since it cannot be conceived that Gentlemen, who live so near to that House as *Charles-Town, South Carolina,* and have daily Opportunities of knowing how the Affair is conducted, should contribute so generously to Mr. *Whitefield,* if they thought his former Collections were not duly applied." The editorial note anticipates Franklin's statement in the *Autobiography:* "Some of Mr. Whitefield's Enemies affected to suppose that he would apply these Collections to his own private Emolument; but I, who was intimately acquainted with him, (being employ'd in printing his Sermons and Journals, &c.) never had the least Suspicion of his Integrity, but am to this day decidedly of Opinion that he was in all his Conduct, a perfectly *honest Man*" (105). *Conclusion*—by Franklin.

84. **On Barclay's *Apology*.** In *Pennsylvania Gazette,* 22 October 1747, p. 3. *Length:* 85 words and 20 lines of iambic pentameter. *Previous attributions:* Suggested by Lemay 1969, no. 865; questioned by Wolf 1972, 588.

The poem, used as part of Franklin's propaganda campaign for the Militia Association, could have been written by Franklin—or by numerous other people. Wolf (1972) questioned whether it was not part of a poem by Matthew Green, *A Copy of Verses wrote by a Gentleman, lately deceased, occasioned by his Reading Robert Barclay's Apology* (Philadelphia: B. Franklin, [1747?]). (See C. William Miller no. 420.) It is not by Green, but there is no good internal evidence for attributing it to Franklin. Richard Peters wrote the Penns on 29 November 1747 that it was "taken as I suppose out of one of the Magazines" (*P* 3:216). *Conclusion*—probably not by Franklin.

85. **The Necessity for Self-Defense.** In (untitled and undated) [Postscript to the *Pennsylvania Gazette,* 29 December 1747, pp. 1–2]. *Note:* This supplement appears in the Rhistoric Publications [later called Microsurance Publications] facsimile reprint (Philadelphia, 1968), 7:336–37, of the *Pennsylvania Gazette* as a supplement to the *Gazette* no. 942 for 30 December 1746. (Both the printed address ["Mr. *FRANKLIN*"] and the size of the paper show that it was intended as a supplement to the *Gazette.*) But it refers to Gilbert Tennent's Sermon of "last *Thursday*" on the lawfulness of self-defense, evidently a reference to Tennent's sermon of Thursday, 24 December 1747, entitled *The Late Association for Defence, Encourag'd, or the Lawfulness of a Defensive War. Represented in a Sermon Preach'd at*

Philadelphia [on Thursday] December 24, 1747 (Philadelphia: W. Bradford, [1748]), Evans no. 6244. Franklin noted in the *Pennsylvania Gazette* for Tuesday, 29 December 1747, page 2: "Thursday last the Reverend Mr. Gilbert Tennent preached an excellent Sermon in the New-Building, on the Lawfulness of War, and on the Usefulness of the Association, into which great Numbers of the Inhabitants of this Province have lately enter'd, and are still entering" (*P* 3:240). The undated and untitled supplement must really be a postscript to the *Gazette* of 29 December 1747, no. 994. C. William Miller does not call for a supplement to either the *Gazette* of 30 December 1746 (Miller no. 397) or the *Gazette* of 29 December 1747 (Miller no. 427). *Length:* 1,760 words. *No previous attribution.*

The sentiments are those of Franklin, as his "Queries" in the *Gazette* for 6 March 1733/4 (no. 55, above) and his pamphlet *Plain Truth*, published in November 1747 (*P* 3:180–204), make obvious. The style too is Franklin's: this author praises Gilbert Tennent's "Sermon last *Thursday* on that Occasion, which is *so* full and clear on the Subject, *so* well supported by Strength of Argument, and carried on with *such* masterly Judgment and Address" (italics added). Compare the *so* . . . *so* . . . *so* . . . *such* structure of the following by Franklin: "This Article therefore cost me *so* much painful Attention and my Faults in it vex'd me *so* much, and I made *so* little Progress in Amendment, and had *such* frequent Relapses" (*Autobiography*, 86, my italics).

In explicating Matthew 26:52, the author displays Franklin's common sense and his fertility of invention. But much more telling is his willingness to rewrite the Bible to make its meaning more explicit. He says:

> The Passage might be enlarged upon; but, in my Apprehension, no Construction appears more clear and easy, than the Text simply pointing out a Contradistinction between the Kingdom of Christ, and those of temporal Princes; carnal Weapons, tho' useful and necessary in the latter, are not only unlawful, but improper and ineffectual for establishing the former; and if Liberty may be taken to vary the concise, comprehensive Stile of Scripture into a familiar Way of Speech, the Sense of those Verses appears much the same as if Christ had said, "*Peter*, put up thy Sword on this Occasion, it is no Time now to use carnal Weapons; My Kingdom is not of this World, is neither capable of being supported, or liable to be subverted by the Sword, to the Dangers of which all earthly Kingdoms are continually exposed: Mine stands on a more sure Foundation, in the Defence whereof, if Force availed, a most powerful Army of Angels would now descend to my Assistance."

Few mid-eighteenth-century authors would take the liberty "to vary the concise, comprehensive Stile of Scripture"; fewer still would obviously prefer "a familiar Way of Speech" to biblical language; and I doubt that anyone else in Philadelphia in the mid-eighteenth century would have written this. But the whole passage is characteristic of Franklin (cf. his biblical parables at *P* 6:114–23, 124–28; and his free use of the Bible at 15:299–303; 20:343–52; Smyth 7:430–43, 432–33; 9:358–59, 698–703; 10:133–34; and cf. nos. 27, 47, 50, 51, and 58). As Aldridge wrote about no. 27: "Franklin crammed his essay with scriptural allusions and quotations, not because he accepted the authority of the Bible, but because most of his readers did. Also, he revised a number of verses to fit the local situation but presented them as direct quotations, not paraphrases. Few writers besides Franklin at this time would have been bold enough to take these liberties" (Aldridge 1967a, 85; cf. no. 57, above).

The essay is obviously part of Franklin's campaign to make the Militia Association a success. *Conclusion*—by Franklin.

86. A Course of Experiments on the newly discovered electrical Fire. In *Maryland Gazette,* 10 May 1749. Reprinted in the *Gentleman's Magazine* 20 (January 1750): 35–35; the *Scots Magazine* 12 (January 1750): 35; and the *South Carolina Gazette,* 28 May 1750. *Length:* 598 words. *Previous attributions:* Lemay 1961, 575–76; 1964, 62–71.

Ebenezer Kinnersley's syllabus of lectures on electricity first published the Franklinian theory of electricity, including the electrical nature of lightning: "Various Representations of LIGHTNING, the Cause and Effects of which will be explained by a more probable Hypothesis than has hitherto appeared; and some useful Instructions given how to avoid the Danger of it." Although the experiments and theories propounded by Kinnersley are mainly Franklin's creation, the order of the topics in these lectures is different from that of the full syllabus published in the *Pennsylvania Gazette,* 11 April 1751 (no. 90 below). In the *Autobiography,* Franklin wrote that he "encouraged" Kinnersley "to undertake showing the Experiments for Money, and drew up for him two Lectures, in which the Experiments were rang'd in such Order and accompanied with Explanations, in such Method, as that the foregoing should assist in Comprehending the following" (153).

The question is, does this earliest advertisement represent an incomplete version of the lectures that Franklin drew up? Probably. But the order is inferior to the *Pennsylvania Gazette* advertisement, and

Kinnersley kept that basic sequence of topics (with some rearrangements and additions) for the rest of his life (Lemay 1964, 117–18). Yet this *Maryland Gazette* syllabus consists primarily of experiments and theories created by Franklin. No doubt Franklin encouraged Kinnersley to undertake the lectures. But if he drew up the systematic series of topics before Kinnersley began his southern tour in the spring of 1749 (and that was, after all, the logical time for him to do so), then Kinnersley rearranged this abbreviated version of the syllabus, probably attempting to give some of the most important new scientific hypotheses along with some of the most eye-catching experiments. He presumably abbreviated the syllabus to save advertising expenses. I therefore believe that these topics were written by Franklin but that the order, omissions, and slight changes, have been made by Kinnersley. *Conclusion*—by Franklin and Kinnersley. (Cf. no. 90.)

87. **News Notes on three Natives of Greenland.** In *Pennsylvania Gazette*, 15 June 1749, p. 2; and follow-up note, 7 September 1749, p. 2. *Length:* 229 words. *Previous attribution:* Aldridge 1962, 79.

Aldridge points out that these Eskimos "made such a profound impression" upon Franklin that almost forty years later he incorporated other details of his conversation with them in a letter to George Whatley of 23 May 1785 (Smyth 9:337). I might add that only the editor of the *Gazette* could conclude the news note with "We may hereafter give our Readers some curious Accounts of *Greenland* from the latest Voyages there." Further, just three years later, Franklin helped sponsor an expedition to find the supposed Northwest Passage (*P* 4:380–84), so information about Eskimos would be interesting to him for practical as well as intellectual reasons. *Conclusion*—by Franklin.

88. **Rules Proper to be observed in Trade.** In *Pennsylvania Gazette*, 20 February 1749/50, p. 1. *Length:* 579 words. Previous attribution: Suggested by Crane 1950, 294, no. "a."

The piece is similar to "Hints for those that would be Rich" (Smyth 2:211–12), "Advice to a Young Tradesman" (*P* 3:304–8), "How to get Riches" (*P* 3:349–50), "The Way to Wealth" (*P* 7:326–50), and to Part 2 of the *Autobiography* (73–91). And Franklin used the "rules" structure in several other writings (see no. 3 and its references).

The first rule begins, "ENDEAVOR to be perfect in the calling you are engaged in." The use of the word *perfect* in such a context, though uncommon (but not extraordinarily unusual in the eighteenth century), was characteristic of Franklin (cf. *P* 1:111, 261; 8:128;

17:395–96; Smyth 8:153–54; and *Autobiography*, 78). The recommendation of "INDUSTRY" as "the natural means of acquiring *wealth*" is the general theme of all the above prudential writings, as well as of "Busy-Body No. 8" (*P* 1:134–39). The second rule (recommending the "golden rule") is a commonplace. The third, "Be strict in discharging all legal debts," is recommended in Franklin's "Advice": "never keep borrow'd Money an Hour beyond the Time you promis'd" (*P* 3:307). Rule 4, "Endeavour to be as much in your shop, or warehouse . . . as possibly you can," echoes Franklin's proverb "Keep thy shop, and thy shop will keep thee" (*P* 2:7 and 7:344). Rule 5, "Be complaisant to the *meanest*, as well as greatest," recommending good manners, is only common sense. Although one may wonder if Franklin would have used the class-conscious dichotomy, the advice itself is egalitarian and may find an echo in the outline of his *Autobiography:* "Costs me nothing to be civil to inferiors, a good deal to be submissive to superiors" (205).

Rule 6, "Be not too talkative," anticipates Franklin's virtue "Silence" (*Autobiography*, 79). The advice "If customers slight your goods, and undervalue them, endeavour to convince them of their mistake, if you can, but do not affront them" recalls the essays on lying shopkeepers (nos. 24–25, above). The good common sense and clear style of the following seems especially Franklinian: "Do not be pert in your answers, but with patience hear, and with meekness give an answer; for if you affront in a small matter, it may probably hinder you from a future good customer. They may think that you are dear in the articles they want; but, by going to another, may find it not so, and probably may return again; but if you behave rude and affronting, there is no hope either of returning, or their future custom." Rule 7, "Take great care in keeping your accounts well," anticipates Franklin's advice "to those young Men who may be employ'd in managing Affairs . . . that they should always render Accounts and make Remittances with great Clearness and Punctuality" (*Autobiography*, 101).

Rule 8, "Deal . . . for ready money," echoes Franklin's "ready Money Plan" (*P* 19:100; 20:333; cf. 15:87; 2:165) and his remarks in the *Autobiography* on the reasons for Keimer's failure (56). The further advice against "making a great figure in your shop . . . [for] Too great an appearance may rather prevent, than engage customers" is echoed by Franklin several times: for example, "In order to secure my Credit and Character as a Tradesmen, I took care not only to be in Reality Industrious and frugal, but to avoid all *Appearances* of the Contrary" (*Autobiography*, 68); compare his cautionary character of David Harry, who was "very proud, dress'd like a Gentleman, liv'd expensively, took much Diversion and Pleasure abroad, ran in debt, and neglected his Business, upon which all Business left him" (*Autobiography*, 68). The final rule, 9, that a *"fair character . . .* will be the best means for advancing your credit, gaining you the most flourishing trade, and enlarging your fortune," anticipates Franklin's advice that "no Qualities were so likely to make a poor Man's Fortune as those of Probity and Integrity" (*Autobiography*, 89).

Although the specific bits of advice contained in these "rules" are generally commonplace, the clear style, good sense, form, and content are entirely Franklinian. *Conclusion*—by Franklin.

89. **Ebenezer Kinnersley's "Course of Experiments on the newly-discovered *Electrical* Fire."** In *Pennsylvania Gazette*, 11 April 1751, p. 2. *Length:* 766 words. *Previous attributions:* Cohen 1941, 130, 404–6; Lemay 1961, 575; 1964, 62–74.

This well-organized syllabus of two lectures on electricity, complete with a demonstration of the way that rods could "secure Houses, Ships, etc., from being hurt by" the "destructive Violence" of lightning, evidently reprints the outline Franklin "drew up for" Kinnersley (*Autobiography*, 153). *Conclusion*—by Franklin (probably with some input from Kinnersley). (Cf. no. 87.)

90. **A New and Mild Method totally to Extirpate the Indians.** In *Weyman's New York Gazette*, 6 February 1764, p. 1. *Length:* 46 lines of iambic tetrameter. *Previous attribution:* Suggested by Lemay 1969, no. 1959.

The poem follows "An Extract of a Letter from South Carolina," reprinted from the *Newport Mercury*, that satirizes American prejudices against Indians and compares the Indians favorably to the Britons and Germans of Caesar's day. An excellent appreciation of Indian culture and values, the essay ironically points out that whites commonly think Indians owe them "Gratitude for the Goods and Rum which hath already produced such happy effects amongst them to the promoting of Quarrels, shortening of their Lives and lessening of their Numbers." Franklin echoes both this ironic passage and the poem's title in his *Autobiography:* "And indeed if it be the Design of Providence to extirpate these Savages in order to make room for Cultivators of the Earth, it seems not improbable that Rum may be the appointed Means. It has already annihilated all the Tribes who formerly inhabited the Seacoast" (121). Lemay connected the poem "written in Philadelphia" with this passage from the *Autobiography*, but he must not have had the poem before him when he suggested that Franklin wrote it.

The poem, poorly written in awkward hudibrastics, attacks Indians and those who befriend him. The essayist prints it to prove how outrageously cruel and vicious whites could be toward Indians. Evidently one of the Paxton boys wrote it. Since Franklin was their foremost opponent (*P* 11:42–69), and since the poem advocates shooting all who "don't our Cause befriend," it calls for Franklin's own death. *Conclusion*—not by Franklin.

91. "*The* VISION *of* Mirza *the son of* Mirza, *translated from the original Arabic*. Said to be written by B———F———, Esq." In *Boston Chronicle*, 13 February 1769, p. 1; rpt. *Newport Mercury*, 27 February 1769, p. 1. *Length:* 619 words. *Previous attribution:* Girouard 191–92n.

Girouard, who did not know that the piece appeared first in the *Boston Chronicle*, says that Solomon Southwick, publisher of the *Newport Mercury*, could have known Franklin but that the initials could also be a ruse. He notes, however, that Silence Dogood No. 4, on Harvard College (*P* 1:14–18) was also a "dream-veiled satiric allegory" and concludes that Franklin's "likely familiarity with Addison's paper [*Spectator* no. 159, 1 September 1711, containing an earlier "Vision of Mirza"] only a decade after the latter's heyday, supports Franklin's authorship."

Nearly all eighteenth-century litterateurs knew the *Spectator*, so the attribution must depend upon the authority of the contemporary published ascription to "B——— F———, Esq." and upon the internal evidence. Unlike two items below (nos. 93 and 95), the ascription is not by an especially knowledgeable contemporary. John Mein and John Fleeming (Loyalist co-publishers of the *Boston Chronicle*) and Solomon Southwick were all apparently unknown to Franklin in 1769. Mein and Fleeming, however, had only six months earlier attributed another work (*Sermons for Asses* by James Murray) to Franklin. Concerning that earlier attribution, William Franklin wrote his father that the publishers no doubt hoped "to give them a Sale" (*P* 16:62). Later, Franklin may have come to know both Mein and Southwick. As "Sagittarius" Mein wrote anti-Franklin propaganda for the North Ministry in the London *Public Ledger* during 1774. And Southwick was appointed deputy postmaster of Newport by the Rhode Island Assembly in 1775 (*P* 22:168). But the 1769 ascription is, at best, without authority.

The internal evidence testifies that the "Vision" is not by Franklin. The piece begins, "On the 3d day of the 10th month, and the 14th hour of the day." But the date and the time are irrelevant to the essay, although they do help set the tone. Such irrelevant details are typical of the loose, rambling structure of the "Vision." It has two parts, but their relation is unclear. The "small Island" in the first half of the essay seems to be England, although the identity of the island's oppressors (the Romans?) and captives (early Britons?) is uncertain—and irrelevant. Since the second part of the Vision makes practically no use of the first part, it might as well be omitted. The "strong nation" that attacks the island in the second part of the essay is presumably France, but the allegory continually breaks down. And in the second half, the "two nations" who are "brothers" seem to be England (the older) and America (the younger), although the brotherhood of the "small Island" (England?) and the "rising land" in the west (America?) has not previously been mentioned.

The whole is a confusing mishmash. Franklin was incapable of writing such a wordy, poorly structured muddle. *Conclusion*—not by Franklin.

92. **The Colonist's Advocate Essay Series.** In the London *Public Advertiser*, 4, 8, 11, 15, 25, and 29 January; 5, 9, 12, and 19 February; and 2 March 1770. Reprinted in Crane 1950, 167–82, 183–86, 192–97, and 201–9; and reprinted in *P* 17:5–8, 14–17, 18–22, 28–30, 33–36, 45–48, 52–55, 58–61, 66–69, 73–75, and 91–92. *Length:* 9,389 words. *Previous attributions:* Crane 1934, 22 and n. 51; Crane 1950, 167ff and 284–86; *P* 17:5; rejected by Hay.

Crane (1934) attributed the essay series to Benjamin Franklin because "the correspondences in ideas, arguments, and phraseology with such other Franklin writings as *The Interest of Great Britain*, the *Examination*, 'The causes of the American discontents,' the letters of 'F.B.,' 'N.N.,' and, even more convincing, Franklin's maginalia and his private correspondence, are so complete and so intricate as seemingly to exclude the possibilities of either independent invention or plagiarism." Crane did, however, conclude note 51 by calling attention to the compliment paid by the essayist to Benjamin Franklin, thus casting doubt upon the attribution. Later (1950) Crane pointed out that a knowledgeable contemporary had attributed the essay series to James Burgh, a friend of Franklin. Besides documenting echoes of Franklin's previously published essays, Crane noted a few vague echoes and anticipations of Franklin's maginalia. He also suggested that the praise of Benjamin Franklin was "possibly evidence of collaboration, presumably by James Burgh" (196n).

The editors of *The Papers of Benjamin Franklin* accept the attribution and state "that Franklin was the principal author, but may have had some assistance from his fellow member of the Club of Honest

Whigs, James Burgh" (*P* 17:5). In a note they add, "We have also pointed out passages that in our opinion are clearly not by BF and hence are presumably Burgh's handiwork" (*P* 17:5 n.5). Specifically, the editors point out that "The Colonist's Advocate" did not know the structure of government in New England (*P* 17:19 n. 6); that his views on charters contradicted Franklin's known views and that, unlike Franklin, he was ignorant of Stuart history (*P* 17:22 n.8); that his use of a string of clichés to describe the American experience was unlike Franklin (*P* 17:28 n.6); that he admiringly praised Franklin (*P* 17:59 n.1); that he showed a knowledge of Blackstone not elsewhere demonstrated by Franklin (*P* 17:67 n.6); and that, unlike Franklin, he was ignorant of the current rate of exchange (*P* 17:74 n.1).

In 1975 Professor Carla Hay argued that Burgh, not Franklin, wrote the series. Hay pointed out that "The Colonist's Advocate" borrowed extensively from Jeremiah Dummer, James Otis, Daniel Dulany, and especially John Dickinson. Indeed, "The Colonist's Advocate" essay series is almost a pastiche of others' work—typical of the method of Burgh and completely unlike Franklin. Hay also notes that "The Colonist's Advocate" misspelled Dickinson's name—and that Burgh used the same misspelling elsewhere (119 n.35). Franklin, of course, knew Dickinson and did not misspell his name. Despite Hay's proof of "The Colonist's Advocate's" extensive borrowing, the editors of the *Papers* think that Franklin "had a hand, though perhaps a lesser one than we supposed, in 'The Colonist's Advocate' "(Hay 124).

The evidence pointed out by the editors of *The Papers of Benjamin Franklin* proves that Franklin did not write all of the essays and did not read over the completed essays before they were published. Professor Carla Hay's evidence proves that Franklin had little, if any, hand in the series. Burgh used more of Franklin's writings than those by any other single person. But that makes good sense on three counts: (1) Franklin wrote more than anyone else on these matters; (2) Franklin's writings are more memorable and striking than those of any American propagandist before Thomas Paine; and (3) Burgh knew and admired Franklin. Finally, the internal literary evidence also suggests that Franklin was not the author. The structure of the various individual pieces and of the whole does not begin to approach the mastery Franklin had attained by the age of sixteen in the "Silence Dogood" essay series. The diction, style, and thought never rise to Franklin's best (except where he is being quoted); and the persona is simple, sober, straightforward, and boring. By age sixteen, Franklin was a superior writer.

One might possibly claim that Franklin supplied Burgh with some materials for the essay series, but Burgh could have composed the series without any help from Franklin. *Conclusion*—not by Franklin.

93. An Act for the more effectual keeping of his Majesty's American Colonies dependent on the Crown of Great Britain and to enforce Their Obedience to all such Acts of Parliament as may be necessary for that Purpose. In *Pennsylvania Journal, Supplement,* 29 June 1774, p. 1; reprinted in *Boston Gazette,* 11 July; *Massachusetts Spy,* 15 July; *Massachusetts Gazette,* 18 July; and *New Hampshire Gazette,* 22 July 1774. *Length:* 1,697 words. *Previous attributions:* Oliver 105–6; cited by Schlesinger 200.

Peter Oliver, a leading Massachusetts Tory who knew Franklin, reported the contemporary gossip that this mock Act was "said to be, and generally believed to be, fabricated by that great Patriot *Dr. Franklin.*"

Additional reasons make one suspect that Franklin wrote the satire. On 16 November 1773, "Britannus," writing in the London *Public Advertiser,* proposed an act prohibiting emigration to America and outlined seven points to be included. Then on 21 December, "Clericus" expressed surprise that no one had followed up the proposal. Sometime after 16 November, Franklin drafted a reply, "On a Proposed Act to Prevent Emigration" (*P* 20:522–28), but he did not send it to the *Public Advertiser* (or the editor did not print it). Then, in the spring of 1774, he wrote two satires quite similar to this one: "An Open Letter to Lord North," 5 April (*P* 21:183–87), and "A Method of Humbling Rebellious American Vassals," 21 May (*P* 21:220–22). I suspect that Franklin wrote the "Act" in May 1774 at about the time he wrote "A Method of Humbling Rebellious American Vassals."

"An Act" begins with a preamble saying that other colonies have "entirely" thrown "off their dependence and subjection" to the "Parent State" and that the British Plantations "in all likelihood, will, if not speedily prevented do so." Franklin, in "A Method," expresses the same thought in similar diction; the American colonies have shown "a mutinous Disposition" that "may, if not timely prevented, dispose them in perhaps less than a Century to deny our Authority." "An Act" next says "*the great* ENCREASE *of People, in said Colonies, has an immediate tendency to produce this effect.*" So too Franklin, in "A Method," goes from the idea of independence to the rapid increase of population in America: "more especially when it is considered that they are a robust, hardy People, encourage early Marriages, and their Women being amazingly prolific, they must of consequence in 100

Years be very numerous." "A Method" concludes by listing as one "advantage" of castrating Americans that "it would effectually put a Stop to the Emigration from this Country now grown so very fashionable" (*P* 21:221–22). This act's provisions are even more outrageous.

Number 6, the high point, requires the mother of every bastard child to pay £50 to the governor of the colony, "and that in case any person, shall hereafter, either with malice prepense, or otherwise kill or destroy any child or children; such killing or destroying shall not henceforth be deemed or adjudged to be murder in any Court or Courts, nor shall such killing be punished in any way or manner whatever." Thus this "Act" is similar to "A Method of Humbling Rebellious American Vassals" in sequence as well as in several details. The grotesque climax recalls Jonathan Swift's "A Modest Proposal," as well as Franklin's earlier use of Swift's satire in "The Speech of Miss Polly Baker," especially the *Maryland Gazette* text, where Franklin directly takes up the murder of bastard children (Lemay 1976, 95 n. "w").

Although the details of the piece and its satire of the proposed act suggest Franklin's authorship, the structure and rhetorical techniques are surprising. In the "Rules by Which a Great Empire May be Reduced to a Small One" (*P* 20:389–400), the satire becomes increasingly severe throughout. But in "An Act," the satire becomes increasingly severe only through article 6. Article 7 merely qualifies article 6 (thus adding to the realism), although this author, like Franklin, cannot refrain from burlesquing the jargon generally used in acts ("any thing in this Act to the contrary in any wise notwithstanding" [cf. his parody of legal jargon, *P* 2:147–49]). But then article 8 changes topics from direct penalties on immigrants to America (and on children born there) to taxes on flour and wheat exported from America. These last articles (8, 9, and 10) satirize the Navigation Acts and the Intolerable Act (as Franklin had done in the "Rules" and in an "Edict" [*P* 20:389–40, 414–19]), but the change from a satire on proposed limitations on emigration to a satire of the Navigation Acts seems to me to weaken the piece. Perhaps Franklin was so bothered by the reality (the existing Navigation Acts) that he thought them more severe than possible threatened acts. He had, after all, campaigned against the Navigation Acts ever since 1731 (see no. 30). At any rate, the general subject of taxes on grains also recalls Franklin's earlier satires (e.g., "and on all Grain and other Produce of the Earth" ["Edict," *P* 20:415]); and the ending of "An Act" (article 10) does rise to a climax. *Conclusion*—by Franklin.

94. **Method of making Salt-Petre.** In *Massachusetts Spy,* 2 August 1775, p. 2; reprinted in *Pennsylvania Magazine* 1 (August 1775): 360; also published by the Continental Congress, *Several Methods of Making Salt-Petre* (Philadelphia: Bradford, 1775), 7–8. *Length:* 590 words. *Previous attributions:* Wolf 1966, 24; Lemay 1983, 148.

In the *Massachusetts Spy,* Joseph Palmer requested the editor to publish "the following method of making it [saltpeter], as practised in Hanover in the year 1766; it is related, in substance, by Dr. Franklin, who saw it, both there and at Paris, where large quantities were made." Franklin was at Hanover on 9 July 1766 (*P* 13:315). Palmer goes on to say, "Both these processes [for making saltpeter] I received from some of our worthy delegates at the American Congress; they have now a Committee upon this business, of which the worthy Dr. Franklin is the Chairman; and it is expected that they will soon publish the most approved method." Palmer corresponded frequently with John Adams and Robert Treat Paine of the Continental Congress, and Paine served on the committee to encourage the manufacture of saltpeter in America (*Journals of the Continental Congress,* 2:86).

If Franklin did not write the description (the words *in substance* say he did not), he supplied the information for it. *Conclusion*—orally from Franklin, though evidently written down by someone else.

95. **The Devices on the Continental Bills.** In *Pennsylvania Gazette,* 20 September 1775, p. 1; reprinted in *Pennsylvania Magazine* 1 (December 1775): 561–63. *Previous attributions:* Suggested by Cafferty 163; argued by Lemay 1983, 147; and by Newman 1983, 2272–273.

Joseph Stansbury, a Philadelphia Loyalist poet, wrote in "The History of Peru" (a satire on the paper currency of the colonies, especially on the Continental currency) that the "Explanation of the Devices and mottos of the Continental Bills of Credit in the Pennsylvania Gazette" was "supposed to be written by Dr. Franklin" (Cafferty 157).

Even without this external evidence, Franklin would be the logical author. He was an authority on emblems and devices (see no. 97). More than twenty-seven years earlier, he had designed at least twenty "Devices and Mottoes" for the flags of the Associator militia companies (*P* 3:267–69). Congress appointed him on 23 June 1775 to a committee "to get proper plates engraved, to provide paper and to agree with printers to print the above bills." Newman (1966) has shown that all but three of the emblems and mottos for the 1775 Continental paper currency were taken from books in Franklin's library. Further, Franklin's original sketch and mottos for two devices (*P* 22: facing 358) prove that two of the exceptions (for the face of the $20 bill and for the back of the $20 and $30 bills) were his original creations. And William Browne (Harvard, 1755) wrote Samuel Curwen on 8 January 1776 that the devices were "the inventions of Dr. Franklin" (Curwen 46).

The explanations and interpretations of the devices and mottoes on the Continental bills appeared in the *Pennsylvania Gazette* at the same time that the bills began to circulate. No one else is so likely to have written this account as the original designer of the bills—Franklin. In addition, the explanations reflect Franklin's characteristic opinions. Thus the comment on the $8 bill (which contains "the figure of a *harp*" and the motto MAJORA MINORIBUS CONSONANT) urges unity and harmony not only between the separate colonies but also between the "various ranks of people" within each. The sentiment echoes Franklin's egalitarian message in the two original figures on the 1748 Associator flags (flag nos. 2 and 11 at *P* 3:268–69; cf. no. 72 above). The comment on the $6 bill (which contains "the figure of a *beaver* gnawing a large tree" with the motto PERSEVERANDO) says "I apprehend the *great tree* may be intended to represent the enormous power Britain has assumed over us, and endeavours to enforce by arms, of taxing us at pleasure *and binding us in all cases whatsoever;* or the exorbitant profits she makes by monopolizing our commerce." These are typical sentiments of Franklin, frequently printed during the preceding decade. Similarly, the comment on the $1 bill (which portrayed the acanthus plant, sprouting on all sides under a weight placed upon it, with the motto DEPRESSA RESURGIT) reflects Franklin's well-known opinions on industry and frugality: "our present oppressions . . . may, by increasing our industry, and forcing it into new courses, increase the prosperity of our country" (e.g., *P* 16:174–75, 177; 17:118, 368; 22:242; cf. McCoy 618–20).

Perhaps the most conclusive single bit of internal evidence occurs in the discussion of the $7 bill, which portrays "*a black heavy cloud,* with the motto, SERENABIT; *It will clear up.*" The writer says, "This seems designed to encourage the dejected, who may be too sensible of present inconveniences, and fear their continuance." Franklin wrote his friend James Bowdoin earlier in this year, "Present Inconveniences are therefore to be borne with Fortitude, and better times expected." This author then gives a quotation from Horace; seven months earlier in the personal letter to Bowdoin, Franklin follows his remark on "Present Inconveniences" with the identical quotation from Horace (*P* 21:507).

Besides echoing Franklin's characteristic opinions and even his diction and sequence of thought, this piece is written in an absolutely clear style and with rhetorical strategies that suggest Franklin's authorship. The pseudonym "CLERICUS" suits the formal and learned tone and contents of the essay. Finally, the essayist inspired the only other American author who was especially interested in the devices on the Continental currency, Francis Hopkinson. Hopkinson consequently wrote an article entitled "On the Use and Abuse of Mottos" for the *Supplement* to the *Pennsylvania Magazine* for 1775 (pp. 587–89), which was reprinted in a shortened and revised form in his *Miscellaneous Essays*, 1:42–46. Although Hopkinson was an interesting writer, any comparison of the two essays will show that "The Account of the Devices" was written by a master. *Conclusion*—by Franklin.

96. The Rattlesnake as a Symbol of America, by an American Guesser. In *Pennsylvania Journal*, 27 December 1775, p. 1. Reprinted by Force 4:cols. 468–69; reprinted from Force in *Naval Documents*, 3:266–68. Redaction printed in Dixon and Hunter's *Virginia Gazette*, 11 May 1776, p. 2; reprinted in *Naval Documents*, 5:56–57. *Length:* 922 words. *Previous attribution:* Lemay 1983, 148.

At the outbreak of the French and Indian War, Franklin created a cartoon illustrating the necessity for the colonies to unite. It featured a snake cut into parts labeled with the initials of the colonies. The motto underneath the snake device read "JOIN, or DIE" (*P* 5:275). Albert Matthews demonstrated the enormous popularity of the device in the prerevolutionary period. And Sinclair Hamilton pointed out that it was "the first device to appear in this country symbolizing or suggesting the union of the colonies" (118). Even earlier, Franklin had used the rattlesnake as a literary symbol of America in "Rattlesnakes for Felons" (*P* 4:130–33). He was no doubt proud of the success of the device, which was widely adopted as a military emblem at the beginning of the Revolution (see Richardson 13–14, 20, 66–67, 86, etc.). And yet, as Albert Matthews showed, the rattlesnake was ridiculed as an emblem by the Loyalists. The essay defends the symbolism of Franklin's emblem.

In addition to the general subject, the diction and details point to Franklin's authorship. The supposedly foolish persona consults a person "learned in . . . heraldry" who says that only " 'the worthy properties of the animal, in the crest-born, shall be considered.' " The unusual diction *crest-born* suggests Franklin's authorship, for he frequently coined words or used them in unusual, though perfectly understandable, ways (see no. 73 and its references).

The first several attributes of the rattlesnake (wisdom, eternity, vigilance, magnaminity, and true courage) reveal a knowledge of the emblem literature possessed by few people other than Franklin in colonial America (cf. no. 95 and its references). And other details in the sixteen interpretations of the rattlesnake's symbolic meanings suggest Franklin's authorship. Number ten, on the future growth of America, recalls his "Observations concerning the Increase of Mankind" (*P* 4:225–34). Number eleven, suggesting that the "half formed additional rattle ... may ... represent the province of Canada" recalls his efforts to secure Canada from at least the time of his 1760 pamphlet *The Interest of Great Britain Considered* (*P* 9:7, 13–14, 61–78; cf. 4:233) until his attempts to have England cede Canada to the United States in his early peace negotiations in 1782 (Smyth 8:472; and see Stourzh 208–11).

The originality of the interpretations also points to Franklin's authorship. The fourteenth interpretation even anticipates the "no entangling alliances" of Washington's Farewell Address. It is the first recommendation of a self-interested isolationism as America's natural foreign policy (cf. Gilbert 34–43): "The Rattlesnake is solitary, and associates with her kind only when it is necessary for their preservation." And the patriotic note of the fifteenth interpretation also suggests Franklin's authorship. The power of fascination attributed to the rattlesnake means "that those who consider the liberty and blessings which America affords, and once come over to her, never afterwards leave her, but spend their lives with her." The sixteenth and last attribute of the rattlesnake is its beauty: "She strongly resembles America in this, that she is beautiful in youth, and her beauty increaseth with her age." Then the author quotes a compound clause (which I suspect that he wrote, for it naturally climaxes the series of attributes). In a heightened style and tone suggesting the emotion of the sublime, the writer stresses the Americans' qualities as fighters and their abililty to retreat into the wilderness continent: "her tongue also is blue and forked as the lightning, and her abode is among impenetrable rocks."

Despite working up to a rhetorical climax in the list of the rattlesnake's attributes, the piece generally contains that inimitable naiveté of tone that John Adams so admired in Franklin's writings (see "On Simplicity," no. 37, and its references). And the contempt expressed for Lord North in the final paragraph echoes Franklin's opinions in "An Open Letter to Lord North" of 5 April 1774 (*P* 21:183–86). Although the essay is ultimately serious, the author concludes (as Franklin so often does) by mocking himself with the pseudonym *"An American Guesser"*—a pseudonym that nevertheless suits the tongue-in-cheek qualities of the most far-fetched interpretations of the snake's characteristics (cf. the references in no. 2). Finally, the series of interpretations could almost seem to parody biblical explications, ranging from allegorical to typological. As a youth of seventeen, Franklin remarked that "the same Passages in the Holy Scriptures or the Works of the Learned, are wrested to the meaning of two opposite Parties, of contrary Opinions" (*P* 1:51), and he elsewhere indirectly satirized the usual techniques of the sermon (cf. no. 40 and its references). *Conclusion*—by Franklin.

CONCLUSION

I reject nineteen items considered above as probably or definitely not by Franklin. They are nos. 5, 7, 10, 12, 20, 23, 28, 44, 45, 65, 67, 68, 75, 77, 80, 84, 90, 91, and 92 (see the Bibliography, part 2). Since two appear in *The Papers of Benjamin Franklin* (nos. 20 and 92) and since the editors of the *Papers* suggest that Franklin may have written two of the others (nos. 7 and 10), it is not surprising that other Franklinists who have ventured attributions have sometimes been wrong in their suggestions.

I attribute seventy-seven items considered above to Franklin (see the Bibliography, part 1), including thirty-nine never before ascribed to him. Of the seventy-seven, the largest number, twenty-two, are news items—notes, hoaxes, or articles (nos. 13, 14, 17, 21, 22, 26, 29, 30, 31, 34, 35, 46, 59, 60, 61, 63, 64, 69, 70, 82, 83, and 87); the second largest number, nineteen, are political or controversial essays (nos. 3, 4, 9, 11, 36, 38, 39, 40, 42, 43, 55, 71, 72, 73, 74, 85, 93, 95, and 96); ten are religious or philosophical pieces (nos. 8, 15, 16, 48, 51, 54, 57, 58, 76, and 78); nine are moral essays (nos. 19, 24, 25, 27, 50, 52, 56, 62, and 88); five are belletristic essays (nos. 37, 41, 47, 49, and 66); five are poems (nos. 1, 18, 32, 53, and 79); three concern science (nos. 86, 89, and 94); one satirizes an opponent's paper (no. 6); one concerns a civic improvement (no. 33); one is a mocking self-satire (no. 2); and one is not literature at all but a map (no. 81). Although some of these classifications are arbitrary (e.g., the satire of an opponent's paper, no. 6, could also be categorized as a news note or a religious satire; and the poem, no. 18, could similarly be grouped with the news notes or with the political essays), they are generally in the genres that we expect of Franklin.

Thirty-eight items have previously been attributed to Franklin, including eleven that have definitively (I believe) been proven to be his since the publication of the relevant volume of the *Papers*. These eleven are nos. 11, 22, 27, 54, 55, 58, 66, 74, 86, 87, and 95. Numbers

31 and 89 were also definitively attributed to Franklin, but that was well before the publication of volume one of the *Papers,* so the editors must have overlooked them, judged the attributions incorrect, or thought them insignificant.

The subjects of the additions complement Franklin's known writings. Indeed, three pieces above belong with Franklin's essay series: nos. 1 and 2, although technically not part of the Silence Dogood series, should be read in conjunction with it; and no. 11 is part of the Busy-Body series. Even in these cases, the pieces add significantly to Franklin's known literary and political interests. The first is a humorous literary criticism; the second a mocking self-satire; and the eleventh marks Franklin's entry into Pennsylvania politics. Religion is a major topic in Franklin's early writings, and the additions concerning religion are especially important. The "Rules" for the *New England Courant* (no. 3 above) contain Franklin's earliest thoroughgoing religious satire and help explain the antiministerial bias that remained with him, though seemingly ever-lessening, throughout his life. The ministers, especially the Mathers, opposed the *New England Courant.* Although Franklin fought with his older brother James Franklin, the youth nevertheless identified with James against the civil and ecclesiastical authorities. Franklin recalled in the *Autobiography* that he "resented" his brother's confinement, "notwithstanding our private Differences" (19). Franklin had satirized the ministers and the New England religious traditions (e.g., the jeremiad) in the Silence Dogood essay series, but he is much more vicious and direct in the "Rules." Nearly eight years later, the hoax in the "Letter of the Drum" (no. 15) and the apology and satire in the follow-up letter (no. 16) continue the earlier antiministerial satires and anticipate the spoofs on credulity found in "A Witch Trial at Mount Holly" (*P* 1:182–83), in the *Autobiography,* and throughout his writings. As Lewis Leary observed, Franklin thought "One man's myth was as good as another's" (35). The early satire of the illogical religious explanations for the "High Tide in Boston" (no. 6) anticipates Franklin's burlesque on Virginia's Governor William Gooch, who strangely connected the burning of the Virginia capitol with the enthusiasm of the "New Lights" (*P* 3:135–40).

The attack by "Portius" in the *Mercury* caused Franklin to engage in a protracted literary quarrel, responsible for six essays in 1732 (nos. 36, 38, 39, 40, 42, and 43). The only personal quarrel in which Franklin wrote more was his 1735 defense of the Reverend Samuel Hemphill. Franklin's "Meditation on a Quart Mugg" (no. 51) anticipates his "Parody of and Reply to a Melancholy Religious Meditation" (no. 58) as a spoof on a popular form. His formal theological question "Whether God concurs with all human Actions or not" (no. 76) reveals that he continued to believe in the underlying satire of his early *Dissertation* (P 1:57–71) and was not really so disgusted with philosophical reasonings as he later claimed (Smyth 7:412). And his consideration of "What is True" in the remarks on Moravianism (no. 78) displays that Melvillean understanding of realilty's different orders that characterize the philosophy of the mature Franklin.

The philosophical essay entitled "The Benevolence as well as Selfishness of Man" (no. 48) nicely complements Franklin's other formal philosophical pieces investigating the basic nature of humanity. One especially original note in the additions to the canon of Franklin is the underlying philosophical considerations brought out by Franklin's news reporting. Having pointed out in the discussion of the "Rules" for the *Courant* (no. 3) that a consciousness of philosophical problems (in this case that the actor's "intention," not the result, "is necessary to denominate any Action good") characterizes Franklin's writings even when they concern everyday subjects, I show that he uses such news reports as "The Trial and Reprieve of Prouse and Mitchel" (no. 13, above; cf. nos. 54, 60, and 69) as the occasion for reflections upon the nature of human beings. These new additions strengthen the arguments made by Schneider, Aldridge (1965; 56–59; 1967a passim), Lemay (1967; 201–4; 1978, 20–33), Lynen, and Shear that Franklin's writings (including his *Autobiography*) have philosophical undercurrents. The news reports also try, like some of his moralistic essays, to influence behavior. Thus the news story "The Compassion of Captain Croak" (no. 69) obviously attempts to influence other captains to save ships in distress, and the essay "Brave Men at Fires" (no. 54) tries to inspire future heroic actions (cf. no. 27, on compassion for the sick).

Even when reprinting the news, the quintessential Franklin sometimes emerges, as when he remarks in "On Exaggerating Bodycounts in Battle Reports" (no. 61) that the supposed facts change according to how "the Writers are affected." News reports also confirm his early interest in—and up-to-date knowledge of—science, natural phenomena, economics, and statistics (on the Aurora Borealis [no. 21], "Death Rates in Boston" [no. 31], on a thunderstorm [no. 59], and "Statistics on Trade in Colonial Ports" [no. 63]). Such information reveals that Franklin was interested in these topics and reading the best scholarly literature long before he made contributions to these sciences. Moral philosophy, too, is a major subject in Franklin's writings and in these additions to his canon. Perhaps my favorite in this category is the essay entitled "Censure or Backbiting" (no. 47), for it gathers together comments that Franklin either hints at or only briefly states elsewhere. It could almost be considered a philosophical essay, for, on one level, it maintains that self-love is a basic aspect of humanity. The essay "A Pertinacious Obstinacy in Opinion" (no. 62) also devotes sustained reasoning to a subject that Franklin touched upon in numerous other places. The underlying view of human nature contained in these two essays, and the worldview that emerges in the companion pieces on the lying of shopkeepers, customers, and wholesale merchants (nos. 24 and 25) are finally pessimistic and bitter—a good corrective to the popular "Poor Richard" view of Franklin. More typical of the Addisonian moral essay is "Rules and Maxims for Promoting Matrimonial Happiness" (no. 19), the rambling imitation of *Tatler* No. 11 by "Chatterbox" (no. 49), the essay on drunkenness (no. 50), and the essay on constancy (no. 56). But of course Franklin's Addisonian essays differ dramatically from those in the *Spectator*. Franklin's style is more colloquial, his tone more familiar and homely, his social attitudes more egalitarian, and his underlying philosophy and worldview more complex.

The personal characteristics of all these essays also complement those associated with Franklin. Humor, of course, is a dominant trait. Those news-note ironic comments on the cowardly braggarts (no. 14); on "an unlucky She-Wrestler" (no. 17); on the weather (no. 26); and on the death of a lion (no. 34); as well as the news-note hoaxes on "a Burnt-Offering" (no. 35); on the threat of a disappointed lover (no. 41); on a sea monster (no. 64); and on the birth of octuplets (no. 70)—all bespeak the varying moods and wide-ranging tones of Franklin's humor—amused, facetious, Olympian, despairing, ironic, savage, bitter, or disgusted. Related to the humor, Franklin's earthy qualities turn up in a few other pieces, as in the Orwellian parable of the farmer's pigs (no. 38) and in the comparison of the monkey climbing the tree (no. 52).

Of course the grotesque poem, "An Apology for the Young Man in Goal and in Shackles" (no. 79), is a consummate example of Franklin's salacious, bawdy, and scurrilous talents, similar to but surpassing in quality his "Frenchman and the Poker" (P 13:182–84), "A Method of Humbling Rebellious American Vassals" (P 21:220–22), "The Sale of the Hessians" (P 23:480–84; and Smyth 7:27–29), and "To the Royal Academy of [*Brussels*]" (Lopez 22–26). Indeed, the twenty lines of "An Apology" will in the future be ranked as a literary achievement with "Old Mistresses Apologue" (P 3:27–31) and only behind "The Speech of Miss Polly Baker" (P 3:120–26), though it is indeed more wonderfully grotesque. Ralph Ellison uses a remarkably similar comparison as a touchstone for the comic grotesque in *Invisible Man*: "Why . . . it would be worse than if I had accused him of raping an old woman of ninety-nine years, weighing ninety pounds . . . blind in one eye and lame in the hip" (201). But the voice underlying the authorial stance of "An Apology" is much more severe and disgusted. In early American poetry, only Robert Bolling's "Neanthe" can approach "An Apology," though some of Franklin's prose satires are as vicious.

"An Apology" and the news report on the murder of a daughter (no. 60) expose the grossest crimes and view them as aspects of the animality of man. Moses Coit Tyler wrote that "The Sale of the Hessians" displays a "monstrous crime against human nature,—a crime which it thus portrays both to the horror and the derision of mankind" (Tyler 2:380). "An Apology" and the news report on the murder of a daughter plumb the same regions of black despair about human nature. The self-deception in the news note on bodycounts in battle reports (no. 61), in Veridicus's "On a Pertinacious Obstinacy in Opinion" (no. 62), and on the lying of customers, shopkeepers, and wholesalers (nos. 24–25) is an aspect of human pride that constantly recurs in the Franklinian vision. The view of the human condition that underlies the essay on the death of infants (no. 57) turns bitter at the end as the author considers what life would be like for infants if they were so *unfortunate* as to live.

No one had more contempt for the basic nature of humanity and for its self-deceptions and vanity than Franklin, but he also had the good sense to know that pessimism and despair were finally self-defeating. He therefore advocated—and tried to practice—optimism. He wrote his favorite sister, Jane Mecom, that she should advise her young son "to be very cheerful, and ready to do every thing he is bid, and endeavour to oblige everybody, for that is the true way to get friends" (*P* 2:448). Franklin's deliberate cultivation of optimism is well represented in several news reports (e.g., no. 54), in the "Rules and Maxims for promoting matrimonial Happiness" (no. 19), and especially in his parody and reply to a melancholy religious meditation (no. 58).

Franklin's egalitarianism appears frequently in these essays. It is the primary subject in Obadiah Plainman's two essays on the dancing assembly (nos. 72 and 73) and in Blackamore's satire of "Molatto Gentlemen" (no. 52). In no attitude is Franklin more fixed than in his belief of the equality of people. His religious opinions range through a bewildering variety of beliefs and possibilities—and he occasionally even mocks the deistic rationales; his philosophic writings on the nature of humanity deliberately espouse first one and then another position (see Aldridge 1965, 57–61)—and he even satirizes, as in no. 36, the tendencies of pyrrhonism; but his belief in a democratic egalitarianism is the rock upon which he builds his faith (see Stourzh 26–30). His attitudes outraged his contemporaries, for he was far ahead of his time. Governor Robert Hunter Morris wrote to Governor William Shirley on 16 June 1755 that Franklin held "very out of the way notions of the power of the People, and is as much a favourer of the unreasonable claims of American Assembly as any man whatever" (*Pennsylvania Archives*, 1st ser., 2:362). Egalitarianism is an important aspect of more than thirty of the essays considered herein, from the early attack by "Juba" (the pseudonym suggests, of course, a black slave [see Addison's *Cato*, 1713]) on the arbitrary proceedings of the Massachusetts General Court (no. 4) to the defense of the rattlesnake as a symbol of America (no. 97).

One aspect of his egalitarianism is Franklin's protofeminism, which shows up clearly when he concludes "Rules and Maxims for promoting matrimonial Happiness" (no. 19) with the statement that they are as proper for husbands to observe as wives. The early dates of his involvement in Pennsylvania politics (nos. 11, 46, 53, and 55) will contradict the published views of some historians. His speech for the New Jersey Assembly (no. 71) and his religious propaganda for the Associators (no. 84) will be new to all.

A number of scholars have puzzled over Franklin's supposed change from monarchist to democrat in 1775. Gerald Stourzh is probably the most careful recent Franklinist who has written on "Franklin's sincere devotion to monarchy" (22), evidently forgetting that Franklin was in a much more conspicuous position than any other American of his time. In fact, his Whiggism, praise of Oliver Cromwell (see no. 56; cf. *P* 3:260), and occasional direct satires of the king (*P* 1:312; 2:7, 219, 3:66 and 248) occur frequently in his early writings. But naturally he was more circumspect in England. No American in public life (and none in private that I know of) advocated democracy before 1775 (see Gipson 6:4–9). To do so was traitorous. From at least the mid-1750s the English suspected that the Americans generally (and Franklin particularly) wanted independence and democracy. If Franklin did sometimes desire independence (and he repeatedly threatened that Great Britain could drive America to independence [e.g., *P* 4:486; 5:443–47; 9:90–91; and 15:3–13]), he knew that advocating independence and democracy would end his usefulness as a public servant, would probably bring infamy upon him, and might even make him a martyr to the idea of democracy—all to no good purpose. As Franklin wrote an unnamed (and imaginary?) correspondent about a manuscript supposedly satirizing religion: "you will not succeed so as to change the general Sentiments of Mankind on that Subject, and the Consequence of printing this Piece will be a great deal of Odium drawn upon your self, Mischief to you and no Benefit to others. He that spits against the Wind, spits in his own Face" (*P* 7:294).

Franklin's supposed pre-1775 monarchism is an anachronistic *ignis fatuus*. In fact, Franklin was the most thorough American patriot long before he began his English mission in 1756. Reading the usual accounts of the rise of Franklin's patriotic American feelings (scholars even sometimes comment on his supposedly greater love for England than for America—thus believing the polite cant he expressed to the English) always makes me realize that the authors of such opinions simply have not carefully read through the colonial newspapers. Franklin's *Pennsylvania Gazette* was the most anti-English, pro-American paper in the colonies from 1729 until he ceased his active involvement with it and sailed for England in 1757. Franklin revealed his Americanism especially in the editorial comment on the earliest New England immigrants (no. 22), in the implied satire of the report on the new North Carolina officials (no. 29), in the perceptive note on the Molasses Bill (and in Franklin's republication of all important news and essays concerning this forerunner of the Stamp Act [no. 30]), in the statistical reports on the increase of the American population (no. 31), in the early plea for a Pennsylvania militia (no. 55), in his pride on the amount of trade passing through the colonial ports (no. 63), in the defense of colonial paper currency (no. 74), in the account and woodcut of Louisburg (no. 82), and in the religious essay on the necessity for self-defense (no. 86). These bits of patriotic propaganda prove that Franklin was a committed American long before the Stamp Act—as everyone should know who reads through the materials printed in *The Papers of Benjamin Franklin*. No one else in the mid-eighteenth century claimed that Americans deserved greater liberties and privileges than the English (*P* 5:447, 451; 6:299); no one else repeatedly satirized the British from the early eighteenth century to the Stamp Act; and no one else wrote so much or such excellent propaganda for the American cause from the Stamp Act to the outbreak of the Revolution.

In assessing the causes of the American Revolution, historians have quarreled over the correct interpretation of the navigation acts (Greene 19–22). But the arguments over the harmful or beneficial economic effects of such acts as the Molasses Act are not so important a cause of the American Revolution as the eighteenth-century Americans' perception of those acts. The newspapers reveal that the Molasses Act excited resentment and hostility from the American colonists (see no. 30). Their resentment was continually reinforced by official acts of the English government throughout the colonial period such as the Iron Act of 1750, which precipitated Franklin's essay "Observations concerning the increase of mankind" (*P* 4:225–34). That "little Paper," he said, was written to show that England's "Jealousies with Regard to Manufactures [by her colonies] were ill-founded" (*P* 6:276). In his satire proposing to send rattlesnakes to Britain in return for the felons sent to America, Franklin disgustedly wrote, "In this, however, as in every other Branch of Trade, she will have the Advantage of us" (*P* 4:133). And his great satire "An Edict by the King of Prussia" (*P* 20:413–19) lists (obviously from memory) dozens of repressive acts over the past century (Simson).

English mercantilism revealed a pervasive colonialism that assumed English dominance and natural superiority to Americans—an attitude that continually irritated the supposedly inferior Americans. The second satire on the transplanted Englishman Portius shows that Franklin, like a number of earlier and later colonials, chafed under the constant assertion that English ways must be best (no. 38). It anticipates his repeated satires and burlesques of English anti-Americanism throughout the pre-Revolutionary period (Crane 1950, passim). Indeed, when Anne Reynolds Phillips (37–39) examined all the American magazines from 1741 to 1789 for patriotic American sentiments, she singled out an essay in the *New American Magazine* for September 1759 as the finest piece on the American character to be published before 1790. She did not know that the essay, signed "A New Englandman," originally appeared in England and was by Franklin (*P* 8:340–56; cf. 7:255–63; 9:59–100, etc.). From 1730 to the Revolution, no one was as patriotically American as Franklin, and no one else wrote so much, or so well, on the subject.

These essays demonstrate the literary techniques and rhetorical knowledge that we associate with Franklin as a great literary craftsman. Just as the seventeen-year-old Franklin reveals a knowledge of the practice of *occupatio* in his "Rules" essay (no. 3), so the mature writer in his satire on Prosit directly mentions that "Figure in Rhetorick by which the Orator seems not to do what he is then doing" (no. 38). He deliberately allows his persona as "Obadiah Plainman" to break down when he defends Plainman's impersonation of "the Public, which you charge as a Crime, tho' it be an allowed Figure of Speech, frequently used, and particularly by those great assertors of Public Liberty ["*Demosthenes*' and *Ciceroes*, . . . *Sidneys* and *Trenchards*"], whose Names I mentioned at the Time." He wrote in "Busy-Body No. 5" that *"drawing too good a Character of any one, is a refined Manner of Satyr that may be as injurious to him as the contrary, by bringing on an Examination that undresses the Person, and in the Haste of doing it, he may happen to be stript of what he really owns and deserves*" (*P* 1:133). His mock praise of opponents is more obvious than "drawing too good a Character"—but it is indubitably a successful rhetorical ploy. And just as Franklin is extraordinarily skilled in rhetoric (and willing to burlesque his opponents' obvious faults, e.g., nos. 36, 38, 39, 42, and 43), so too he was an extraordinary logician, not only fertile and able to carry an argument far beyond the usual or expected conclusion (e.g., nos. 3, 75, 77, and 94) but also willing to burlesque or burst the bubble of false or absurd reasoning (e.g., nos. 6, 36, 58, 70, 73, and 93). And occasionally he allows his technical knowledge of logic to peep through, as when he comments on the relation between logic and digressions (no. 42) or on the "Laws of Argument" (no. 73).

His personae too demonstrate those skillful, playful, savage, and ironic abilities that one associates with an eighteenth-century rhetorical master. As Larzer Ziff has observed, "Franklin's brilliant creation of the appropriate *persona* for the literary task at hand is a feature of almost every piece he wrote" (xx–xxi). "Philomusus," "A, B, C, &c.," "Juba," "Timothy Wagstaff," "Abigail Twitterfield," "Philoclerus," "Betty Diligent," "Mercator," "Marcus," "Prosit," "A Quaker Lady," "Y.Z.," "Chatterbox," "Blackamoor," "Pennsylvanus," "Veridicus," "Philomath," "Obadiah Plainman," "Theophilus," "one of the Moravian Brethren," "an American Guesser," and a host of anonymous personae all contribute to the particular purposes of individual essays, hoaxes, skits, poems, or satires that they ostensibly author. Just as no other eighteenth-century writer has so many moods and tones or so wide a range of correspondents, interests, and abilities in his personal letters, so no other eighteenth-century writer has so many different personae or so many different voices as Franklin. All the above personae are notable additions to the canon, though I especially admire the witty, ironic, Olympian, contemptuous, and disgusted anonymous persona of "An Apology for the Young Man in Goal and in Shackles" (no. 79).

Of course these additions to the canon also shed light upon the biography and personality of Franklin. He engaged in more personal quarrels than has been known. He was committed earlier and more vigorously to political positions than scholars have appreciated. Not only the specific writings but even the patterns of alternating commitments shown in these new writings illuminate fundamental traits of Franklin's mind. He seems almost incapable of not realizing what could be said for an opposing point of view. After burlesquing superstitious ministers and their shenanigans at a convention (no. 15), he reverses himself and defends their important role in society (no. 16). When he writes an essay on censure or backbiting, implicitly defining people as selfish, vain animals who cannot bear to hear their contemporaries praised (no. 47), he turns around and writes a philosophical defense of the benevolence as well as the selfishness of human beings (no. 48). And after he bitterly assesses the wicked design of Providence, complains of the death of infants, and ends by condemning the thorough unpleasantness of life (no. 57), he about-faces and parodies a melancholy religious meditation, substituting a cheerful and happy meditation in its stead (no. 58). Thomas Jefferson appreciated Franklin's extraordinary ability to see all sides of an issue and judged that this quality was especially responsible for making him a great diplomat: "He possessed the confidence of that government [the French] in the highest degree, insomuch, that it may truly be said, that they were more under his influence, than he under theirs. The fact is, that his temper was so amiable and conciliatory, his conduct so rational, never urging impossibilities, or even things unreasonably inconvenient to them, in short, so moderate and attentive to their difficulties, as well as our own, that what his enemies called subserviency, I saw was only that reasonable disposition, which, sensible that advantages are not all to be on one side, yielding what is just and liberal, is the more certain of obtaining liberality and justice" (Jefferson 10:117–18).

Even one piece judged not to be Franklin's sheds light upon a characteristic of his mind and upon an often-misunderstood passage in the *Autobiography*. Franklin evidently recalled "A New and Mild Method totally to Extirpate the Indians" (no. 91) when he wrote: "And indeed if it be the Design of Providence to extirpate these Savages in order to make room for Cultivators of the Earth, it seems not improbable that Rum may be the appointed Means" (121). Just as Franklin undercuts the Reverend Charles Beatty by having him distribute rum just before saying prayers (148), so he implicitly satirizes the basic nature of a Providence that would use rum as "the appointed Means" to kill off the Indians. Setting this passage from the *Autobiography* in the context of his satire on Providence in the essay "Drunkenness" (no. 50) and recalling that the "New and Mild Method" calls for Franklin's own death because he is an "Indian Lover," one can see that it is not, as Leslie Fiedler (57) and others have thought, a statement of "bland assurance" about the annihilation of the Indians. It is instead a bitterly ironic comment on the nature of God and mankind.

Finally, this book demonstrates, I hope, that Franklin wrote more than we knew before—and more, no doubt, then we know now.

But I cannot conclude without paying tribute to the excellent scholarship of Alfred Owen Aldridge and the editors of *The Papers of Benjamin Franklin*. Of the items herein attributed to Franklin, twenty-two (nos. 15, 16, 18, 22, 24, 25, 26, 27, 31, 33, 36, 38, 39, 49, 54, 55, 58, 66, 72, 73, 74, and 87) have previously been ascribed (definitively, in eight cases) to Franklin by Professor Aldridge. Furthermore, he has previously removed one from the canon that was printed in *The Papers of Benjamin Franklin* (no. 20). And Leonard W. Labaree, William B. Willcox, Whitfield J. Bell, Jr., Claude-Anne Lopez, and the other editors, past and present, of *The Papers of Benjamin Franklin* have done a splendid job in their editorial decisions and comments. Even in the case of the essay series that I believe they mistakenly attribute to Franklin (no. 93), my opinion depends in great part upon the painstaking evidence given in their notes. This study of Benjamin Franklin's canon relies upon the *Papers* in nearly every sentence. And it could not be expected that in cases of such great intrinsic doubt as the anonymous and pseudonymous periodical publications of Benjamin Franklin, that either the editors of *The Papers of Benjamin Franklin* or any other scholar could be infallible.

APPENDIX

Since this book was written and the complete work (except the index) set in pages, I have read a new study that attributes two additional essays to Franklin. Mitchell Robert Breitwieser, in *Cotton Mather and Benjamin Franklin: The Price of Representative Personality* (Cambridge: Cambridge University Press, 1984), assumes that Franklin wrote the lead essays in the *New England Courant* of 8 April and 9 September 1723. I will therefore add a brief discussion of these new attributions here.

97. **The degenerating Times.** In *New England Courant,* 8 April 1723, p. 1. *Length:* 650 words. *Previous attribution:* Breitwieser 183–84.

Breitwieser believes that this is a mock jeremiad, satirizing the common lamentations of the Puritan ministers, and therefore attributes it to Franklin. But he writes in conclusion, "It is not clear whether this missive . . . is actual or a pastiche, though the pleonasm ('Why is this People of Jerusalem slidden back, by a perpetual backsliding?') suggests pastiche, a bemused and ironic observation that conservative authority will deride change as decline" (184). Since the piece is entirely serious, it cannot be a mock jeremiad. The writing has none of the genius of Franklin: the biblical quotations are all straightforward, the diction is sometimes poor and certainly repetitious, the verbs are usually passive, the author uses several sentence fragments, the syntax is sometimes awkward, and the straightforward persona is that of a scolding Puritan preacher.

Even if the piece were a mock jeremiad, I would not necessarily think that it must be by Franklin. Nathaniel Gardner, after all, wrote a mock jeremiad in the *Courant* for 6 November 1721 and burlesqued Increase Mather's style on 20 November 1721 (W. C. Ford 351; see also Perry Miller 358). If Franklin wrote this and if it were a mock jeremiad, I would expect it to have an extraordinary complexity of thought, flashes of bawdy humor, a mocking persona and an excellent prose style. But this actual jeremiad is clearly by some second-rate hack. It is not up to the standard of Nathaniel Gardner. The only reason for anyone to suspect that it is a mock jeremiad is that it appeared in the *New England Courant*, but straightforward religious pieces appeared even in the early numbers of the *Courant* (cf. no. 10) and they became more common later. The Couranteers could have thought that this piece was so wretched an example of the jeremiad that it was in itself a satire on the genre. Or it could be a pastiche, but if so, I see no reason to think that Franklin, rather than some other Couranteer, put it together. *Conclusion*—not by Franklin.

98. **On New England Church Discipline.** In *New England Courant*, 9 September 1723, p. 1. *Length:* 1,150 words. *Previous attribution:* Breitwieser 184–85.

On 6 May 1723, the *Boston Gazette* published an essay claiming that New England Congregational churches were historically composed of separatists. In reply, "Miso-Schismaticus" in the *Boston News Letter* for 30 May 1723 argued that the earliest religious leaders in New England "were very far from censuring and condemning those who" conformed to the Church of England, but only wanted their own "purer worship." The anonymous author of this *Courant* essay continues the discussion. Like Franklin in no. 8 above (pp. 38–39), he begins by commenting on "the Power and Influence of Custom and Education." And he writes well: "A Pin for Platforms say I, while we are only amus'd with the empty Name, the Sound and Shadow, instead of the Substance and Reality."

But unlike Franklin, this author is interested in the history of New England church government and in "the true Apostolical Constitution." He knows the history of the Cambridge platform. He cites Benjamin Colman's early attack on the old doctrines. He refers to Increase Mather's attack on Solomon Stoddard's position on the administration of communion, *Dissertation Wherein the Strange Doctrine* (Boston, 1708). Like John Wise, he thinks that some New England ministers (the Mathers are evidently suggested) "have cloath'd the Priesthood with more absolute Authority, and divested the Fraternity of most of the Immunities which the Platform secures to them." The theological subject matter familiar to this author simply did not interest Franklin. Further, despite the essay's relatively well-written prose, I see little internal evidence for thinking that Franklin wrote it. The persona does not have his mocking humor or self-satire, and the content nowhere suggests Franklin's subtlety or complexity. Of the known Couranteers, Nathaniel Gardner is a more likely author than Franklin. But, partly because of the time lag (three months) for this response to the *Boston News Letter* essay, I suspect that someone other than a local Bostonian wrote it.

Biography further weakens the attempted attribution. The essay appears in the penultimate *Courant* (9 September) in Franklin's own file of the paper (W. C. Ford 340). Franklin ceased working for his brother James one week later and sailed for New York on 25 September. Franklin makes it clear in the *Autobiography* that his departure followed a series of difficulties (18). He explains, "At length a fresh Difference arising between my Brother and me, I took upon me to assert my Freedom, presuming that he would not venture to produce the new Indentures" (19–20). It seems unlikely that Franklin would have written for the *Courant* one week before breaking off his apprenticeship to his brother. *Conclusion*—not by Franklin.

BIBLIOGRAPHY

1. Items Attributed to Franklin

Note: Items marked with an asterisk are printed in the Library of America's *Benjamin Franklin: Writings*.

* 1. Philomusus to Dr. John Herrick on his incomparable Elegy, 25 June 1722
* 2. Hugo Grim on Silence Dogood, 3 December 1722
* 3. "A, B, C, &c." suggests "Rules" for the *New England Courant*, 28 January 1722/3
* 4. Juba to "Your Honour" [Samuel Sewall], 4 February 1722/3
* 6. High Tide in Boston, 4 March 1722/3
* 8. Timothy Wagstaff on the Influence of Education and Custom, 15 April 1723
* 9. Abigail Twitterfield replies to the Sin of Barrenness, 8 July 1723
*11. Suppressed Addition to Busy-Body No. 8, 27 March 1729
*13. The Trial and Reprieve of Prouse and Mitchel, 23 December 1729 and 20 January 1729/30
*14. News Note Jeu d'Esprit on "a gallant Duel," 10 February 1729/30
*15. The Letter of the Drum, 23 April 1730
*16. Philoclerus on that odd Letter of the Drum, 7 May 1730
*17. News Note Jeu d'Esprit on an unlucky She-Wrestler, 23 July 1730
 18. Poem on the Rats and the Cheese, 24 September 1730
*19. Rules and Maxims for promoting matrimonial Happiness, 8 October 1730
*21. News Report on the Aurora Borealis, 29 October 1730
*22. Why the earliest New Englanders came to America, 5 November 1730
*24. The Lying of Shopkeepers, 19 November 1730
*25. Betty Diligent and Mercator on the Lying of Shopkeepers, 3 December 1730

26. An ironic Comment on Astrology, 8 December 1730
*27. Compassion and Regard for the Sick, 25 March 1731
*29. English Officials for America, 27 May 1731
*30. The Effects of the Molasses Bill, 17 June 1731
31. Death Rates in Boston, 26 August 1731
32. Apollo and Daphne, A Dialogue, 4 November 1731
33. Hints on Fairs, 27 November 1731
*34. News Note Jeu d'Esprit on a Lion, 25 January 1731/2
*35. News Note Jeu d'Esprit on a Burnt-Offering, 15 February 1731/2
36. Marcus burlesques Portius, 30 March 1732
*37. Simplicity, 13 April 1732
38. *"This is the Practice at Home"*: a second Satire on Portius, 20 April 1732
39. Prosit satirizes Prosit, 4 May 1732
40. A glorious Passage in Persius, 25 May 1732
41. A Quaker Lady on a Lover's Threat, 25 May 1732
42. A Discourse on Argumentations from California or the Moon, 1 June 1732
43. On Declamation, 1 June 1732
*46. Praise for William Penn, 14 August 1732
*47. Censure or Backbiting, 7 September 1732
*48. "Y.Z." on the Benevolence as well as Selfishness of Man, 30 November 1732
49. Chatterbox on the Family of Boxes, 11 January 1732/3
50. On Drunkenness, 1 February 1732/3
*51. A Meditation on a Quart Mugg, 19 July 1733
*52. "Blackamore" on Molatto Gentlemen, 30 August 1733
53. Poem by Pennsylvanus against Party-Malice, 28 September 1733
*54. Pennsylvanus on brave Men at Fires, 20 December 1733
*55. "Queries" urging establishing a Pennsylvania Militia, 6 March 1733/4
*56. On Constancy, 4 April 1734
*57. The Death of Infants, 20 June 1734
*58. Parody of and Reply to a melancholy religious Meditation, 8 August 1734
*59. Note on a Thunderstorm, 25 September 1734
*60. Report on the Murder of a Daughter, 24 October 1734
*61. Exaggerating Body Counts in Battle Reports, 19 December 1734
*62. Veridicus on a pertinacious Obstinacy in Opinion, 27 March 1735

Bibliography

  63. Statistics on Trade in Colonial Ports, 8 April 1736
*64. Report of a Sea Monster, 29 April 1736
*66. Philomath on the Talents requisite in an Almanac Writer, 20 October 1737
*69. News Note on the Compassion of Captain Croak, 10 August 1738
*70. News Note Jeu d'Esprit on Octuplets, 24 November 1738
  71. The New Jersey House of Representatives' Address to Governor Lewis Morris, 28 April 1740
*72. Obadiah Plainman defends the Meaner Sort, 5 May 1740
*73. Obadiah Plainman to Tom Trueman, 29 May 1740
*74. Paper Currency in the American Colonies, February 1741
*76. Letter from Theophilus, Relating to the Divine Prescience, March 1741
  78. Introduction and "Remark" on "What is True?" 24 February 1742/3
*79. An Apology for the young Man in Goal and in Shackles, 15 September 1743
*81. Cut of Louisburg, 6 June 1745
*82. Appreciation of George Whitefield, 31 July 1746
*83. George Whitefield's financial Accounts, 23 April 1747
*85. The Necessity for Self-Defense, 29 December 1747
  86. A Course of Experiments on the newly discovered electrical Fire, 10 May 1749
  87. News Notes on three Natives of Greenland, 15 June and 7 September 1749
*88. Rules Proper to be observed in Trade, 20 February 1749/50
*89. Ebenezer Kinnersley's "Course of Experiments on the newly-discovered Electrical Fire," 11 April 1751
*93. An Act for the more effectual keeping of his Majesty's American Colonies Dependent on the Crown of Great Britain, 29 June 1774
  94. Method of making Salt-Petre, 2 August 1775
*95. The Devices on the Continental Bills, 20 September 1775
*96. The Rattlesnake as a Symbol of America, by an American Guesser, 27 December 1775

2. Items Rejected from the Canon

  5. Proceedings against the *Courant*, 26 February 1722/3
  7. On Tattlers and Talebearers, 18 March 1722/3
10. Bridget Bifrons on Lecture Day Visiting, 19 August 1723
12. Burlesque Ballad Criticism, 16 December 1729

20. On Conversation, 15 October 1730
23. On Swearing, 12 November 1730
28. The Conduct of Common Life, 1 April 1731
44. Philanthropos on helping young Men, 26 June 1732
45. Belinda on a too-bashful Suitor, 26 June 1732
65. David's Lamentation, 22 September 1737
67. The Origin of the English Constitution, 30 March 1738
68. "A.B." writes "Dear Ned" on Pennsylvania Politics, 4 May, 6 July, 12 October 1738; 29 March and 5 April 1739
75. Theophilus Misodaemon on the Wandering Spirit, February 1741
77. An infallible Receipt to make a new Kind of a Convert, by Esculapius, June 1741
80. The New Jersey House of Representatives' Address to Governor Lewis Morris, 18 April 1745
84. On Barclay's *Apology*, 22 October 1747
90. A New and Mild Method totally to Extirpate the Indians, 6 February 1764
91. The Vision of Mirza, 27 February 1769
92. The Colonist's Advocate Essay Series, 4 January to 2 March 1770

3. Scholarly References

Adams, Charles F., ed. 1850–60. *The Works of John Adams.* 10 vols. Boston: Little, Brown.

Adams, John. *Diary and Autobiography of John Adams.* Edited by Lyman H. Butterfield et al. 1962. 4 vols. Cambridge: Harvard University Press.

Aldridge, Alfred Owen. 1949a. "Franklin as Demographer." *Journal of Economic History* 9:25–44.

———. 1949b. "Franklin's 'Shaftesburian' Dialogues Not Franklin's: A Revision of the Franklin Canon." *American Literature* 21:151–59.

———. 1950. "Franklin and the Ghostly Drummer of Tedworth." *William and Mary Quarterly,* 3d ser., 7:559–67.

———. 1957. *Franklin and His French Contemporaries.* New York: New York University Press.

———. 1960. Review of *The Papers of Benjamin Franklin*, vol. 1. *American Literature* 32:208–10.

———. 1962. "Benjamin Franklin and the *Pennsylvania Gazette.*" *Proceedings of the American Philosophical Society* 106:77–81.

———. 1964. "A Religious Hoax by Benjamin Franklin." *American Literature* 36:204–9.

———. 1965. *Benjamin Franklin: Philosopher and Man.* Philadelphia: Lippincott.

———. 1967a. *Benjamin Franklin and Nature's God.* Durham, N.C.: Duke University Press.

———. 1967b. "Form and Substance in Franklin's *Autobiography.*" In *Essays on American Literature in Honor of Jay B. Hubbell,* edited by Clarence Gohdes. Durham, N.C.: Duke University Press.

The Autobiography of Benjamin Franklin: A Genetic Text. 1982. Edited by J. A. Leo Lemay and P. M. Zall. Knoxville: University of Tennessee Press.

Bier, Jesse. 1958. "Franklin's *Autobiography:* Benchmark of American Literature." *Western Humanities Review* 12:57–65.

Bigelow, John, ed. 1887–89. *The Complete Works of Benjamin Franklin.* 10 vols. New York: G. P. Putnam's.

Blair, Walter. 1980. "Franklin's Massacre of the Hessians." In *Toward a New Literary History: Essays in Honor of Arlin Turner,* edited by Louis J. Budd, Edwin H. Cady, and Carl L. Anderson. Durham, N.C.: Duke University Press.

Blair, Walter, and Hamlin Hill. 1978. *America's Humor.* New York: Oxford University Press.

Brodwin, Stanley. 1979. "Strategies of Humor: The Case of Benjamin Franklin." *Prospects* 4:121–67.

Cafferty, Pastora San Juan. 1971. "Loyalist Rhapsodies: The Poetry of Stansbury and Odell." Ph.D. diss., George Washington University.

Cappon, Lester J., ed. 1959. *The Adams-Jefferson Letters.* 2 vols. Chapel Hill: University of North Carolina Press.

Cohen, I. Bernard, ed. 1941. *Benjamin Franklin's Experiments: A New Edition of Franklin's Experiments and Observations on Electricity.* Cambridge: Harvard University Press.

Cook, Elizabeth Christine. 1950. *Literary Influences in Colonial Newspapers 1704–1750.* New York: Columbia University Press.

Crane, Verner W. 1934. "Certain Writings of Benjamin Franklin on the British Empire and the American Colonies." *Papers of the Bibliographical Society of America* 28:1–27.

———. 1950. *Benjamin Franklin's Letters to the Press, 1758–1775.* Chapel Hill: University of North Carolina Press.

Curwen, Samuel. 1842. *Journals and Letters 1775–1784.* New York: C. S. Francis. (The modern edition of Curwen's *Diary* does not quote the letter from William Browne to Curwen.)

Davy, Francis X. 1958. "Benjamin Franklin, Satirist: The Satire of Franklin and its Rhetoric." Ph.D. diss., Columbia University.

DeArmond, Anna Janney. 1949. *Andrew Bradford: Colonial Journalist.* Newark: University of Delaware Press.

Duane, William, ed. 1861. *Memoirs of Benjamin Franklin . . . Augmented by much matters not contained in any former edition.* 2 vols. New York: Derby.

Duniway, Clyde A. 1906. *The Development of Freedom of the Press in Massachusetts.* Cambridge: Harvard University Press.

Eddy, George Simpson, ed. 1928. *Account Books Kept by Benjamin Franklin. Ledger 1728–1739, Journal 1730–1737.* New York: Columbia University Press.

Eliot, John. 1798–99. "A Narrative of the Newspapers Printed in New England." *Collections of the Massachusetts Historical Society* 5 (for 1798):208–16; and "Continuation," 6 (for 1799):64–77.

Ellison, Ralph. 1952. *Invisible Man.* New York: Modern Library.

Evans, Charles. 1903–59. *American Bibliography: A Chronological Dictionary . . . 1639 . . . to 1800.* 14 vols. Chicago and Worcester: Evans and American Antiquarian Society.

Fiedler, Leslie A. 1968. *The Return of the Vanishing American.* New York: Stein and Day.

Force, Peter, ed. 1843. *American Archives,* 4th series, vol. 4. Washington, D.C.: M. St. Clair Clarke and Peter Force.

Ford, Paul Leicester. 1889. *Franklin Bibliography: A List of Books Written by or relating to Benjamin Franklin.* Brooklyn, N.Y., n.p.

Ford, Worthington Chauncey. 1923–24. "Franklin's *New England Courant.*" *Proceedings of the Massachusetts Historical Society* 57:336–53.

Franklin, William Temple, ed. 1817–18. *Memoirs of the Life and Writings of Benjamin Franklin.* 3 vols. London: H. Colburn.

Gilbert, Felix. 1961. *To the Farewell Address: Ideas of Early American Foreign Policy.* Princeton: Princeton University Press.

Gipson, Lawrence Henry. 1936–70. *The British Empire Before the American Revolution.* 15 vols. New York: Alfred A. Knopf.

Girouard, Robert. 1982. "A Survey of Apocryphal Visions in Late Eighteenth-Century America." *Proceedings of the Colonial Society of Massachusetts* 59:191–219.

Goldberg, Joseph Philip. 1962. "The Eighteenth-Century Philadelphia Almanac and Its English Counterpart." Ph.D. diss., University of Maryland.

Granger, Bruce Ingham. 1964. *Benjamin Franklin: An American Man of Letters.* Ithaca, N.Y.: Cornell University Press.

Greene, Jack P., ed. 1968. *The Reinterpretation of the American Revolution 1763–1789.* New York: Harper & Row.

Griffith, John. 1976. "Franklin's Sanity and the Man behind the Masks." In *The Oldest Revolutionary: Essays on Benjamin Franklin,* edited by J. A. Leo Lemay. Philadelphia: University of Pennsylvania Press.

Hall, Max. 1960. *Benjamin Franklin and Polly Baker: The History of a Literary Deception.* Chapel Hill: University of North Carolina Press.

Hay, Carla H. 1975. "Benjamin Franklin, James Burgh, and the Authorship of 'The Colonist's Advocate Letters.'" *William and Mary Quarterly,* 3d ser., 32:111–124. (The essay concludes with a letter from William B. Willcox, editor of *The Papers of Benjamin Franklin,* defending the attribution to Franklin.)

Hamilton, Sinclair. 1948–49. "The Earliest Device of the Colonies and Some Other Early Devices." *Princeton University Library Chronicle* 10:117–23.

Havens, Raymond D. 1953. "Simplicity, a Changing Concept." *Journal of the History of Ideas* 14:3–32.

Jefferson, Thomas. *The Writings of Thomas Jefferson.* Edited by Paul Leicester Ford. 1892–99. 10 vols. New York: Putnam's.

Jorgenson, Chester E. 1934. "Sidelights on Benjamin Franklin's Principles of Rhetoric." *Revue Anglo-Americaine* 11:208–22.

Jorgenson, Chester E., and Frank Luther Mott, eds. 1962. *Benjamin Franklin: Representative Selections.* New York: Hill & Wang. (A reprint of the Mott & Jorgenson 1936 edition, with the annotated bibliography brought up to date.)

Journals of the Continental Congress. Edited by Worthington C. Ford et al. 1904–37. 34 vols. Washington, D.C.: U.S. Government Printing Office.

Journals of the House of Representatives, Vol. 4, 1722–1723. Edited by Worthington C. Ford. 1923. Boston: Massachusetts Historical Society.

Keill, John. 1698. *Examination of Dr. Burnet's Theory.* Oxford: Theatre.

Kellogg, Thelma L. 1929. "Early American Social Satire Before 1800, with especial reference to social satire in the early American Almanac." Ph.D. diss., Harvard University.

Leary, Lewis. 1975. *Soundings: Some Early American Writers.* Athens: University of Georgia Press.

Lemay, J. A. Leo. 1961. "Franklin and Kinnersley." *Isis* 52:575–81.

———. 1964. *Ebenezer Kinnersley: Franklin's Friend.* Philadelphia: University of Pennsylvania Press.

———. 1965. "Franklin's Suppressed 'Busy-Body.'" *American Literature* 38:307–11.

———. 1967. "Franklin and the *Autobiography:* An Essay on Recent Scholarship." *Eighteenth-Century Studies* 1:185–211.

———. 1969. "A Calendar of American Poetry in the Colonial Newspapers and Magazines and in the Major English Magazines Through 1765." *Proceedings of the American Antiquarian Society* 79 (1969): 291–392; 80 (1970): 71–222, 353–469. (Reprinted, with minor revisions, separately, 1972.)

———. 1972. *Men of Letters in Colonial Maryland.* Knoxville: University of Tennessee Press.

———. 1975. Review of *Benjamin Franklin and the Zealous Presbyterians,* by Melvin H. Buxbaum. *Early American Literature* 10:222–26.

———. 1976. "The Text, Rhetorical Strategies and Themes of 'The Speech of Miss Polly Baker.'" In *The Oldest Revolutionary: Essays on Benjamin Franklin,* edited by Lemay. Philadelphia: University of Pennsylvania Press.

———. 1978. *The Renaissance Man in the Eighteenth Century: Papers Read at a Clark Library Seminar 9 October 1976.* Los Angeles: William Andrews Clark Memorial Library.

———. 1983. Review of *The Papers of Benjamin Franklin, vol. 22, March 23, 1775 through October 27, 1776,* edited by William B. Willcox et al. *Pennsylvania Magazine of History and Biography* 107:146–49.

Levin, David. 1964. "The *Autobiography* of Benjamin Franklin: The Puritan Experimenter in Life and Art." *Yale Review* 53:258–75.

Lopez, Claude-Anne, ed. 1967. *The Bagatelles from Passy.* New York: Eakins Press.

Lynen, John F. 1965. *The Design of the Present: Essays on Time and Form in American Literature.* New Haven: Yale University Press.

McCoy, Drew R. 1978. "Benjamin Franklin's Vision of a Republican Political Economy for America." *William and Mary Quarterly,* 3d ser., 25:605–28.

McMaster, John Bach. 1887. *Benjamin Franklin as a Man of Letters.* Boston: Houghton, Mifflin.

Mather, Cotton. 1710. *Bonifacius: An Essay upon the Good.* Boston: B. Green. (Better known by the running title "Essays to Do Good.")

———. 1702. *Magnalia Christi Americana.* Edited by Thomas Robbins. 1853–55. 2 vols. Hartford, Conn.: Andrus & Son.

———. 1721. *Silentiarius. A Brief Essay on the Holy Science.* Boston: S. Kneeland.

Matthews, Albert. 1906–7. "The Snake Device, 1754–1776, and the Constitutional Courant, 1765." *Publications of the Colonial Society of Massachusetts* 11:409–53.

Miller, C. William. 1974. *Benjamin Franklin's Philadelphia Printing 1728–1766: A Descriptive Bibliography.* Philadelphia: American Philosophical Society.

Miller, Perry. 1953. *The New England Mind: From Colony to Province.* Cambridge, Mass.: Harvard University Press.

Morris, Richard B. 1949. "Spotlight on the Plowmen of the Jersies." *Proceedings of the New Jersey Historical Society* 67:106–23.

———. 1975. "Dr. Franklin and Mr. Jay: Conversations in Paris." *Columbia University Library Columns* 24:10–17.

———, ed. 1980. *John Jay: The Winning of the Peace. Unpublished Papers 1780–84.* [Vol. 2 of *The Papers of John Jay.*] New York: Harper & Row.

Mott, Frank Luther. 1957. *A History of American Magazines 1741–1850.* Cambridge: Harvard University Press.

Naval Documents of the American Revolution. Edited by William Bell Clark et al. 1964———. Washington, D.C.: U.S. Government Printing Office.

Newman, Eric P. 1966. "Continental Currency and the Fugio Cent: Sources of Emblems and Mottoes." *Numismatist* 79:1587–98.

———. 1983. "Benjamin Franklin and the Chain Design." *Numismatist* 96:2271–84.

Nevill, Samuel. 1746. "Speech to the House of Representatives of the Colony of New Jersey, on the Second Reading of the Petition from a Number of Persons stiling themselves Inhabitants chiefly of the Northern Part of New Jersey, on Saturday the 26th of April, 1746." *New York Post Boy,* 19 and 26 May.

Nicolosi, Anthony. 1969. "Colonial Particularism and Political Rights: Jacob Spicer II on Aid to Virginia, 1754." *New Jersey History* 87:69–88.

Oliver, Peter. *Peter Oliver's Origin & Progress of the American Revolution.* Edited by Douglass Adair and John A. Schutz. 1961. San Marino, Calif.: Huntington Library.

OED. Oxford English Dictionary. Edited by James A. H. Murray. 1933. 13 vols. London: Oxford University Press.

P = *Papers of Benjamin Franklin.* Edited by Leonard W. Labaree, William B. Willcox, Whitfield J. Bell, Jr., Claude-Anne Lopez et al. 1959– . 23 vols. to 1984. New Haven: Yale University Press.

Parton, James. 1864. *Life and Times of Benjamin Franklin.* 2 vols. Boston: Osgood and Company.

Pennsylvania Archives. 1874–1919. 119 vols. in 9 series. Philadelphia: J. Severs & Co., 1852–56; Harrisburg, 1874–1919.

Pennsylvania Gazette, 1728-1789: A Reprint Edition. 1968. 25 vols. Philadelphia: Rhistoric Publications.

Phillips, Anne Reynolds. 1953. "Expressions of Cultural Nationalism in Early American Magazines, 1741–1789." Ph.D. diss., Brown University.

Pitt, Arthur Stuart. 1942. "The Sources, Significance, and Date of Franklin's 'An Arabian Tale.'" *PMLA* 57:155–68.

Pritchett, V. S. 1941. Review of Franklin's *Autobiography, New Statesman and Nation* 22 (27 September): 309.

Reilly, Elizabeth Carroll. 1975. *A Dictionary of Colonial American Printers' Ornaments and Illustrations.* Worcester: American Antiquarian Society.

Richardson, Edward W. 1982. *Standards of the American Revolution.* Philadelphia: University of Pennsylvania Press.

Roach, Hannah Benner. 1960. "Benjamin Franklin Slept Here." *Pennsylvania Magazine of History and Biography* 84:127–74.

Rossiter, Clinton. 1952. "The Political Theory of Benjamin Franklin." *Pennsylvania Magazine of History and Biography* 76:259–93.

Rush, Benjamin. 1948. *The Autobiography of Benjamin Rush, Together with his Commonplace Book for 1789–1813.* Edited by G. W. Corner. Princeton: Princeton University Press.

Sappenfield, James A. 1973. *A Sweet Instruction: Franklin's Journalism as a Literary Apprenticeship.* Carbondale: Southern Illinois University Press.

Schlesinger, Arthur M. 1966. *Prelude to Independence: The Newspaper War on Britain 1764–1776.* New York: Alfred A. Knopf.

Schneider, Herbert W. 1925. "The Significance of Benjamin Franklin's Moral Philosophy." In Columbia University, Department of Philosophy, *Studies in the History of Ideas* 2:291–312.

Seed, David. 1983. "Projecting the Self: An Approach to Franklin's *Autobiography.*" *Etudes Anglaises* 36:385–400.

Sewall, Samuel. *Diary.* Edited by M. Halsey Thomas. 1973. 2 vols. New York: Farrar Straus and Giroux.

Seward, William. 1740. *Journal of Voyage from Savannah to Philadelphia.* London: J. Oswald.

Shear, Walter. 1962. "Franklin's Self-Portrait." *Midwest Quarterly* 4:71–86.

Simson, George, 1960–61. "Legal Sources for Franklin's 'Edict.'" *American Literature* 32:152–57.

Smyth, Albert Henry, ed. 1905–7. *The Writings of Benjamin Franklin.* 10 vols. New York: Macmillan Co.

Spiller, Robert E. 1942. "Benjamin Franklin: Student of Life." *Journal of the Franklin Institute* 233:309–29.

Sparks, Jared, ed. 1836–40. *The Works of Benjamin Franklin.* 10 vols. Boston: Hilliard, Gray & Co.

Spicer. *See* Nicolosi.

Stourzh, Gerald. 1969. *Benjamin Franklin and American Foreign Policy.* 2d ed. Chicago: University of Chicago Press.

Thomas, Isaiah. *The History of Printing in America.* Edited by Marcus A. McCorison. 1970. New York: Weathervane Books.

Tourtellot, Arthur Bernon. 1977. *Benjamin Franklin: The Shaping of Genius: The Boston Years.* Garden City, N.Y.: Doubleday & Co.

Tyler, Moses Coit. 1897. *The Literary History of the American Revolution 1765–1783.* 2 vols. Reprint ed., New York: Ungar, 1957, 1963.

Van Doren, Carl. 1938. *Benjamin Franklin.* New York: Viking.

Vaughan, Benjamin, ed. 1779. *Political, Miscellaneous, and Philsophical Pieces . . . Written by Benjamin Franklin.* London: J. Johnson.

Wages, Jack D. 1973. "Father Benjamin and the Ladies: Chauvinist or Champion?" *Proceedings of Conference of College Teachers of English of Texas* 38:38–42.

Wainwright, Nicholas B. 1949. "Nicholas Scull's 'Junto' Verses." *Pennsylvania Magazine of History and Biography* 73:82–84.

Ward, John William. 1963. "Who was Benjamin Franklin?" *American Scholar* 32:541–53.

Weber, Max. 1930. *The Protestant Ethic and the Spirit of Capitalism*. Translated by Talcott Parsons. London: Allen & Unwin.

Wheat, James Clements, and Christian F. Brun. 1978. *Maps and Charts Published in America before 1800: A Bibliography*. Rev. ed. London: Holland Press.

Wilson, F. P., ed. 1970. *Oxford Book of English Proverbs*. Compiled by William Smith. 3d ed. Oxford: Clarendon Press.

Wolf, Edwin, II. 1966. *Annual Report of the Library Company of Philadelphia for 1965*. Philadelphia: Library Company of Philadelphia.

———. 1972. Review of *A Calendar of American Poetry in the Colonial Newspapers and Magazines and in the Major English Magazines through 1765*, by J. A. Leo Lemay. *New England Quarterly* 45:587–89.

Ziff, Larzer. 1959. "Introduction." *Benjamin Franklin's Autobiography and Selected Writings*. New York: Holt, Rinehart and Winston.

INDEX

Note: BF is used throughout for "Benjamin Franklin."

"A. B.," 93–94
Adams, John, 45, 61, 83, 122, 125
Addison, Joseph, 51; *Cato*, 83, 132; *Spectator*, 117, 130; *Tatler*, 76, 130
Ad hominem argument: as uncharacteristic of BF, 104
Aesop, 48, 82
Aesthetic, 49, 62
Aldridge, Alfred Owen, 108–9, 136–37; *BF and Nature's God*, 45, 66, 69, 75, 97, 101, 113, 129; "BF and the *Pa. Gazette*," 16–17, 46, 51, 53, 71, 75–76, 82, 91, 102, 114; *BF: Philosopher and Man*, 75, 91–92, 129; "Form and Substance in Franklin's *Autobiography*," 63; *Franklin and His French Contemporaries*, 28; "Franklin and the Ghostly Drummer of Tedworth," 42, 43, 58, 62, 64; "Franklin as Demographer," 22, 57, 75; "Franklin's 'Shaftesburian' Dialogues Not Franklin's," 75; "A Religious Hoax by BF," 48, 78, 84, 86, 89; review of *The Papers of BF*, vol. 1, 18, 50, 51, 52, 70, 71, 79, 81
Alfred (king of England), 35, 36
Allen, Dr. John, 77
Alleyne, John, 70–71
Almanac writing, 91
Americanism. *See* Patriotism; Proto-nationalism
American Revolution, 124, 132, 134
American Weekly Mercury, 106; anticlerical and antichristian essays in, 69; its editorial against James Franklin, 37; "An Essay on Envy, Philosophical and Political" ("Civicus"), 72; imitates BF essay on slippery sidewalks, 76; "Marcus Verus" attacks "Prosit" in (#39), 68; "Portius" attacks BF and Alexander Hamilton in, 58–59, 128; "Portius" replies to "Marcus" in (#37), 62, 128; "Prosit" replies to #38 in, 64; refuses to print "T. Scrub" letter, 70; as rival to *Pa. Gazette*, 20; "S.H." attacks BF's "Marcus" essay in (#39), 65; "Tom Trueman" replies to "Obadiah Plainman" in (#72), 99–102
Amplification, 69–70, 76. *See also* Periphrasis
Anecdote, 23, 42, 45, 63, 67, 81; savage, 58
Anti-Christianity: charged against BF, 110
Anti-clericism, 23, 30–31, 39, 42–45, 65–66, 69, 128, 135. *See also* Religious satire
Anti-feminism: as atypical of BF, 54, 73. *See also* Proto-feminism
Antimetabole, 23, 30
Anti-pacifism, 82–83, 133. *See also* Militia Association
Anti-provincialism, 30, 67
Aphorisms, 61, 74, 85. *See also* Proverbs; Sententiae
Appearance vs. reality, 23, 61–62, 101, 105, 115
Aristocracy, 98, 101. *See also* Social hierarchy
Associators. *See* Militia Association
Astrology: burlesque of, 23, 53

152

Index

Astronomy, 36, 50
"Athanasius Wildfire," 60
Atheism, 46, 67–68. *See also* Infidelity; Religious satire
Attribution: external evidence for, 19–21; internal evidence for, 21–24
Aurora borealis, 50–51
Avarice, 46
Avery, John: death of, 30

Bache, Sarah Franklin, 97
Baender, Paul, 45
Bagatelles, 47
Baker, Henry, 40, 50
Barbadoes, 55
Barclay, Robert, 111
Bawdy. *See* Salaciousness
Beatty, Rev. Charles, 78, 136
Belcher, Gov. Jonathan, 46, 51
Bell, Whitfield J., 137. See also *Papers of BF*
Benjamin Franklin: Representative Selections (Jorgensen and Mott), 22, 65, 74–75, 78
Bermuda, 91
Bible: Apocrypha, 52; Dives, 84; Exodus, 32; Hebrews, 91; Judges, 82; Lazarus, 84; Proverbs, 40; Psalms, 35; revision of, 112–13; Saul and the Witch of Endor, 43
Biblical allusions, 113, 126; comparisons, 82; explications, parodied, 126; imitations, 22; parables, 113. *See also* Religious references
Bickerstaff, Isaac, 75–76
Bier, Jesse, 62
Bigelow, John, 15–16
Bills of mortality, 84
Blackstone, Sir William, 119
Blount, Sir Thomas Pope, 39
Bolling, Robert, 108, 130
Boston Chronicle, 117
Boston Gazette, 36, 120, 139
Boston News Letter, 35, 37, 57, 140
Bowdoin, James, 123
Bowman, William, 60
Bradford, Andrew, 37, 58, 70, 76. See also *American Weekly Mercury*
Bradford, William, 109
Breintnall, Joseph, 19
Breitwieser, Mitchell Robert, 138–40

"Bridget Bifrons," 39
Brodwin, Stanley, 28
Browne, William, 123
Burgh, James, 118–19
Burlington, N.J., 95–96, 103
Burnet, Gov. Gilbert, 46
Burnet, Thomas, 38
Burrington, Gov. George, 55
Butler, Samuel: *Hudibras*, 32
Byles, Mather, 29

Caesar, Julius, 116
Cafferty, Pastora San Juan, 122
California, 69
Cambridge Platform, 139
Canada: BF tries to secure for U.S.A., 125
Cappon, Lester J., 45
"Case of the British Northern Colonies, The," 56
"Case of the British Sugar Colonies, The," 56
"Cassettie," 76
Cato's Letters (Trenchard and Gordon), 33
Cawtawba Indians, 41
Censure, 72–74. *See also* Scandal
Charles II (king of England), 84
Charles XII (king of Sweden), 83
Charles, Robert, 94
Charleston, S.C., 90, 110–11
Chattin, James, 80
Chiasmus, 39
Cicero, 102, 134
Circumlocution, 76
"Civicus," 72, 102, 134
Class consciousness. *See* Egalitarianism; Social hierarchy
Classical examples, 52
Clichés, 29
Club of Honest Whigs, 118–19
Cohen, I. Bernard, 116
Colden, Cadwallader, 63
Collins, John, 77
Colman, Benjamin, 139
"Colonists' Advocate" essay series, 118–20
Commerce: as cheating, 53. *See also* Trade
Common man, 98, 107. *See also* Egalitarianism

Compassion: of man, 23, 40–41, 53, 88, 91, 94. *See also* Human nature
Condescension: of English for Americans, 62–63, 65, 134. *See also* Patriotism; Proto-nationalism
Conduct, 49
Confucius, 69
Consensus gentium argument, 69
Constancy, 47, 83, 130
Cook, Elizabeth Christine, 17, 53, 58, 62
Cook, William, 109
Cooper, Joseph, 95–96, 109
Copernicus, 36
Coulter, William: trial of, 106–7
Crane, Verner W., 16, 28, 29, 64, 118
Creech, Thomas, 49
Cromwell, Oliver, 84, 132
Currency, paper, 76, 102, 122–24, 133
Curwen, Samuel, 123

Darrell, John (undersheriff), 34
Davy, Francis X., 27, 46, 78, 91, 93
DeArmond, Anna Janney, 59
"Dear Ned" essays: BF not the author of, 21, 93–94
Death. *See* Mortality
Deism, 39, 43–45, 60, 69, 99–100, 131. *See also* Religious satire
Democratic sentiments, 49, 79, 97–98, 131–32. *See also* Egalitarianism
Demosthenes, 102, 134
Denham, Thomas, 53
Descartes, René. *See* Logic: cartesian
Devices. *See* Emblems, devices, and mottoes
Dichotomization: as uncharacteristic rhetorical strategy for BF, 54
Dickinson, John, 119
Diction, 23, 28, 50, 61, 82–83, 89, 96–97, 101, 119–20, 124; colloquialisms, 23, 130; jargon, burlesque of, 23, 121; learned, 52; originality of, 55, 76, 101; precision of, 23, 108; Quaker, 66–67, 82–83; repetition of words and phrases, 22; specialized vocabularies, 23, wordplay and coinages, 23, 38, 55, 124. *See also* Words
Digressions, 67, 135. *See also* Logic
Disputes, 48
Drinking, 76–78, 87–88, 130, 135; of clergymen, 42

Duane, William, 15–16, 52
Dudley, Gov. Joseph, 33
Dulany, Daniel, Jr., 119
Dulany, Daniel, Sr., 59–60
Dummer, Jeremiah, 119

Economics, 23, 90, 129. *See also* Trade
Editorial disclaimer, 23, 45, 46, 57, 64, 80, 86
Editorial note, 20, 27, 45, 46, 52, 57, 64–65, 77, 80, 86, 88, 97, 99, 102
Egalitarianism, 24, 32, 38, 49, 54, 68, 80, 81, 97–100, 115, 123, 130–32; and simplicity, 61. *See also* Common man; Democratic sentiments; Law; Social hierarchy
Electricity, 113–14, 116
Eliot, Jared, 72
Eliot, John, 37
Ellison, Ralph, 130
Emblems, devices, and mottoes, 122–24
Emigration, 92, 120–21
England: as shopkeeping nation, 53
English. *See* Condescension
Epigraphs, 49, 52, 63, 65, 79, 83
Eskimos, 114
"Essay Upon the Nonsense of the Bar, An," 70
"Essay Upon the Nonsense of the Pulpit, An," 70
Experimental method: applied to beliefs, 45. *See also* Open-mindedness
Exports. *See* Trade
"Extract of a Letter from South Carolina, An," 116

Facts: BF's freedom with, 57, 108
Farmar, Col. Thomas, 95
Fast Day sermons: BF's parable on, 48
Feminism. *See* Proto-feminism
Fiedler, Leslie, 136
Fleeming, John, 117
Force, Peter, 124
Ford, Paul Leicester, 16
Ford, Worthington Chauncey, 71, 138, 140
France, 118
Franklin, Benjamin: his ability to see both sides of issue, 135–36; as apprentice shopkeeper for Thomas Denham, 53; as cartoonist, 124; as clerk of Pennsylvania Assembly, 21; defends *Penn-*

Franklin, Benjamin *(con't.)*
sylvania Gazette, 43; designs emblems for Associator Flags, 122–23; early involvement of, in politics, 132; as Indian lover, 117; learns foreign languages, 75; leaves Boston, 45–46, 140; marries Deborah Read, 20, 50; organizes Associators, 20; personal quarrels of, 128; as popular leader, 99; prints Whitefield's *Journals and Sermons*, 111; his reputation as punster, 59, 65; his reputation for religious satire, 99–100; speaks at Constitutional Convention, 38, 90; as temporary editor of *New England Courant*, 45, 48; writes preface to Galloway's *Speech*, 105; writes speech for N.J. Assembly, 19, 132. *See also* Pseudonyms of BF; Rhetorical strategies and devices; Subjects and attitudes in writings of BF; Writings of BF
Franklin, Deborah (Read), 20, 49–50, 103
Franklin, Francis Folger (son of BF), 86, 101; illness of, 20
Franklin, James (brother of BF), 27, 30, 140; arrest and imprisonment of, 31–35, 37, 128, 136; as author, 71; as not an author, 28; as possible author, 40. *See also New England Courant*
Franklin, John (brother of BF), 103
Franklin, Sarah (daughter of BF), 101
Franklin, William (son of BF), 61, 101, 117
Franklin, William Temple (grandson of BF), 15–16, 21, 100
Free Briton, 56
Free will: and God, 103–4. *See also* Religious satire
French (language), 75
French and Indian War, 124; threatened, 82
Frugality, 123

Galloway, Joseph, 105
Gardner, Nathaniel, 27, 32, 138–40; attacks Samuel Shute in *Courant*, 34; burlesques the jeremiad, 31; as not an author, 29; as possible author, 37, 39–40, 138–40; writes essay on religious hypocrites, 34–35, 139
General Magazine, 103–4
Georgia, 110–11

Germany, 92, 104, 116
Gilbert, Felix, 125
Gipson, Lawrence Henry, 132
Girouard, Robert, 117
God: as mad clockmaker, 44, 84–85; as mechanic, 100; as responsible for evil as well as good, 103; as unjust and cruel, 77, 136. *See also* Providence; Religious satire; Spirits
Goldberg, Joseph Philip, 91
Golden rule, 115
Gooch, Gov. William: BF burlesques, 128
Gordon, Gov. Patrick, 56
Gordon, Thomas. *See Cato's Letters*
"Grand Maitre," 93
Granger, Bruce I. 37–39
Great Awakening, 103
Great Chain of Being, 89
Green, Joseph, 108
Green, Matthew, 111
Greenland, 114
Grotesque: BF's, 107–8, 121, 130

Hall, Bishop Joseph, 38
Hall, Max, 36
Hamilton, Andrew, 55, 58–59, 66, 71, 79, 93–94
Hamilton, Sinclair, 124
Hanover, Germany, 122
Happiness, 48
Harry, David, 115
Harvard College, 117, 123
Havens, Raymond D., 62
Hay, Carla, 118–19
Hemphill, Rev. Samuel, 62, 128
Henderson, Rev. Jacob, 59–60
"Hercules and the Wagoneer" (Aesop), 48
Heroism, 81, 129
Herrick, Dr. John, 27
Hobbes, Thomas, 74–75. *See also* Hobbes vs. Locke
Hobbes vs. Locke: on natural state of man, 41, 74–75. *See also* Philosophical issues
Hopkinson, Francis, 124
Horace, 49, 123
House of Commons, 55–56
House of Lords, 56
Human nature, animality of, 45, 87–88,

Human nature (con't.)
106–8, 130–31; benevolence of, 74–75; disdain for, 44–45, 46–47, 73–74, 108; imperfection of, 105; insight into, 41, 129–31; satirized, 116, 117; virtue of, 8. See also Compassion; Infallibility; Pessimism; Pride; Vanity
Hume, David, 43, 101
Humility, 54
Humor, 23, 28, 39, 54, 67, 73, 76, 96, 107, 130; BF criticized for, 65. See also Irony; Puns

Imitation, 63, 79
Independence: of America, 132
Indians: American prejudice against, 116–17, 136
Industry, 76, 115, 123
Infallibility: BF's scorn for, 90
Infidelity, 58–60. See also Religious satire
Intolerable Act: BF satirizes, 121
Iron Act, 134
Irony, 23, 35, 41–42, 46, 67, 78, 83, 89, 91, 116, 130; dramatic, 52; and extraordinary orginality, 104; and extravagant praise, 23, 27, 59, 135; in personae, 23, 28, 49, 52–53, 74, 79, 104; in puns, 66, 81; savage, 107–8, 130–31. See also Self-satire
Isolationism, 125
Italian (language), 75

Jay, John, 19, 95, 109
Jefferson, Thomas, 136
Jeremiad: BF burlesques, 31
Johnston, Col. Andrew, 96
Jorgensen, Chester E., 22. See also *Benjamin Franklin: Representative Selections*
Junto, 46, 69, 71, 75, 77, 84–85

Keill, Dr. John, 37
Kellogg, Thelma L., 91
Kinnersley, Ebenezer, 19, 113–14, 116
Kittle, Mehitabel, 27, 59

Labaree, Leonard W., 137. See also *Papers of BF*
Langhorne, Jeremiah, 94
Language. See French; German; Spanish; Words

Law: favors rich, 78
Law of nature, 87
Lawrence, Robert, 109
Lawyers. See Amplification
Leaming, Aaron, 95
Leary, Lewis, 128
Leeds, Titan, 65, 91
Lemay, J. A. Leo, cited: *A Calendar of American Poetry*, 27, 46, 51, 67, 71, 79, 80, 108, 111, 116; *Ebenezer Kinnersley*, 114; "Franklin and Kinnersley," 113; "Franklin and the *Autobiography*," 17, 18, 42–43, 67, 78, 129; "Franklin's Suppressed 'Busy-Body,'" 40, 80; *Men of Letters in Colonial Maryland*, 33, 46, 60; *Renaissance Man in the Eighteenth-Century*, 48; review of *BF and the Zealous Presbyterians*, 58, 77, 102; review of *The Papers of Benjamin Franklin*, vol. 22, 122, 124; "The Text . . . of Miss Polly Baker," 36, 53, 65, 121
Levin, David, 45, 90
Libel, 102
Library Company of Philadelphia, 68, 100, 101
Life: as misery. See Pessimism
Lightning: electrical nature of, 113, 116
Locke, John, 38, 44, 67, 74. See also Hobbes vs. Locke
Logan, James, 93–94
Logic, 23, 29, 39, 58, 67, 96–97, 101, 128, 135; Cartesian, 54; Ramistic, as unlike Franklin, 54; ratiocinative, 39, 58. See also Reasoning; Rhetoric
London Magazine, 94
Lopez, Claude-Anne, 137. See also *Papers of BF*
Louisburg: BF's woodcut of, 109–10
Low, John, 95, 109
Loyalists, 124
Lucan, 83
Lynen, John F., 129

"Mack," 76
McMaster, John Bach, 16–18, 25, 40, 47, 51, 52, 75, 78, 91
Mandeville, Bernard de, 46, 74–75. See also Shaftesbury vs. Mandeville
"Marcus-Porcus," 64
"Marcus Verus," 59

Maryland Gazette, 114, 121
Maryland Tobacco Act, 60
Massachusetts Gazette, 120
Massachusetts General Court, 32; BF satirizes, 37, 132
Massachusetts Spy, 120, 122
Mather, Cotton: denounces James Franklin in *New England Courant*, 30; satirized, 30, 93, 128
Mather, Increase, 128; condemns James Franklin, 36
Mather, Samuel, 29
Matrimony: state of, 47, 66
Matthews, Albert, 124
Mecom, Jane, 15, 83, 86, 131
Mein, John, 117
Meiosis: earthy, 63. See also Scurrility
Melville, Herman, 105, 129
Mercantile Acts. See Navigation Acts
Meredith, Hugh, 77
Merrewether, James: BF's obituary on, 61, 98
Metaphors: BF's, 32, 47, 78; for death, 84, 85; of God as a clockmaker, 44, 84–85; mixed, 65; for racial relations, 126; of ship voyage, 83; of shipwreck, 32; of shopkeepers and shopkeeping, 52, 53, 115, 130–31
Metaphysics, 23, 103. See also Philosophical issues; Truth
Metempsychosis, 45
Meteorology, 86–87
Miles gloriosus type, 41
Militia Association, 82, 111, 113, 132
Miller, C. William, 96, 99, 110, 111–12
Miller, Perry, 32, 138
Ministers: satire of. See Anti-clericism
Miracles, 79
"Mirza," 117–18
"Misodaemon." See "Theophilus Misodaemon"
Mitchel, James, 40–41, 74
Mock panegyric poetry, 27
Molasses Bill, 55–57, 133
Monarchy: BF's supposed devotion to, 132–33. See also Patriotism
Morality: and religion, 43–44, 69, 85
Moravian Church, 104–6, 129
Morgan, Rev. Joseph, 104
Morris, Gov. Lewis, 95–96, 109
Morris, Richard B., 109

Morris, Gov. Robert Hunter, 132
Mortality, 84–86, 131
Mott, Frank Luther, 22, 104. See also *Benjamin Franklin: Representative Selections*
Mottoes: BF's, for militia companies, 122–23
Murray, James, 117

Natural law, 88
Nature of man. See Compassion; Human nature
Naval Documents of the American Revolution: cited, 124
Navigation Acts, 56, 133–34; BF's satire of, 121
Nevill, Samuel, 96
New American Magazine, 134
New England Courant, 16, 18–19, 138–40; BF defends paper, 28–29, 128; BF as temporary editor of, 27; BF writes "Silence Dogood" for, 22, 46, 71; James Franklin forbidden to publish, 37; its reputation for irreligion, 40
New Hampshire Gazette, 120
New Jersey, 55, 94–96, 109
Newman, Eric P., 122
Newport Mercury, 116–17
Newton, Sir Isaac, 44
New York Gazette, 55
New York Weekly Post Boy, 109
Norman Conquest, 98
North, Frederick, Lord, 125. See also North Ministry
North Carolina, 55, 132
North Ministry, 117. See also North, Frederick, Lord
Northwest Passage, 114

Occupatio, 65, 134
Old South Church (Boston), 36
Oliver, Peter, 120
Open-mindedness, 88–90, 135–36. See also Experimental method
Optimism, 23, 29, 41, 48, 86, 131. See also Pessimism
Original sin, 77. See also God
Orthography: BF's, 108–9
Orwell, George, 63, 130
Otis, James, 119

Paine, Robert Treat, 122
Paine, Thomas, 119
Palmer, Joseph, 122
"Paper-Money the Conqueror," 76
Papers of Benjamin Franklin, The (Labaree, Willcox, et al.), 16–22, 24, 28, 33, 46, 57, 71–72, 75, 78, 109–10, 118–19, 127–28, 132, 136–37
Paralipses, 23, 43
Parenthesis, 37
Parker, James, 109
Parton, James, 16–18, 38
Patriotism, 67, 125, 132–34. *See also* Condescension; Proto-nationalism
Paxton boys, 117
Penn, John, 72, 111
Penn, Thomas, 71, 99–100, 111
Penn, William, 71–72, 93, 97, 111
Pennsylvania Assembly, 57, 97
Pennsylvania Gazette, 16, 18, 20–22, 40–41, 50, 55, 56, 59, 62–66, 68–69, 70, 72, 74, 77, 81, 84, 88, 90, 97–102, 106–14, 122–23, 133
Pennsylvania Journal, 106, 120, 124
Pennsylvania Magazine, 122, 124
Periphrasis: burlesque of, 23, 51. *See also* Amplification
Persius, 65–66, 69
Personae, 28, 29, 42, 46, 49, 67–68, 74, 77, 79, 91, 97, 99, 101, 107, 119, 124–25, 132, 135; feminine, 49; Quaker, 66–67, 82–83; self-deluding, 45, 52, 59, 64–65. *See also* Pseudonyms of BF; Self-satire
Personification, 101–2
Perth Amboy, N.J., 95, 109
Pessimism, 53, 73, 86, 88, 130–31. *See also* Optimism
Peter (czar of Russia), 98
Peters, Richard, 100–101, 111
"Petit Maitre," 93
Petty, Sir William, 84, 86
Philadelphia, 80, 82, 87, 90, 96–97, 105, 107, 110, 113, 116, 122
"Philanthropos," 70–71
Phillips, Anne Reynolds, 134
Philosophical issues, 23, 29, 55, 58, 81, 129–30, 136. *See also* Free will; God; Hobbes vs. Locke; Human nature; Metaphysics; Relativism; Religious satire; Shaftesbury vs. Mandeville; Truth

Philosophical Transactions, 50–51
Physico-ideology, 85
Pitt, Arthur Stuart, 89
Platonic idealism, 45
Political shrewdness, 23
Pope, Alexander, 63, 81, 91
Population, 92–93, 125
"Portius," 58–59, 62–64, 68–70, 128, 134
Pragmatism, 43, 44, 49, 81, 86
Prichett, V. S., 89
Pride: contempt for, 23, 44–45, 54, 68, 131. *See also* Human nature; Vanity
Priestley, Joseph, 57, 79, 88
Primitivism: and simplicity, 61
Proto-feminism, 38, 47–49, 132. *See also* Anti-feminism
Proto-nationalism, 23, 51, 55, 132–33. *See also* Condescension; Patriotism
Prouse, James, 40–41, 74
Proverbs, 23, 42, 47–48, 51, 72, 79, 81, 98. *See also* Aphorisms
Providence: satire of, 73, 136. *See also* Religious satire
Provinciality: burlesqued, 30, 67
Pseudonyms: common in 18th century, 15; use of another person's, 64
Pseudonyms of BF: "A, B, C, &c," 28, 135; "Abigail Twitterfield," 39, 135; "Alice Addertongue," 72, 74, 80–81; "An American Guesser," 125, 135; "Anthony Afterwit," 49; "Betty Diligent," 52, 135; "Blackamore," 78–79, 131, 135; "Britannus," 120; "Busy-Body," 19, 39, 42, 61, 65, 73, 76, 80, 115, 128, 134; "the Casuist," 28; "Cato," 61, 98; "Chatterbox," 75–76, 130, 135; "Clericus," 46, 120, 124; "F.B.," 118; "Great Person" ("Cravenstreet Gazette"), 28; "Homespun," 68, 99; "Hugo Grim," 28; "Johannes Clericus," 46; "JUBA," 35–36, 132, 135; "Leather Apron Man," the, 68; "Marcus," 58–59, 62–64, 68, 135; "Mercator," 52, 135; "Mr. *Courant*," 27; Mrs. Dogood (*see* "Silence Dogood"); "A New Englandman," 134; Obadiah Plainman," 96–102, 131, 134–35; "Pecunia," 66; "Pennsylvanus," 81–82, 135; "Philocleris," 43–46, 135; "Philomath," 91, 135; "Philomusus," 27, 135; "Polly Baker," 28, 53, 59, 88; "Poor Richard," 28, 46, 48–49, 53, 54, 59–62, 65, 73, 76,

Index

Pseudonyms of BF *(con't.)*
78, 80–81, 86, 88, 98, 130; "Prosit," 59, 64–65, 68, 134–35; "A Quaker Lady," 135; "Silence Dogood," 19–20, 22, 27–28, 29, 30, 33, 42, 46, 52, 59, 71, 74, 77, 91, 104, 107, 117, 119, 122; "Theophilus," 103–4, 135; "Timothy Scrubb," 70; "Timothy Wagstaff," 38–39, 135; "Veridicus," 88–90, 131, 135; "Y.Z.," 135
Ptolemy, 36
Public Advertiser (London), 118, 120
Public Ledger (London), 117
Puns, 27, 78, 101; BF's skill in, 59; ironic, 66, 81; sexual, 32, 47, 52. *See also* Humor
Pyrrhonism, 45, 58, 131
Pythagoras, 49

Quakers, 83. *See also* Diction: Quaker
Quotations: use of unusual, 23

Rabelais, François, 32
Racial relations, 79, 132
Ramus, Petrus, 54
Ratiocination, 39. *See also* Logic
Rattlesnake, 124–26, 132, 134
Read, Deborah. *See* Franklin, Deborah (Read)
Reader: and attempt to influence, 82; emotions of, and benevolence, 41, 74–75, 81
Reasoning, false: satire of, 52, 135. *See also* Logic
Reductio ad absurdum, 23, 37, 58
Reilly, Elizabeth Carroll, 110
Relativism, 23, 38, 88, 105. *See also* Philosophical issues
Religion: usefulness of, 43–44. *See also* Morality
Religious debates, 64
Religious meditations, 78, 136
Religious references, 77. *See also* Biblical allusions
Religious satire, 23, 29, 38, 39, 42–43, 48, 58–59, 62–63, 73, 77, 78, 86, 89, 99, 100, 126, 128. *See also* Anti-Christianity; Anti-clericism; Atheism; Deism; Free will; God; Infidelity; Providence; Theology
Reputation: concern for, 54
Rhetoric: knowledge of, 23, 65–66, 102,
134–35. *See also* Logic
Rhetorical strategies and devices of BF. *See* Amplification; Anecdote; Antimetabole; Aphorisms; Apothegms; Bagatelles; Biblical allusions; Biblical comparisons; Biblical imitations; Biblical parables; Chiasmus; Classical examples; Clichés; *Consensus gentium* argument; Diction; Digressions, Editorial note or disclaimer; Epigraphs; Humor; Irony; Logic; Metaphors; Mock panegyric poetry; *Occupatio;* Paralipses; Parenthesis; Periphrasis; Personae; Proverbs; Puns; Quotations: use of unusual; *Reductio ad absurdum;* Religious meditations; Religious references; Rhetoric: knowledge of; Scurrility; Self-satire; Sententiae; Structural techniques; Synecdoche
Rhode Island Assembly, 117
Richardson, Edward W., 124
Rush, Benjamin, 42

"Sagittarius," 117
Salaciousness, 32, 47, 51, 57, 107–8, 130
Salem witchcraft, 36
Saltpeter, 122
"Sandbox," 76
Sappenfield, James A., 104
Scandal, 72, 81; personal, not in newspapers, 102. *See also* Censure
Schlesinger, Arthur M., 120
Schneider, Herbert W., 129
Scientific trends and speculations, 31, 50–51, 86–87, 113–14, 129
Scots Magazine, 113
"Scots Traveller, The," 42
Scurrility, 23, 32, 76, 79, 130. *See also* Meiosis
Seed, David, 90
Selfishness, 41, 136
Self-satire, 28, 39, 54, 68, 70, 74, 91, 125, 128. *See also* Irony
Sententiae, 23, 36, 51, 79, 82, 85–86. *See also* Aphorisms
Sermon: techniques of, satirized, 66, 126
Several Methods of Making Salt-Petre, 122
Sewall, Samuel: BF satirizes, 20–21, 32–34, 35–37; opposes sermons on science, 31; his role in Salem witchcraft trials, 36

Seward, William, 97, 100
"S. H.," 65
Shaftesbury, Anthony Ashley Cooper, third earl of, 74–75; *Characteristics*, cited, 58, 70
Shaftesbury vs. Mandeville, 41, 74–75. *See also* Philosophical issues
Shear, Walter, 129
Shields, David S., 80
Shirley, Gov. William, 132
Shute, Gov. Samuel, 34
Sidney, Algernon, 93
Sidney, Sir Philip, 102, 134
Simplicity, 60–62
Simson, George, 134
Sincerity, 47, 54
Skepticism, 105
Smith, Albert Henry, 16, 28, 47–48, 50, 68, 71, 79, 83, 85, 98, 114
Smith, Richard, 109
Social hierarchy: opposition to, 24, 38, 51, 54, 79, 80, 115. *See also* Aristocracy; Egalitarianism
Social relations, 98
Society of the Cincinnati: BF satirizes, 97
Souls: as not worth saving, 44. *See also* Religious satire
South Carolina, 56, 76, 90, 110–11
South Carolina Gazette, 76, 86, 90
Southwick, Solomon, 117
Spanish (language), 75
Sparks, Jared, 15–16
Spectator, 117, 130
Spicer, Jacob, II, 96
Spiller, Robert E., 45
Spirits: probability of existence of, 44. *See also* God
Stacy, Mahlon, 95–96
Stamp Act, 133
Stansbury, Joseph, 122
Statistics, 23, 57, 84, 129. *See also* Trade
Steele, Richard. See *Spectator*; *Tatler*
Stevenson, Mary, 58
Stiles, Ezra, 44
Stoddard, Solomon, 139
Stourzh, Gerald, 89, 132
Strahan, William, 63
Structural techniques, 112; framework, 23, 43; ironic queries, 23, 83; "receipt," 104; "rules," 23, 29, 32, 47–49, 114–16, 128–29, 134
Stuarts, 119

Styles: variety of BF's, 22, 66, 70
Subjects and attitudes in writings of BF. See Anti-clericism; Anti-pacifism; Anti-provincialism; Appearance vs. reality; Aristocracy; Astrology: burlesque of; Astronomy; Atheism; Avarice; Censure; Common man; Compassion; Condescension: of English for Americans; Conduct; Constancy; Currency; Deism; Democratic sentiments; Drinking; Economics; Egalitarianism; Electricity; Emblems; Frugality; Great Chain of Being; Heroism; Human nature; Humility; Imitation; Industry; Infallibility; Infidelity; Isolationism; Jeremiad; Metaphysics; Metempsychosis; Meteorology; Miracles; Morality; Moravian Church; Mortality; Natural law; Northwest Passage; Optimism; Original sin; Patriotism; Pessimism; Philosophical issues; Platonic idealism; Political shrewdness; Pragmatism; Pride: contempt for; Primitivism; Proto-feminism; Proto-nationalism; Providence: satire of; Pyrrhonism; Racial relations; Relativism; Religious debates; Religious satire; Reputation: concern for; Scandal; Scientific trends and speculations; Selfishness; Simplicity; Sincerity; Skepticism; Social hierarchy: opposition to; Social relations; Statistics; Success; Theology; Utilitarianism; Vanity; Vice; Virtue; Whiggism
Success, 51
Sugar Islands, 55–57
Superstition: satire of, 42, 128
Susquehanna Indians, 41
Swift, Jonathan, 78, 93, 121
Symmes, Rev. Thomas, 38–39
Synecdoche, 94

Tatler, 76, 130
Taylor, Capt. Christopher, 35, 37
"T. E." ("The Extinguisher"), 59–60
Tennent, Gilbert, 111–12
Thanksgiving Day: BF's parable of origin, 48
Theology, 103–4, 128–29. *See also* Religious satire
"Theophilus Misodaemon," 102–3

Thomas, Gov. George, 93
Thomas, Isaiah, 37
Thompson, Emma, 60
Tindal, Matthew, 66
"Tinderbox," 76
"Tom Trueman," 99, 101
Tories, 88, 105, 120
Tourtellot, Arthur Bernon, 32–34, 37
Trade, American, 55–56, 90; and population, 92; rules for, 114–16; West Indies, 56. See also Commerce; Economics; Statistics
Treasure hunting: satire of, 76
Trenchard, John, 102. See also Cato's Letters
Truth: kinds of, 105
Tully, Alan, 93–94
Tyler, Moses Coit, 131

Universal Spectator, 40, 50
Utilitarianism, 43–44

Van Doren, Carl, 16–17, 63
Vanity, 45, 54, 59, 65, 67, 131, 135; as reason for censure, 72. See also Human nature; Pride
Vaughan, Benjamin, 15
"Verus," 68
Vice, 61
Virginia Gazette (Dixon & Hunter), 124
Virtue, 61, 66, 81, 105, 115–16
Virtues: list of, 47

Wainwright, Nicholas B., 46
Walsh, Williams, 67
Warren, Erasmus, 38
Washington, George: Farewell Address of, 125
Webbe, John, 93
Wesley, John, 104, 106
Weyman's New York Gazette, 116
Whatley, George, 114
Whiggism, 23, 32, 71–72, 102, 132
Whigs, 88, 105
Whiston, William, 38
Whitefield, George, 69, 97, 99–100, 103, 104, 110; involvement of, with Georgia orphanage, 103, 110–11
Whitehall Evening Post, 55
Whitemarsh, Pa., 106
Whitisin, William, 67
Whitmarsh, Thomas, 41, 76

Willcox, William B., 137. See also Papers of BF
Williams, Jonathan, 61, 79
Wolf, Edwin, II, 122
Words: difficulty of knowing meaning of, 99, 105. See also Diction
Writings of BF: "Advice of a Pretty Creature," 83; "Advice to a Young Tradesman," 114; "Advice to Youth," 80; "Apology for Printers," 45, 69; "Articles of Belief and Acts of Religion," 44, 85, 89; "Art of Virtue," 83; "Aurora Borealis: Suppositions and Conjectures," 50; Autobiography, passim; "Busy-Body" essay series, 19, 39, 42, 61, 65, 73, 76, 80, 115, 128, 134; "The Captivity of William Henry," 18–19; "Catalogue of the Principal Kings and Princes in Europe with the Time of their Births and Ages" (Poor Richard), 57; "The causes of the American discontents," 118; Dissertation on Liberty and Necessity, Pleasure and Pain, 44, 84, 103–5, 129; "The Drinker's Dictionary," 22, 52, 101; "An Edict by the King of Prussia," 46, 121, 134; Editorial comments, 20; "The Elysian Fields," 68; "The Ephemera," 68; Essay on slippery sidewalks, 76; Examination, 118; "Frenchman and the Poker," 130; "golden Extract from a favourite Old Book," 18; "The Handsome and Deformed Leg," 48; "Hints to those that would be Rich," 114; "How to get Riches," 114; "Information to Those who would remove to America," 63; The interest of Great Britain Considered, 118, 125; "I Sing my plain Country Joan," 47–48; "Letter to the Royal Academy," 101; "The Lighthouse Tragedy," 27; "A Man of Sense," 61; "Martha Careful and Caelia Shortface," 83; "A Method of Humbling Rebellious American Vassals," 120–21, 130; A Narrative of the Late Massacres, 52, 66; The Nature and Necessity of a Paper Currency, 66, 80; "New Lights," 128; News items, 20; "Observations Concerning the Increase of Mankind," 84, 92, 125, 134; "Old Mistresses Apologue," 22, 47, 107–8, 130; "On a Proposed Act to Prevent Emigration," 120;

Writings of BF *(con't.)*
"On Literary Style," 62, 66, 70; "On Simplicity," 125; "On the Providence of God in the Government of the World," 69, 84–85; "An Open Letter to Lord North," 120, 125; "The Palatines Appeal" (translation), 75; "A Parable against Persecution," 22, 107; parable of man in a fog *(Autobiography)*, 90; "A Parable on Brotherly Love," 22, 107; parable on Fast Day sermons, 48; parable on origin of Thanksgiving, 48; "Petition of the Left Hand," 49; "Petition to the Pennsylvania Assembly regarding Fairs," 57; *Plain Truth*, 48, 80, 82, 112; *Poor Richard's Almanac*, 29, 30, 43, 47, 51, 53–54, 57–58, 71, 83–84, 91; "Proclamation for a General Fast," 66; "Project of arriving at moral Perfection" *(Autobiography)*, 83; "Rattlesnakes for Felons," 63, 124; "Reply to a Piece of Advice," 47–48; "Rules by Which a great Empire May be Reduced to a Small One," 30, 121; "Rules for Making Oneself a Disagreeable Companion," 30; "The Sale of the Hessians," 18, 130–31; "Silence Dogood" essay series, 19–20, 22, 27, 29, 33, 42, 59, 71, 74, 77, 91, 104, 107, 117, 119, 122; "The Speech of Miss Polly Baker," 22, 36–37, 45, 49, 58, 66, 77, 87, 107, 121, 130; "The Taking of Teach or Blackbeard the Pirate," 27; "To the Royal Academy," 130; "Verses on the Virginia Capitol Fire," 22, 107; "The Way to Wealth," 43, 66, 91, 114; "A Witch Trial at Mount Holly," 42, 128

Wycherley, William, 70

Young, William, 66

Zenger, John Peter, 95
Ziff, Larzer, 46, 135